Gendered Transitions

Gendered Transitions

Mexican Experiences of Immigration

Pierrette Hondagneu-Sotelo

UNIVERSITY OF CALIFORNIA PRESS
Berkeley · Los Angeles · London

University of California Press
Berkeley and Los Angeles, California

University of California Press, Ltd.
London, England

© 1994 by
The Regents of the University of California

Library of Congress Cataloging-in-Publication Data

Hondagneu-Sotelo, Pierrette.
   Gendered transitions : Mexican experiences of immigration /
Pierrette Hondagneu-Sotelo.
     p.   cm.
   Includes bibliographical references and index.
   ISBN 0-520-07513-7. — ISBN 0-520-07514-5 (pbk.)
   1. Mexicans—United States—Social conditions. 2. Women
immigrants—United States. 3. United States—Emigration and
immigration. 4. Mexico—Emigration and immigration.   I. Title.
JV6895.M48H66   1994
325′ .272′0973—dc20

                            93-33289
                            CIP

Printed in the United States of America
9 8 7 6 5 4

The paper used in this publication meets the minimum requirements of American National Standard for Information Sciences—Permanence of Paper for Printed Library Materials, ANSI Z39.48-1984.

For my parents

Contents

Acknowledgments

I could not have written this book without the generous help of many people. First and foremost, I am grateful to the people in the "Oakview" community who allowed me into their private lives and histories. Not only did I learn a lot from them, but my life has been enriched by their friendship, and I regret that they must remain anonymous. As I conducted the field research, Violeta Ortega, Consuelo Sánchez, Beatríz Soto, Aurora Vega, and the late Alberto Sánchez inspired my deep respect for community activism, and their support facilitated my investigation. I am also grateful to Stephen Carey, director of bilingual education in the "Oakview" school district, for making school documents available to me.

This project began as a Ph.D. dissertation in the Department of Sociology at the University of California at Berkeley. Michael Burawoy, whose reputation for providing challenges to graduate students is well earned, served as chair of the committee. He guided the organization of my initial thinking on this subject, and I benefited immeasurably from his wisdom and his penchant for asking difficult questions. Arlie Hochschild was the first person to encourage me to look seriously at the relationship between gender and immigration, and she provided constructive comments in the early stages of this project, as did historian Alex Saragoza, who also taught me much of what I know about effective teaching. I am grateful to all of them for helping me to put the pieces together.

Several institutions gave me valuable support. The Department of Sociology at U.C. Berkeley and the Business and Professional Women's Foundation supported part of the research. The process of writing was facilitated by my one-term reduced teaching schedules in the sociology departments at California State University at San Bernardino and at the University of Southern California, and by a Visiting Research Fellowship at the Center for U.S.-Mexican Studies, located at the University of California at San Diego. Betsy Amster, Nazli Kibria, Eun Mee Kim, Barbara Laslett, Ruth Milkman, and Carol Zabin read and commented on parts of the manuscript, and María Patricia Fernández-Kelly, Michael A. Messner, Barrie Thorne, María de Lourdes Villar, Carol A. B. Warren, and Maxine Baca Zinn read the entire manuscript and made many helpful suggestions. The book is vastly improved because of their input, though I did not always heed their advice. A wonderful spirit of collegiality prevails among researchers in Mexico and the United States who are studying various facets of Mexican immigration. The following people readily shared their work with me: María Blanco, Leo Chavez, Wayne A. Cornelius, Katharine M. Donato, María Patricia Fernández-Kelly, Mercedes González de la Rocha, Luin Goldring, Sherri Grasmuck, David M. Heer, Gail Mummert, Orlandina de Oliveira, Roger Rouse, Rubén Rumbaut, Maurice D. Van Arsdol, and Ofelia Morales Woo. I appreciate the help of Naomi Schneider, Scott Norton, and Carl Walesa, whose expertise allowed me to transform the manuscript into a book, and of Gloria Gonzalez, who kept me honest with the accent marks.

I am fortunate to have received much support and encouragement from friends, neighbors, and family. My good friends Leticia Alcántar and Marianne Hunt regularly listened to my ramblings about this project, and their company provided enjoyable and much needed distractions. Ana Ruth cared for my children with great patience and kindness during many hours when I worked on this book. My parents, Pierre and Maria Inés Hondagneu, strongly supported this long project. To my parents I owe special thanks for allowing me to live in their home while I carried out most of the field research. Besides caring for many of my daily needs during this time, my mother occasionally accompanied me in the field. Dedicating this book to my parents seems a small token in light of their lifetime dedication to me. I was also very lucky to have my brother Michel come through for me on a moment's notice to meticulously and painstakingly proofread the entire manuscript. Although they were born after I conducted the primary research, my sons Miles (better known as Lito) and Sasha rewarded me with countless moments of joy during subsequent stages of writing. I reserve my final expression of gratitude for Michael A. Messner, who from the inception of this project listened as I aired out ideas and alternative courses of direction. He read nearly everything more than once, and agilely delivered critical comments with his inimical sense of humor. I was most impressed when he began reciting passages of the text in unexpected venues. He has given me a decade of loving companionship that has enhanced my work and the quality of my day-to-day life, and I am grateful to him for all of it.

Introduction

On a weekday evening in November 1986, I attended a public forum held at a community center where I'd once worked. Over three hundred people, adults and children, had crammed into the multipurpose room to learn about the then–recently passed Immigration Reform and Control Act. The audience sat on folding chairs or stood in the aisles and back corridors, listening attentively and murmuring among themselves the questions for which they had come seeking answers. Would they qualify for *la amnistía,* the much-publicized but as yet poorly understood amnesty-legalization program, and could they confidently expect to get their "papers" through this program? What types of documents would they need to prove their history of undocumented residence and work in the United States, and how should they go about gathering them? What were the consequences if they did not meet the criteria for legalization? Or worse, what if submitted applications were rejected by the Immigration and Naturalization Service? Would they or their family members then face deportation? Would employer sanctions leave them jobless and without an income?

On that evening I accepted an invitation to join a small, grass-roots community group that was forming to deal with these questions, and during the next year and a half I immersed myself, as an activist and as a researcher, into family and community life in this barrio. The women, men, and children who came to the multipurpose room that November evening expressed the aspirations and anxieties shared by many other Mexican immigrants who, without the benefit of legal status, had set down roots in other communities in California and elsewhere in the United States. I conducted this study because I wanted to find out why more women and entire families were participating in undocumented migration and settlement, and because I wanted to understand the relationship between gender relations and these processes. So I too entered the picture with a series of questions. How does gender organize and shape this migration? What are the implications for gender relations among these newcomers to U.S. society? And finally, what are the defining features of settlement, and how do women help to establish family and community life in the United States? To answer these questions, I spent a year and a half conducting semistructured interviews, observing and participating with Mexican immigrants in many social settings. The majority of these people were undocumented at the time of the study, although many of them did eventually obtain legal status.

The Immigration Reform and Control Act of 1986 (IRCA) had a more profound impact on undocumented immigrants than any other piece of legislation ever passed in the United States. For those who qualified for legalization, it presented the overwhelming "paper chase" task of securing obscure pieces of evidence (receipts of utilities and rent payment from years before, notarized letters, etc.), and then the risk of presenting these documents to the authorities, from whom the immigrants had always had to hide all indicators of "illegal" status. For those ineligible for legalization, it required the development of innovative responses to new employment and survival problems. I assisted in both endeavors, and my field research dovetailed with community work, political activism, and personal assistance. IRCA, then, affected both undocumented immigrants and the way I conducted the study. Furthermore, I believe this legislation represented a direct reaction to the phenomenon this study focuses on—undocumented immigrant settlement.

While the media portrayed IRCA as a liberal and generous immigration law because of legalization provisions, the primary impulse behind it was immigration restriction.[1] Each of the various bills leading to IRCA featured as the centerpiece employer sanctions—that is, penalties for employers who knowingly hire unauthorized immigrant workers—and as such, these legislative initiatives reflected the xenophobia of the 1970s and the 1980s. During the recession of the early 1980s, politicians and newspaper editorials commonly scapegoated immigrants for causing a lagging economy. Restrictionist lobby groups achieved national prominence, while their leaders warned that the new immigrants and refugees were causing a host of domestic social problems ranging from high taxes and crime to California's traffic jams and air-pollution problems. Even language became a target of attack, as the well-funded national organization U.S. English campaigned against the implementation of bilingual education programs and election ballots. Outside the law, the new nativism assumed more violent, vitriolic, and blatantly racist manifestations.

IRCA codified this xenophobia. The xenophobia of this period, however, represented less a response to undocumented migration per se than to undocumented immigrant settlement. While many U.S. citizens welcomed the labor services performed by immigrants, they remained more apprehensive about the permanent incorporation of Asian and Latin American immigrants and refugees in the United States. Claims of an impending white baby "birth dearth," of the "minoritization," "Mexicanization," or *reconquista* (reconquest) of California, sometimes animated this discourse. Meanwhile, in an attempt to quell this resurgent xenophobia, liberal scholars and journalists concentrating on the subject of immigration often underlined the large proportion of sojourners among the Mexican immigrant population. "They aren't really staying," they seemed to argue, but in fact, many indicators pointed to the contrary.

The xenophobic scapegoating which ushered in the new immigration legislation targeted settled immigrants and centered around three claims. First, immigrants were blamed for stealing the jobs of U.S. citizens and depressing wage levels. These allegations of job competition intensified during the recession of the early 1980s, when plant closures, unemployment, and the declining number of manufacturing jobs were foremost in the public's eye, and they again surfaced with the severe recession and economic restructuring processes of the early 1990s. Second, immigrants were accused of draining the U.S. economy through their consumption of social services. The accusations included claims that immigrants come to the United States to obtain welfare payments, that they do not pay taxes, and that their children and families constitute a growing underclass, as they drain medical and educational resources in the United States. Finally, immigration restrictionists mimicked the allegations voiced by their predecessors about Southern and Eastern European immigrants in the early twentieth century, arguing that the new immigrants from Asia and Latin America were after all "too different," that they were ultimately unassimilable. Accordingly, further immigration signaled, as Senator Alan K. Simpson put it, the cultural and linguistic "Quebec-ization" of the United States. This investigation examines the group most visibly singled out by these attacks: Mexican undocumented immigrants.

THE SETTING

I conducted this study in an unincorporated area of what I shall call Oakview, a city that lies along a metropolitan corridor in the San Francisco Bay area, and when I began my fieldwork, I returned to a place that was at once familiar and new to me. I grew up ten minutes from the Oakview barrio, and as a child I regularly visited family friends there with my parents—who are immigrants from, respectively, Chile and France—and my brother. After graduating from college I worked in a nonprofit immigration legal-services agency and then in a bilingual-education program in the Oakview barrio.

Since the mid-1960s, this area, like others in California, has become transformed into what is primarily a Mexican immigrant barrio. The most graphic indicator of the recency with which Mexican immigrant families have settled in Oakview comes from surveys conducted in the three area elementary schools. As recently as 1964, Spanish-surnamed students accounted for only 15 percent of the student body, but by 1987 they made up 81 percent of local public elementary school children.[2]

Central Avenue, a half-mile strip lined with commercial establishments, serves as the barrio's main artery. It is filled with grocery stores stocked with tortillas and various Mexican products, as well as *carnicerías* (butcher shops), *panaderías* (Mexican bakeries), "Mexicatessens," jewelry and bridal-gown shops, bars, barber shops, beauty salons, record and tape stores, repair shops, and notary-public offices. In most of these establishments, transactions regularly occur in Spanish. As in many poor neighborhoods, banks and major supermarket chains are conspicuously absent along the avenue. A community center well decorated with graffiti, a nonprofit medical clinic and senior center, an elementary school, check-cashing centers, taco-vending trucks, and a Catholic church also populate the avenue, and by day, women, men, and children walk along the sidewalks that flank the four-lane thoroughfare. At night the sidewalks are vacant, except for a three-block stretch of bars where mostly men, occasionally accompanied by strolling mariachis, congregate.

The Oakview barrio remains one of the poorest areas in an otherwise affluent county, posing a stark contrast to surrounding municipalities. Well-established physical boundaries once outlined the barrio, but by the late 1980s, the perimeters around the Mexican immigrant neighborhood had become increasingly elastic as residents stretched outward to nearby areas, renting homes and apartments along the highway off-ramps and across the railroad tracks and wide avenues that had once served as de facto residential enclosures. High rents, crowding, and problems associated with drugs and crime encouraged some Mexican immigrant families to move away from the barrio to nearby neighborhoods. While nearly all of the people in this study lived within the barrio, four families had moved from these confines to nearby neighborhoods: one couple and their child lived rent free in a garage of an estate home; another family rented a house from kin in a predominantly African American neighborhood; and two families had managed to purchase homes in predominantly Anglo neighborhoods. These families still came to the barrio to worship, shop, cash checks, and visit kin. (In Chapter 3, I present a more extensive description of the Oakview barrio and its evolution.)

The Oakview barrio provides an advantageous research site for examining processes of settlement because it is a relatively nascent yet thriving Mexican immigrant community. Although crews of Mexican railroad workers and cannery workers labored in the Oakview area in the late nineteenth and early twentieth centuries, it was not they who proved to be the pioneers of the contemporary immigrant community, but rather the Mexican immigrants who began arriving in the 1950s and who established a more forceful presence by the 1960s. As an immigrant community in formation, the Oakview barrio provides an ideal vantage point for developing an understanding of the ongoing processes of gender as they relate to migration and settlement.

THE STUDY PARTICIPANTS

Most of the families who participated in this study lived in residences near Central Avenue, renting modest-sized, unattached, single-level houses or units located in small apartment buildings. The 1990 census counted nearly four thousand household units and fourteen thousand people, the majority of them "Mexican-origin," in this one-square-mile unincorporated area of Oakview.[3] The many one-level houses and duplexes, punctuated by occasional four-story apartment buildings, together with the lack of sidewalks on some streets, contribute to the barrio's distinctively suburban and spread-out spatial quality, one very unlike the densely packed urban neighborhoods typical in eastern cities or in nearby San Francisco. The buildings are fairly new, post–World War II stucco constructions, and although residents often grow vegetables and brightly colored flowers in their yards, the structures already show signs

of deterioration, and landlords are not always quick to replace malfunc-
tioning plumbing fixtures and heaters. Given the high monthly rents—
one-bedroom apartments cost five hundred to seven hundred
dollars—many of the families live in small, crowded dwellings. A family
of six living in a one-bedroom apartment is not uncommon.

Still, many of these people consider themselves to be quite fortunate
in their living arrangements, especially when they compare themselves
with their more recently arrived, undocumented immigrant peers. While
more-recent newcomers are forced to make do with sleeping niches on
someone else's living-room sofa or in a garage, the people in this study
had achieved a modicum of residential stability. Most of them lived in
modified nuclear-family households, although it was not unusual for
them to share *their* living space—generally for a fee—with kin or friends.

The achievement of residential stability reflects the fact that at the
time of the study—1986 to 1988—all of the participants had lived in the
U.S. for a minimum of three years. In soliciting participants for this
study, I had determined three years of residence as a minimum indicating
long-term settlement. Many of the respondents had been in the United
States for much longer: the average number of years of U.S. settlement
was nearly thirteen. All of these forty-four women and men form part of
a much larger group of Mexican immigrants who are spending prolonged periods of time in the U.S., a group sometimes referred to as
"permanent settlers." Table 1 lists the study participants' names (all
pseudonyms), ages, current occupations, number of children, and years
of residence in the U.S.

When I met them, most of these women and men were living and
working in the U.S. without legal authorization. With the exception of
four families who had achieved legal status after entering the country
without official authorization, the respondents lacked "lawful permanent
resident" status when this study was conducted.[4] These are some of the
people commonly described, in popular vernacular, as "illegal aliens."

I recruited study participants by asking people I knew for names of
others who might participate in the study. In spite of my use of this
snowball technique, which often yields a homogenous group, the persons
in this study represent a diverse group with respect to class, occupational
background, and place of origin in Mexico. Their heterogeneous characteristics indicate the wide range of Mexican immigrants settling in the
U.S. today, and so belie the stereotype that all undocumented immigrants
from Mexico are poor, illiterate, landless peasants. Nearly two-thirds of
the respondents had in fact worked as *campesinos* (peasants) in rural

places which share long traditions of U.S.-bound migration, in states such as Zacatecas, Michoacán, and Jalisco. This is no surprise; these Mexican regions are among the traditional sources for undocumented migrants bound for California (Dagodag, 1975).

A substantial concentration of the Mexican immigrants in the Oakview barrio hailed from a particular rural *municipio* (county area) in the state of Michoacán. The pioneer migrants who settled in Oakview during the 1950s and 1960s came principally from this region, and although the subsequent migration of their kin resulted in the numerical predominance of their *paisanos*, they did not dominate local social affairs when I conducted the research. In fact, people from this area sometimes lied about their place of birth, as they were harshly stigmatized by other, more recently arrived Mexican immigrants, who tended to view them as backward hillbillies prone to committing acts of violence.

During the late 1970s and the 1980s, U.S.-bound undocumented migrants came from more diverse points of origin in Mexico, increasingly from cities (Cornelius, 1992). Some of the study's participants who had migrated during the 1970s and 1980s hailed from Mexico's large urban centers—Guadalajara, Puebla, and the Federal District's sprawling megalopolis—where they had last worked as small entrepreneurs, secretaries, bus drivers, and factory workers. During the 1980s, as Mexico's economic crisis worsened, Mexican undocumented immigrants were more likely than before to come from professional middle-class sectors located in Mexico's largest cities. Since I conducted the study in the late 1980s, and because I designed it in order to examine the experiences of long-term settlers, only a few of the subjects came from middle-class backgrounds.

Most of the study participants had first migrated in their twenties and thirties, and as the chart listing the study participants shows, at the time of the research, many were middle-aged. To my knowledge, all of them were heterosexual, although several spoke of gay family members. The majority were married or living in consensual unions, and were parents of children who had attended or were attending U.S. schools. The respondents' own levels of education varied: many of them had attended three to six years of elementary school, but two men held teaching credentials in Mexico, and one man and one woman had received enough education or on-the-job training to work as accountants. Several of the respondents had received less than one year of formal schooling, but the finesse with which they maneuvered their daily activities rarely betrayed their lack of formal education.

These men and women displayed varying degrees of English proficiency, ranging from no facility to fairly sophisticated colloquial usage. They generally preferred Spanish to negotiate commercial and bureaucratic transactions and to communicate with kin, friends, and neighbors; all of my discussions and interviews with them occurred in Spanish. Most of them held jobs that required minimal English-language skills. Although four of the families had purchased homes in Oakview, many of the respondents could be accurately described as "working poor," struggling each month to scrape together enough cash to pay rent, utilities, and other bills.

METHODS

Over the course of eighteen months, forty-four women and men in twenty-six families allowed me to gather data using participant-observation methods, in-depth tape-recorded interviews, and informal conversations that occurred during my visits to their homes and other sites of shared activities. A tape-recorded group interview with Latina immigrant women participating in a co-dependency group, and my ongoing interactions with the larger immigrant community in the Oakview barrio, also inform this study. These qualitative methods allowed me to assess complex social dynamics related to migration and settlement as they occur in family and community groups.

I used chain or snowball referrals to select a nonrandom sample of forty-four study participants.[5] The majority of these people were undocumented when they entered the U.S., but many of them became successful applicants for legalization. As I was primarily interested in long-term residents, as opposed to sojourner migrants, I recruited study participants who had resided in the U.S. for a minimum of three years. Other studies of Mexican immigrants (Massey et al., 1987; Chavez et al., 1989) also use the three-year-residency criterion as an indicator of long-term settlement.

All of my field interactions and interviews occurred in Spanish. I learned Spanish from my mother, but that language was prohibited when I began first grade in Catholic school, and like many second-generation children, I rejected Spanish as a second-class language. I made subsequent efforts to improve my fluency, and although my Spanish isn't perfect, it served me well enough in the field.

In addition to the interviews, I engaged in participant observation in homes, public meetings, and offices, and at social events. Over the course of eighteen months, I regularly visited most of the twenty-six families in their homes. With some families, this took the form of an informal afternoon or evening visit on a biweekly or, for some periods, a weekly basis, while with other families, I visited as few as three times. During these visits, I observed daily family interactions and conflicts, participating in meals and meal preparation, viewing television and videos, and talking with my informants. I was particularly interested in observing the household division of labor. While my presence in people's homes modified behavior, direct observation yields a more accurate portrayal of peoples' lives than do methods of self-report. As Hochschild (1989) found in a study of working parents, what women and men *say* about the household division of labor or decision making, for example, may be quite different from what they actually *do*.

In addition to these many informal conversations, I tape-recorded and fully transcribed interviews with thirty-eight of the forty-four study participants. The interviews consisted of open-ended questions about life history, with specific questions regarding family and community relations in the migration and settlement process. In some instances, by the time I actually did an interview, I knew elements of the respondent's biography well enough to interject reminders about omissions, or to note discrepancies with what the respondent had previously related. Whenever possible, I interviewed husbands and wives separately. Some respondents, older women in particular, were reluctant to be tape-recorded, and in those cases, I rapidly wrote notes during the interviews, trying to capture as many verbatim quotes as possible. Although all respondents initially agreed to an interview, three men avoided the interview, stating that they were too busy with work schedules, or simply "forgetting" our appointments. Perhaps they distrusted me and my intentions, either because of their legal status or because I bonded too closely with their wives.

The ways that I went about soliciting research subjects varied, but in all cases, either I had an introduction or I waited until some relationship had been established before asking people to serve as participants in the study. I told everyone that I was a student gathering information for a research project, and through community work, I established a visible profile throughout the barrio and gained the acquaintance and, I think, the trust of a wide number of people. Although I was living apart from my husband in order to conduct the study—an arrangement viewed disapprovingly or with pity by many of the study participants—the fact that I was living with my parents minimized the gravity of this error. I sometimes brought my mother to informal gatherings in the park, baby showers, and Mass, and I recruited her to help with child care for several public forums. People saw me, to some extent, in the context of my own family relations. Finally, the timing of my project also assisted my research, as the new immigration legislation effectively made undocumented immigrants "come out," and I became a community activist and personal helper. On a typical day, I drove people to a collections agency or a doctor appointment, visited another family in the afternoon, and attended an evening meeting. Although I explained to those who asked that I studied sociology, some people thought I was studying social work—a likely conclusion, since I seemed to be practicing it.

All of the study participants verbally consented to serve as "human subjects," but before they did so, many of them interviewed me about my background and beliefs. I recall most vividly one man, the father of several adolescent girls, asking me about my religious commitments and my premarital sexual practices. I tried to answer vaguely, but I failed that quiz miserably. Still, he and his wife allowed me to interview them and regularly visit at their household.

As I did community work and personal favors, some people thanked me for my assistance. One woman compared me with a public-health nurse she had known, and another referred to me as a "saint" for helping poor people. Although initially flattered, I grew uncomfortable with these rituals of deference. The results of my help were minimal, and although it seemed cold and calculated of me to do so, I tried to remind people that they were helping me with my project too. Some of the most revealing information I collected was disclosed to me in the context of being a friend, as people enmeshed in explosive family conflicts or problematic decisions often produced unedited but reflective outpourings of emotions and intimate details of their lives. In these instances, I generally did not remind research participants that they were producing "data," but instead reciprocated as an empathetic friend.[6]

WHY AN ETHNOGRAPHY OF SETTLEMENT?

Some readers may wonder why we need an ethnography of settlement. Settlement is not simply the result of an individual deciding to stay permanently in the United States. Even if immigrants are committed to remaining in the U.S., unanticipated events in Mexico—family illness, death of a parent, or the inheritance of property—can quickly sidetrack such plans. For this reason, a research strategy based on simply asking respondents about their settlement intentions has serious limitations.

Immigrants may live and work for many years in the United States while simultaneously keeping alive the dream to return and buy a ranch or a small business in Mexico. Many do return, but as time passes, immigrant women and men become more integrated into economic, social, and cultural life in the United States. While being undocumented may retard acquisition of these ties, undocumented immigrants also make these important connections (Massey et al., 1987). They develop ties to jobs, financial institutions, churches, schools, and to friends and neighbors, and these ties anchor many of them to the U.S.

The ethnographic material assembled in chapter 6, for example, illustrates features of undocumented immigrants' lives that are not easily captured through interview or survey methods. I looked at undocumented immigrants' everyday activities to see how these mundane practices actively construct settlement—an outcome that has important macro-level implications. Settlement, as observers have noted, is an ongoing process that unfolds over time, and ethnographic methods are uniquely suited to capture what people actually do and how this changes over time. Unlike large-scale surveys based on probability samples, intensive participant observation and interviews conducted in an area like Oakview enable one to gain insights into the everyday activities, meanings, and motives of immigrant women and men, so that knowledge is derived from the perspectives of the principal actors as well as established theory.

The goal of this study is not to arrive at a set of universal generalizations, predictions, or propositions regarding immigration, but rather to elucidate the dynamics of a neglected analytic category—gender—in processes of immigration and settlement. The study's findings and analyses complement and enhance those based on survey and demographic research.

ORGANIZATION OF THE BOOK

This study analyzes how the intersection of micro and macro forces shapes the migration and settlement of Mexican undocumented immigrant women and men in a northern California community. Chapter 1 begins by situating the study in the literature from various disciplines, drawing from theories about migration and adaptation, feminist scholarship on gender and inequality, and analyses of settlement.

Chapter 2 provides a brief historical overview and highlights legal and economic arrangements that have set the structural parameters and pressures for the permanent integration of Mexican immigrant families in the

United States. Transformations in political economy set the stage, but do not write the script, for U.S.-bound migration and settlement. Immigrants respond to opportunities created by macro-level forces, but they do so in a social context, and it is the explication of this social context that Chapter 4 addresses.

Chapter 3 introduces in greater depth the people involved in the study, and describes the evolution of the Oakview barrio in the San Francisco Bay area. This chapter also includes biographical sketches of people in five families, and introduces a typology I use to classify migration patterns: family stage migration, where husbands precede the migration of their wives and children; family unit migration, where intact nuclear families migrate together; and independent migration, where unmarried men and women migrate independently.

Chapter 4 focuses on how gender relations in families and social networks shape diverse migration patterns for women and men. While larger forces provide pressures, resources, and opportunities, it is patriarchal gender relations in family and community, together with generation, class, and culture, that determine how those pressures and opportunities lead to particular patterns of migration and settlement. Patriarchal gender relations mediate between broad economic and political factors and actual patterns of migration.

Chapter 5 examines how immigrant women and men in the U.S. reconstitute gender relations. Immigration and resettlement patterns tend to weaken familial patriarchy, as indicated by changes in the gender division of household labor, decision-making power within the family, and women's and men's spatial mobility. While there is a general trend toward the establishment of more gender-egalitarian familial relations, this occurs in a heterogeneous fashion that varies according to the three patterns of migration.

The new gender arrangements forged in these families motivate immigrant women to prolong settlement. Chapter 6 examines how women engage in activities—employment, securing public and private forms of assistance for their families, and building a social nexus of community— that ultimately serve to consolidate family settlement. Through participation in these activities, undocumented immigrant women strengthen their own position in the family, further deepening their commitment to settlement. While Mexican men often play an important part in initiating migration, women play an important part in solidifying settlement. The concluding chapter returns to the initial research questions and suggests the broader implications of the study.

TABLE OF STUDY PARTICIPANTS

I. Family Stage Migration

	Year of Departure[1]	Years in U.S.	Age	Current Occupation	Number of Children
Marcelino Ávila	1957	30	40s	janitor	6
Dolores Ávila	1962	25	50s	laundry worker	
Arturo Barrios	1952	37	60	janitor	7
Isabel Barrios	1964	23	50s	apartment manager	
Raymundo Carbajal	1954	33	50s	janitor/gardener	7
Rebecca Carbajal	1970	17	50s	cafeteria cook	
Manuel Galván	1950	37	70s	retired cook	0
Sidra Galván	1957	30	70s	retired laundry worker	
Pedro Morales (ill)	1964	(23)	60	disabled cook	8
Griselia Morales	1976	11	50s	unemployed	
Rubén Sánchez	1952	35	50s	painter	15
Isa Sánchez (in Mexico)	1983	(1)	—		
Luis Bonilla	1973	14	50	gardener	7
Tola Bonilla	1975	12	40s	domestic worker	
Gerardo Duarte (in Mexico)	1977	—	—	—	4
Delia Duarte	1981	6	30s	domestic worker	
Alberto Gándara	1983	4	30s	warehouse employee	3
María Gándara	1984	3	30s	homemaker/occasional domestic worker	
Eudoro Ibarra	1980	7	40s	auto dismantler	7
Teresa Ibarra	1981	6	30s	domestic worker	
Patricio Macías	1978	9	30s	cook and janitor	3
Blanca Macías	1979	8	30s	homemaker, disabled	
Héctor Valenzuela	1966	21	40s	nursery worker, disabled	9
M. Teresa Valenzuela (deceased)	1974	—	—		

TABLE (continued)

II. Family Unit Migration

	Year of Departure[1]	Years in U.S.	Age	Current Occupation	Number of Children
Ignacio Cerritos	1980	7	30s	baker	6
Jovita Cerritos			30s	baker/domestic worker	
Roberto Melchor	1979	8	30s	box loader	2
Francisca Melchor			30s	plastics polisher	
Ausencio Mendoza	1982	5	40s	self-employed vendor	6
María Mendoza			30s	domestic worker	
Jesús Oseguera (deceased)	1978	9	—	—	
Filomina Oseguera			60s	in-home child care	5
Felipe Palacios	1979	8	30s	dishwasher	2
Trinidad Ochoa			30s	homemaker	(+3)
Jorge Ramírez	1976	11	30s	welder	3
Josefa Ramírez			20s	homemaker	

III. Independent Migration (single at time of migration)

	Year of Departure[1]	Years in U.S.	Age	Current Occupation	Number of Children
María del Carmen Ochoa single	1979	8	50s	domestic worker/ factory assembler	0
Anabel Mesa Castrillo living w/R. Castrillo (R)[2]	1981	6	20s	homemaker/ occasional domestic worker	1
Marisela Ramírez de Hernández married to C. Hernández (R)	1981	6	20s	homemaker/occasional baby-sitter	3
Milagros Aguilar widowed	1978	9	70	home care for elderly	9
Mariana Viñas-Valenzuela (stepmother of 9) married to H. Valenzuela (R)	1977	10	30s	hospital cleaner	0
Margarita Cervantes married to L. Cervantes	1975	12	30s	self-employed vendor	0
Rosario Quiñones married to E. Quiñones	1976	11	30s	domestic/laundry worker	3
María Alicia Navarro living with A. Sánchez	1984	3	30s	domestic worker	3

TABLE (continued)

The Men:

	Year of Departure[1]	Years in U.S.	Age	Current Occupation	Number of Children
Gerónimo López single	1979	8	20s	factory assembly	1
Reynaldo Castrillo living with A. Mesa Castrillo (R)	1971	16	30s	gardener	1
Carlos Hernández living with M. Ramírez de Hernández (R)	1979	8	30s	cement pourer	3
Pablo García single	1980	7	20s	gardener	0
Fidencio Flores living with L. Gonzalez		5	30s	dishwasher	2

1. Year of departure refers to date when noninterrupted stay in the U.S. began (excepting vacations and visits to Mexico). In most cases, this refers to the last year of departure from Mexico. Some of the respondents had departed for and arrived in the U.S. earlier, but had remained temporarily and returned to Mexico. For example, Eudoro and Teresa Ibarra had come to Oakview in 1969 and 1970, respectively, but had returned within a year or two, and did not migrate again until 1980 and 1981, respectively.

2. (R) indicates study participant.

CHAPTER ONE

Immigration, Gender, and Settlement

I came in 1975 just to stay for a spell, at least that's what I thought. One thinks that it's so easy to come, make a little money, and then return to Mexico to put up a little store and maintain oneself with that—that was my thinking when my sister invited me to join her. I wanted to get out from my father's thumb, to make something for myself, but my idea was not to leave forever or to stop helping the family. But once here, it was initially difficult for me to find work, and later I became locked up in the routine of work at the motel. And at first I did not want to learn English out of fear that immigration authorities would catch us, but yes, eventually I did learn English. Now I have my little [flower vending] business, but it is here, not in Mexico. I have my husband, and most of my brothers and sisters are here too. My life, my sorrows and my joys, they are all here now.

Margarita Cervantes

Settlement has a funny way of creeping up on immigrant workers who intend to stay only a short while. With the Immigration Reform and Control Act of 1986, more than 2 million formerly undocumented Mexican immigrants applied for legal status, but many other Mexican immigrants and their families are staying in the United States despite their inability to secure permanent legal residence status, and in spite of their original intentions to remain only a short while.[1] This trend toward staying for prolonged periods of time was well under way by the 1970s and 1980s, signaling the establishment of permanent or "settled-out" immigration.[2] The consequences are visible to even the most casual observer in California, the preferred place of destination for Mexican immigrants, where the surge of marketing efforts directed at Spanish-speaking consumers, and the proliferation of Mexican immigrant communities, are difficult to ignore. The permanent settlement of Mexican immigrants is a principal factor driving the so-called Latinization of California.[3]

1

Among these long-term Mexican immigrant settlers in California and other states, there is a significant presence of women and entire families.[4] In fact, the Mexican undocumented settler population appears to be nearly evenly composed of women and men (Cardenas and Flores, 1986; Passel, 1986), a sharp contrast with the temporary Mexican migrant population, where men predominate.[5] In other words, the well-established, long-staying undocumented immigrant population reflects a balanced sex ratio.

Perhaps the most significant recent development in Mexican immigration to the United States is the concurrent increase in undocumented settlement and the participation of women and entire families in undocumented migration and settlement. As I studied these developments in a California community, I came to see that gender is a fundamental category of analysis for developing theories of immigration and settlement, and that in turn, immigration and resettlement experiences are vital to our understanding of how new immigrants reconstruct gender relations. I also developed a view of settlement that highlights how women's activities advance undocumented immigrant settlement. My aim in this book is to show how gender and immigration are reflexively intertwined. Gender relations shape immigration patterns, and in turn, migration experiences reshape gender relations.

THE INTERSECTION OF IMMIGRATION, GENDER, AND SETTLEMENT

Before looking at the theoretical legacies and implications of these perspectives, it is useful to ask why themes of gender and settlement have been neglected in the immigration literature. Feminist scholarship has shown that gender—that is, the social and cultural ideals, practices, and displays of masculinity and femininity—organizes and shapes our opportunities and life chances. Yet the concept of gender as an organizing principle of social life has encountered resistance and indifference in both mainstream sociology (Stacey and Thorne, 1985) and immigration scholarship conducted in various disciplines (Beuchler, 1976; Brettell and Simon, 1986; Crummet, 1987; Glenn, 1986; Morokvasic, 1984). There is now research on the topic of women and migration sufficient to yield substantive review essays (Pedraza, 1991; Tienda and Booth, 1991), but gender is typically considered in migration theory only when women are the focus.[6] In this book, I argue that gender is an analytical tool equally relevant to our understanding of men's migration as it is to our understanding of women's migration.

Since men predominated in many periods of U.S.-bound Mexican migration, most immigration research has ignored questions of gender altogether, as if men were without gender. This study begins with the premise that an appropriate research strategy requires more than either examining men's gender in isolation or simply "adding" women to the picture. Gender is not simply a variable to be measured, but a set of social relations that organize immigration patterns. The task, then, is not simply to document or highlight the presence of undocumented women who have settled in the U.S., or to ask the same questions of immigrant women that are asked of immigrant men, but to begin with an examination of how gender relations facilitate or constrain both women's *and* men's immigration and settlement. As Joan Acker (1992:568) aptly states, "The relevant question becomes not why are women excluded but to what extent have the overall institutional structure, and the character of particular institutional areas, been formed by and through gender?" Gender is exercised in relational and dynamic ways, and in this study I examine how the social relations of gender contour women's and men's immigration and settlement experiences.

Over the last two decades, a lively literature has debated the nature of patriarchal subordination and domination under capitalism. In an effort to avoid viewing gender as secondary to class inequality, Heidi Hartmann (1976, 1981) conceptualized patriarchy as an independent system of domination rooted in the division of labor and predating capitalism. Critics, however, have argued that this type of dual-systems scheme suggests that patriarchy is a monolithic, ahistorical system where all men have equal interests and privileges, and all women are equally disadvantaged. More recently, this universalizing view has been modified by a framework emphasizing that gender inequality is produced simultaneously with hierarchies of class and race (Collins, 1990; King, 1988; Zinn et al., 1986). Race, class, and gender shape immigrant women's and men's life experiences, and this study also shows how legal status is an important factor in shaping these experiences as well.[7]

Building on these aforementioned works, I define patriarchy as a fluid and shifting set of social relations where men oppress women, in which different men exercise varying degrees of power and control, and in which women collaborate and resist in diverse ways. While patriarchal gender relations are simultaneously constructed and exercised in different arenas, such as the labor market and the state, and through mass

media, I suggest that important elements of patriarchal power and meanings are constructed in family relations, and that macro-level economic
and political transformations such as those that produce mass immigration are key to the social construction of patriarchy. Examining connections of family-based patriarchal relations and broader global processes
may offer a dynamic view of women's subordination and resistance that
goes beyond the public/private dichotomy.[8]

I prefer to conceptualize patriarchal gender relations within family
relations rather than in the "household" or the "domestic sphere of
reproduction," as others have, because a focus on family relations draws
attention to the ideological and cultural meanings embedded in families.
Moreover, family relations may span household units which simultaneously exist in two different countries. For years feminist scholarship has
focused on the domestic unit of reproduction precisely in order to avoid
dealing with the family, which anthropologist Rayna Rapp (1978) identified as an ideological and normative construct.[9] A consequence of this,
as sociologist Sherri Grasmuck (1991:2) has pointed out in a discussion
of women's subordination in Latin America, is that because of the analytic emphasis on the reproductive sphere and the household, "the
autonomous role played by kin structures in regulating social life has
been underestimated." My approach in this study is to focus on the social
relations that people identify as the most experientially salient in their
lives. This book, then, examines how immigrant husbands and wives,
mothers, fathers, sons and daughters, siblings, and extended kin enact
and reconstruct patriarchal gender relations in families. Another important institution for the social construction and expression of gender relations is social networks. Patriarchal gender relations are contextually
expressed and contested in families and social networks.

Historical, conceptual, and methodological factors explain the neglect, until very recently, of settlement in the study of Mexican immigration. Historically, much of Mexican immigration to the U.S. was
dominated by male migrants on temporary sojourns, and hence researchers focused on sojourner migration, not settlement. Undoubtedly,
political agendas also exerted influence, as many U.S. politicians and
employers found Mexican immigration more palatable when defined as
temporary labor migration. Conceptually, settlement remains an impre-
cise and indiscrete category, further discouraging research and analysis
(Massey, 1986; Chavez, 1988; Rouse, 1992). Finally, there is a methodological obstacle to studying settlement when undocumented immigrants
are concerned, as people with "illegal" status are naturally reluctant to

expose themselves to scrutiny while attempting to maintain an established, settled life in the U.S. For this reason, many studies of undocumented immigrants have been exclusively or primarily conducted in Mexico, where return migrants are surveyed in their place of origin; for research done in the U.S., apprehended undocumented immigrants have served as the research subjects. As many observers have pointed out, these methodological strategies effectively undersample and underestimate the presence of both long-term settlers and women.[10] This study attempts to join the two relatively neglected areas of analysis—gender and immigrant settlement—in the examination of Mexican undocumented immigrants in a California community.

TOWARD A THEORY OF MIGRATION AS A SOCIAL PROCESS

Theories based on macrostructural transformations or "push-pull" analyses cannot explain the immense variety of socially distinct migration routes. Take, for example, the familiar pattern whereby husbands migrate before their wives. Why does this pattern continue when there is now a well-documented, objective demand for immigrant women's labor? Why do some families continue to follow this route while others do not? In order to answer such questions, one needs to consider the immediate social context in which migration occurs. This social context is often lost in the two competing theoretical frameworks which dominate the study of immigration: the orthodox, equilibrium perspective; and the macrostructural approach.

Derived from neoclassical economics and congruent with modernization theory, the orthodox perspective, alternately called the equilibrium or "push-pull" model, posits migration as an individual response to negative "push" factors at the point of origin and positive "pull" factors at the point of destination (Lee, 1966; Todaro, 1969, 1976). At its most extreme, this perspective casts the individual migrant as a purely self-interested economic agent, as an actor who compares present income with potential earnings in alternative locations. This analysis yields a one-dimensional view of human action, flattening complex social processes into a random composition of generic, individual calculations.[11] Moreover, the voluntarist assumptions embedded in this paradigm ignore the contingent social structural factors that shape migration, so that individual calculus occurs in a vacuum devoid of history and political economy. The conditions which give rise to "push" and "pull" factors

are not investigated, but are assumed to derive from distinct, uncon-
nected societies or, more distortingly, from universal conditions.

Macrostructural approaches to the study of migration developed in
opposition to the neoclassical model, and redirected the research focus
to the structural and historical factors that make labor migration possible.[12] Unlike the orthodox model, the structural model conceptualizes
migration as a phenomenon internal to one global "world system," not
as the movement between two autonomous spheres.

Research informed by macrostructural and comparative historical approaches illuminates how broad structural factors induce and support
migration, offering a necessary corrective to the orthodox views by providing the missing "big picture" focus. Yet in explaining the origins of
migration and the functions that labor migrations play in the development and maintenance of modern capitalism, the social dimensions of
immigration are neglected. Conspicuously absent from the macrostructural perspective is any sense of human agency or subjectivity. Rather
than human beings, immigrants are portrayed as homogeneous, nondif-
ferentiated objects responding mechanically and uniformly to the same
set of structural forces.

This study views immigrants as active participants in the process of
migration, not as victims of structural forces or as robots computing cost
benefits of their moves. A complementary research strategy to this perspective requires some attention to the diversity of immigration patterns.
Beyond broadly defined categories of border commuters, seasonal or
sojourner migrants, and settlers, which catalog outcomes more than
social patterns, variations of gender, generation, class, and culture in
immigration remain obscured in the macrostructural theories. These
variations should be unveiled.

In the late 1970s and early 1980s, immigration researchers addressed
some of these issues by focusing on more intermediate units of analysis:
the household and immigrant social networks. These efforts, however,
remained flawed by several unexamined assumptions. Analyses presented the household as a unified collectivity, ignoring divergent and
conflicting interests, and thus continued to obscure gender and generation as social relations influencing immigration. And while studies high-
lighted the importance of transnational social networks in encouraging
Mexican immigration and showed how the networks incorporate demographic diversity as they mature, research did not explore how gender
may regulate these social networks. Just as the household model assumes
that all resources are shared equally among household and family mem-

bers, studies focusing on networks imply, for example, that married women automatically benefit from the resources and expertise located in their husbands' social network. Chapter 4 begins with a more in-depth look at how the household model and approaches focusing on immigrant social networks have unwittingly masked the power of gender in shaping migration.

AN ALTERNATIVE PERSPECTIVE

Although the origins of undocumented Mexican immigration lie in the political and economic transformations occurring both within the United States and Mexico and in linkages between the two countries, it is the immediate context of family and community relations (such as social networks) that shape how people will respond to pressures exerted by structural transformations. With the objective of further understanding how this intermediate level shapes migration, the approach developed in this book examines families and immigrant social networks as gendered institutions. Gender relations in families circumscribe migration options and decisions. Together with age, class, and marital status, gender places various constraints on individuals.

Migration opportunities are also circumscribed by transnational social networks. While the immigration literature underscores the importance of these social networks, insofar as they provide important resources and connections, most of the literature either ignores the gender-based character of these networks or assumes that male-dominated immigrant networks are natural and do not need further inquiry.[13] An exception here is the analysis by Sherrie A. Kossoudji and Susan I. Ranney (1984), based on data collected from a Mexican national survey, that suggests the formation since the 1970s of immigrant networks by young single Mexican women. Although survey data do not lend themselves to the probing of the character of network supports and dynamics, Kossoudji and Ranney's observation serves as a meritorious point of departure for exploring the internal dynamics of these networks.

This study begins with the assumption that we must question and investigate the gender-based character of immigrant social networks in order to understand immigration patterns. We cannot assume, for example, that women are automatically accorded access to male-dominated immigrant networks, or that women necessarily migrate with the help of other women. The task, then, is to consider not only the separate spheres of women's and men's immigrant networks and cross-gender ties, but also the dynamics of gendered activities and relations within the networks.

Understanding the gendered patterns of migration requires an examination of the internal organizational features of family and community relations. Specifically, this requires attention to the power relations of gender in immigrant social networks and in families, as they constrain or facilitate migration for women and men. Gender relations in family and community help determine how the opportunities and limits of broader political and economic forces translate into different migration patterns. This is not a one-way street. As I point out in the next section, political and economic transformations in Mexico and the United States are also affecting gender relations.

GENDER RELATIONS: ADAPTATION, PERSEVERANCE, OR TRANSFORMATION?

Sociological studies of immigrants have traditionally focused on immigrant responses to the new social environment in the country of destination. In this regard, much of the research has been grounded in, and limited by, the language of assimilation, adaptation, and acculturation. While these concepts improved upon late nineteenth- and early twentieth-century eugenic notions that proclaimed the biological inferiority of immigrants, the sociological imagination was confined to examining only how immigrants fail or succeed in becoming more like the U.S.-born.

These concepts were developed through the studies conducted by Chicago School sociologists in the late nineteenth and early twentieth centuries. Informed by the classical theory of urbanism, these studies revealed negative implications about immigrants' lives in the cities. At their most optimistic, these studies concluded that accommodation would be attained after a period of social disorganization, transience, and anomie. According to this "breakdown" perspective, redemption is predicated on a long process of immigrant settlement, during which secondary associations replace the disintegrated primary groups and traditional values (Wirth, 1938; Gordon, 1964).[14]

Social historians in the late 1960s and 1970s challenged the view of immigrant adaptation as breakdown with claims that the perseverance of pre-migration culture and norms characterizes immigrant life (Thompson, 1966; Gutman, 1977; Yans-McLaughlin, 1977). The proponents of this paradigm of cultural continuity argued that pre-migration culture provides a rich source of support for political resistance in the new society.[15]

While neither the breakdown nor the cultural-continuity paradigm focuses on the changing character of gender relations among new immigrants, these theoretical traditions provide a point of departure for an analysis of gender and immigrant settlement. If we translate these theoretical stances to the realm of gender, the following questions emerge: Do traditional gender relations disintegrate once they are immersed in the new urban society? Or do they remain intact, with patriarchal cultural legacies continuing as before? The answer lies somewhere between these absolutes, but answering these questions first requires specification of traditional gender relations among Mexican immigrants.

When looking at Mexican and Chicano families, Anglo observers have often confused an ideal type family, which resembles a caricature of submissive, self-sacrificing women and dominant, aggressive, tyrannical men, with what is a more varied social reality. Buttressed more by negative and ethnocentric stereotypes than by research, the Anglo gaze casts the Chicano family—and by extrapolation, the Mexican family—as a static, homogeneous entity where patriarchy and pathology reign (Ybarra, 1983; Zinn, 1979). An extensive body of research on Chicano and Mexican families in the U.S. indicates that these families are not all characterized by a uniformly extreme type of patriarchy, although patriarchal ideologies and divisions of labor certainly endure.[16] Looking at Mexican cultural traditions and societal transformations provides some clues to identifying the character of Mexican patriarchal relations.

MEXICAN PATRIARCHAL TRADITIONS

Well-defined gender ideals prescribe behavior for masculine and feminine behavior in traditional Mexican society. Machismo calls for men to be sexually assertive, independent, and emotionally restrained, to wield absolute authority over their wives and children, and to serve as family breadwinners.[17] The ideological corollary for women, which some commentators refer to as *marianismo* (marianism), is modeled on the Catholic Virgin Madonna, and prescribes dependence, subordination, responsibility for all domestic chores, and selfless devotion to family and children (Stevens, 1973; Mummert, 1990; Soto, 1986).

Machismo and *marianismo* are ideological constructs that may inform people's actions, but they are not themselves actual patterns of behavior.[18] In the United States, distinctions between Mexican cultural legacies and contemporary lived realities are easily ignored, as Mexico is popularly viewed as the epitome of patriarchal domination, and Mexican rural society as home to the most exaggerated manifestations of patriarchy. But to what extent do patriarchal cultural ideals and stereotypes coincide with everyday practices in contemporary Mexican society?

Examining rural traditions is a good place to begin. Gail Mummert's (1990) research in rural Michoacán indicates that until the 1960s, gender relations in peasant society were indeed characterized by clear-cut divisions of authority, a sharp household division of labor by gender, and different spatial sites for men's and women's activities. Men served as the undisputed patriarchs in family life, and with the help of their oldest sons, they took responsibility for supporting the family. Women cared for the home and the children, remaining cloistered in the domestic sphere, and emerging only to fetch water, attend Mass, or wash clothes in the river. While men were allowed autonomy, young single women's spatial mobility and courtship were highly restricted in order to avoid violent abductions by men seeking wives (Arizpe and Aranda, 1981). Upon marriage, newly wedded couples lived with the husband's parents until they became economically independent (de la Peña, 1984), and in these patrilocal arrangements, which resemble the classic patriarchy of Asian and Muslim societies, daughters-in-law experienced subordination to their parents-in-law, especially their mothers-in-law (Arias and Mummert, 1987).[19] Traditionally, informal polygamous arrangements were not unusual in Mexican families of various socioeconomic classes. Some observers have noted that the mother-child bond, not the husband-wife link, served as the emotional core of family life in Mexico (Romanucci-Ross, 1973; LeVine, 1993).

RECENT CHANGES IN MEXICAN PATRIARCHY

Twentieth-century urbanization, industrialization, and migration have profoundly transformed Mexican society. The daily lives of contemporary rural peasants and of working-class and middle-class urban dwellers in Mexico do not rigidly conform to traditional patriarchal cultural ideals, or even to the practices that seemed firmly in place only a few decades ago. The emergence of women in the Mexican political arena may be one indicator of these changes.[20] By the 1980s, Mexican women made up 80 percent of active participants in territorially based urban movements; they composed a high proportion of the rank-and-file members in the teachers', nurses', and garment workers' trade unions, and 1982 witnessed the first female presidential candidate (Carrillo, 1986, 1990). While women's political activism is often based on their identities and needs as mothers, a role imbued with a double-edged reverence in Mexican society, their movement into the public sphere of politics is significant.[21]

During the mid–twentieth century, migration transformed Mexico from a rural nation to an urban one. As in many parts of Latin America, in Mexico women predominated in rural-urban migration, and women contributed significantly to the building of new urban communities.[22] Urbanization is an important factor because it is associated with the increase in women's education and employment. Although Mexican women work in commercial export agribusiness in rural areas,[23] employment opportunities for women concentrate in cities. In addition, the expansion in educational and health-care systems during the 1970s has also altered the lives of Mexican women, especially urban women (LeVine, 1993). National fertility rates declined during the 1970s and 1980s; the average number of children a Mexican woman bore declined from 6.7 in 1970 to 3.46 in 1989 (UNICEF, 1991, cited in LeVine, 1993:197).

In spite of traditional patriarchal ideals that mandate against women working, Mexican women's labor-force participation increased more than 50 percent during the 1970s, a period when men's labor-force participation increased less than 10 percent (Pedrero and Rendón, 1982; García and Oliveira, 1984, cited in Oliveira, 1990:33). In the 1970s, job demand came from the tertiary sector, where relatively educated single women took jobs as teachers, medical assistants, and secretaries and in administrative positions (Oliveira, 1990), and from the informal sector, where poor women, many of them rural-urban migrants, took jobs as paid domestic workers and street peddlers (Arizpe, 1977). Multinational *maquiladora* export assembly plants along Mexico's northern border, supported by the Mexican Border Industrialization Program, also account for the dramatic increase in women's employment.[24] During the 1970s, women accounted for 75 to 90 percent of *maquiladora* factory workers, and most of them were young, single, childless women (Fernández-Kelly, 1983).

While in the 1960s and 1970s it was primarily single women who sought wage work in Mexico, with the economic crisis of the 1980s, financial needs propelled married women with small children into the labor force (Benería and Roldán, 1987; Escobar Latapí and González de la Rocha, 1988; Chant, 1991; Oliveira, 1990; González de la Rocha, 1988).[25] As the dynamism of the tertiary sector diminished in the 1980s, more women concentrated in informal-sector jobs—in manual occupations where they were self-employed, worked part-time, or did some type of income-earning activity in the home (Benería and Roldán, 1987; Oliveira, 1990). Many types of unregulated, informal-sector work—for example, vending or doing assembly in the home—allow women to still assume child-rearing and domestic responsibilities in the home (Arizpe, 1977; Benería, 1992). The concentration of Mexican women—especially older, married women with children—in the informal sector both underscores that Mexico's pattern of development has not created sufficient employment for women, and testifies to the tenacity of patriarchal divisions of labor in the home, which mandate that mothers take primary responsibility for their home and children.

Male migration to the United States is another factor that has accelerated women's employment in Mexico. Meager remittances and the prolonged absences of migrant husbands, starting during the bracero program (1942–64)[26] and continuing in recent decades, often propelled women into the labor force, in agricultural occupations previously defined as male, and in newly created occupations where labor is exclusively or primarily female, such as jobs in packinghouses, in *maquiladoras*, and in shoe, clothing, textile manufacturing, and home-work assembly.[27]

Have Mexican women's increased levels of employment challenged traditional patterns of domestic patriarchy? While women's incorporation into the paid labor force has eroded men's positions as sole family providers, women's labor does not necessarily signal women's emancipation either in the public sphere or in the domestic sphere. As is the case in the U.S., women in Mexico earn significantly less than men do, and they are subject to occupational segregation and sex discrimination and harassment.[28] And just as in the United States, the inferior earnings of Mexican women are often justified by patriarchal assumptions that men deserve wages large enough to support their families, and that women are necessarily secondary or supplementary earners and thus deserve less pay (Ortega, 1988).[29]

Research conducted by Fernández-Kelly (1983) in the *maquiladora* factory plants reveals that the employment of daughters, wives, and mothers has neither eroded domestic patriarchy nor enhanced women's positions in families. Husbands and fathers, when they are present, still maintain family authority, and employed women still take primary responsibility for domestic household chores. One arena of control that does appear to be affected by women's employment in the *maquiladoras* is women's enhanced spatial mobility and concentration in new public spaces; Fernández-Kelly reports that in their leisure hours, young women congregate in discotheques and the all-female *cervezerías* (beer bars).

When women's employment occurs in regions of Mexico marked by U.S.-bound male migration, patriarchal gender relations may show more receptiveness to change. Gail Mummert's (1990) research in the rural villages surrounding Zamora, Michoacán, where young, single women entered wage labor in the mid-1960s, underlines how women's employment in commercial agriculture, in conjunction with male wage labor in the U.S., has brought about rapid and significant changes in gender relations. Female employment has shifted from being a stigmatized rarity to a virtual rite of passage, an expectation for all young, single women that will allow them to escape household drudgery and isolation. Initially, recruitment efforts focused on obtaining parental permission by assuring parents that their daughters would be properly chaperoned. Today, young women are no longer cloistered in the home, but walk about with their friends, with whom they take buses outside the village to the fields and packinghouses. While the first generation of female workers turned over their entire earnings to their parents, young women now either keep all of it, or contribute only part of their paychecks to their families and spend the rest as they please, usually on clothes and cosmetics. Even when working daughters compliantly turn over their salary to parents, young women have acquired more decision-making power in the domestic arena (Arias and Mummert, 1987). Courting patterns are more open, and in less than two decades there has been a shift away from patrilocality to matrilocality or neolocality, as mothers and daughters pool their earnings to purchase the new couple land, and thus avoid the subordination a newly married daughter suffers when living with parents-in-law (Arias and Mummert, 1987; Mummert, 1990; Rosado, 1990).

In Los Altos de Jalisco, a region with a long tradition of U.S.-bound migration, women are frequently sighted driving trucks that transport cattle fodder, and they earn income by selling, and by embroidering, sewing, or knitting, products in their home (Alarcòn, 1988). Research conducted by Mercedes González de la Rocha (1989) in this region indicates that many young women no longer see patriarchal authority as legitimate. In particular, the working daughters of fathers off on long-term sojourns in the U.S. now refuse to submit to their fathers' patriarchal control, and when fathers return, daughters "obey" them only symbolically. As one young woman in her twenties related: "My father was like a stranger to my sisters and me. He left when I was two years old and returned when I was seven—well, what kind of father is that? . . . We grew up without him and we learned to decide ourselves, just with our mother. So we more or less do what we want." (González de la Rocha, 1989, translated by Hondagneu-Sotelo).

Young, single women are not the only ones who undergo these transformations. In a Zapotec village in Oaxaca, Stephens (1991) found that men's migration during the bracero era allowed women to branch out into commercial spinning and weaving. As one married mother recalled: "I first got to be independent when my husband went to work in the United States in 1952. He was gone most of the time from 1952 to 1964, from two to twelve months per year. The whole time he was away he only sent money twice—about twenty dollars. I didn't spend this money, I saved it until he returned. I had six children born during that period. When he left the first time, I already had two little ones. . . . You know the whole time I worked like a mule" (Stephens, 1991:114).

It would be misleading to overstate these transformations in domestic patriarchy. Although women may "take the reins" during men's long-term absences by making decisions, securing employment, and venturing beyond the domestic sphere, their behavior often remains subject to strong double standards. Sexual infidelity, for example, may be tolerated in a man, who is traditionally allowed to maintain a *casa chica* with a second woman and children, but a woman left alone by her sojourning husband is often under the watchful eyes of other villagers, and any contact with an unrelated man may be cause for suspicion (Cárdenas, 1983, cited in Alarcon, 1988). Yet young women's acceptance of these double standards may be eroding.[30] Moreover, among the urban working class and lower middle class, informal polygamous arrangements appear to be declining due to the growing acceptability of divorce and because it is simply too expensive for a man to help support more than one household (LeVine, 1993:92).

There is indeed ample evidence that Mexican gender relations are patriarchal. Yet urbanization, women's increased participation as income earners, and immigration have begun to erode men's dominance over women in Mexican families. Patriarchy exists in Mexican families, but it endures in varying degrees.[31] This premise warns against treating "the Mexican family" as a monolithic entity, as a subject always preceded by a singular article.

Do traditional forms of patriarchy break down or continue in the U.S.? First, there is little evidence of social chaos or anomie as postulated by theories of breakdown. Affectual, primary groups, such as family and kin, constitute one of the principal spheres where patriarchy is exerted, and these ties do not wither away but may, in fact, be fortified by the exigencies of migration and resettlement.[32] On the other hand, the cultural-continuity model wrongly assumes that there is a uniform, static patriarchal culture that immigrants carry from the old country. In reality, patriarchal relations in Mexican families, as the literature above illustrates, take various forms and are modified by a range of pressures. This study specifies this range, examining the contingencies and complexities of gender in migration and settlement.

In this study I use an interactionist view that acknowledges the initiative and agency of members of both sexes, as well as the fluidity of culture and social structure. The new environment in which immigrants settle is in a state of flux, in part due to the growth and maturation of the immigrant community. Men and women together uphold, even as they alter, patriarchal institutions.

In their daily lives and actions, immigrants draw upon social norms and traditional cultural frameworks, but they do so in this new, changing social environment. Immigrants arrive with cultural and ideological baggage, but in the new society, as they unpack and rearrange it, they discard elements and adopt new ones; women, for example, may take up new activities such as working for wages, attending meetings in the evenings, and driving, and they may exert authority over family matters previously out of their control. Women and men may not always agree on these arrangements. Traditional social relations and cultural resources neither disintegrate nor continue intact, but are reshaped through processes of migration and resettlement.

In short, the cultural legacies of patriarchy are selectively reproduced and rearranged through migration and resettlement in the new society. Family and community relationships, the maturation of the immigrant community, and the ways these intersect with the local economy form a constellation that reconstructs gender relations.

TOWARD A WOMEN-CENTERED
THEORY OF SETTLEMENT

In the book *Birds of Passage* (1979), economist Michael J. Piore laid the foundation for most contemporary thinking on immigrant settlement with his two-stage model, which focuses on the immigrant's shifting locus of social identity from the community of origin to the new society.[33] While a number of studies confirm Piore's general propositions regarding sociopsychological transitions, the framework itself does not tell how these shifts arise, but instead lapses into an easy, if not very useful, circular logic. At its most succinct, the logic maintains that the longer immigrants stay, the less likely they are to deliberately live in extreme frugality and to work as many hours as possible, and hence the more likely they are to permanently settle. This sort of tautological reasoning tells us little about how settlement is socially constructed. Certainly incorporation into the new society occurs gradually, with the accumulation of time and experience (Bohning, 1972; Piore, 1979), but what exactly does settlement entail, and how does it unfold?

Studies of Mexican undocumented immigrant settlement identify family formation as an important key to settlement (Browning and Rodríguez, 1982, 1985; Chavez, 1988).[34] When immigrant workers form families, they are more likely to become enmeshed in a myriad of community institutions, such as schools, medical institutions, churches, and clubs. And as children of Mexican immigrants are born and raised in the United States, they grow attached to their surroundings and peers, and are increasingly reluctant to return to Mexico.[35]

Family formation strengthens ties to the new society, and working from this observation, Douglas S. Massey (1986) proposes a model of settlement that involves interpersonal, institutional, and economic dimensions. The interpersonal refers to social ties immigrant families establish with each other and with citizens; institutional integration refers to participation in social clubs and public institutions, such as school attendance for children; and economic integration refers to patterns of employment and consumption. Beyond these indices of integration, how exactly is settlement or integration established?

The question is easily posed, but less simply answered. As Massey (1986) has noted, settlement is a "slippery" concept, as the permanency of one's stay in a country is never fully established until death. Due to the geographical proximity of Mexico, this is especially true of Mexican immigrants. Even immigrants who insist they are permanently committed to staying in the U.S. may in fact be drawn back by unanticipated events, such as the death or illness of a parent or the return migration of a spouse. Similarly, immigrants who say they wish to depart to their home country may in fact remain in the U.S. a lifetime, as months and then years pass and they become more integrated into economic, social,

and cultural life in the United States. Settlement is usually posed dichoto-
mously with sojourner migration. In reality, Mexican immigrant settlement often derives from sojourner or circular migration, and hence
settlement cannot be confidently treated as a discrete condition (Massey,
1986). Moreover, migration creates new transnational communities
(Goldring, 1993; Rouse, 1989, 1992). Taking a more comparative view
may highlight some of the fundamental differences that distinguish settlement from circular or sojourner migration.

In circular migrant labor, migrants live in the country of destination
only while employed, and when not employed they return to their country of origin, where their families remain. This system of migration is
characterized by the physical separation of employment and family home
residence, as well as by the physical separation of the costs of maintaining and renewing labor (Burawoy, 1976). Immigrant workers receive the
resources necessary for daily subsistence or maintenance in the country
of destination, but the workers are renewed in their country of origin.

Settlement is characterized by both family reunification or formation
and the joining of maintenance and renewal in the new country. In
settlement, the resources needed for daily subsistence—what Burawoy
(1976) calls "maintenance costs"—are provided only in one country.
Settled immigrant workers no longer enjoy ready access to resources
generated by their families in Mexico. The resources for daily sustenance
derive from the U.S., and immigrant families discover that they must
purchase daily sustenance in an economy with higher prices. What hap-
pens to settled undocumented immigrants who are not accorded the
basic protections and entitlements of U.S. citizens, and who in general
earn a smaller income than U.S. citizens do?

The early stages of household or family settlement are particularly
expensive for undocumented immigrants (Browning and Rodríguez,
1982), and those involved in such settlement may initially undergo
downward social mobility (Briody, 1987). Immigrants respond by putting forth multiple wage earners, and by devising shared living arrangements during the initial period of settlement. Several incomes can better
accommodate a family's increased needs, so multiple wage earners, including women and teenage children, enter the labor force in order to
provide resources sufficient for the family's daily needs. In those families
where women were previously not employed in the wage-labor force, the
exigencies of daily maintenance in the U.S., coupled with with an increase in job opportunities, prompts the relaxation of patriarchal ideology that says women should not work (Briody, 1987; Browning and

Rodríguez, 1982, 1985). Meager incomes are also stretched when several families, kin, and unrelated individuals share the same residence.

One may look at settlement as a series of microprocesses related to household and family establishment, or one may take a macro view that emphasizes the reunification of labor maintenance and renewal. From either angle, it is clear that the presence of women and entire families is key to settlement. Close attention to gender dynamics deepens understanding of these processes. In *Issei, Nisei, Warbride* (1986), a study of Japanese immigrant and Japanese-American women, Evelyn Nakano Glenn offers three promising points of departure for developing a theory of immigrant settlement that encompasses families and highlights women's contributions.

First, Glenn notes that the employment of Japanese immigrant women provided crucial earnings that allowed for the establishment of their families' economic position in the new society. Second, women's work encompassed a wide range of reproductive activities necessary to maintain family members in the work force. And third, Glenn highlights how Japanese immigrant women played an important role in settlement by creating and perpetuating group culture for the family.

Settlement, as defined by the unification in one country of family residence and employment, and the maintenance and reproduction of labor, hinges on the presence of immigrant women and entire families. Acknowledging these patterns raises news questions about immigrants: What are the defining features of settlement, and what role do women play in constructing these elements? How do gendered practices and meanings enter into these processes?

CHAPTER TWO

The History of Mexican Undocumented Settlement in the United States

Early in my research in the Oakview barrio I heard a poignant cliché: "It's not Mexicans but California that migrated to the United States." This simple statement refers to the fact that prior to 1848, Mexico included what is today the southwestern region of the United States, so that subsequent Mexican immigrants and their descendants found themselves living and working in conquered territory. In fact, one could argue that California migrated north "illegally." Another popular saying refers to contemporary Mexican immigration as *la reconquista* (the reconquest). Although the large Chicano or U.S.-born population of Mexican descent is indeed largely the outcome of post-1848 immigration, the term *reconquista* misrepresents the legacy of labor exploitation and racial subordination that Mexican immigrants and Chicanos have endured in the United States.[1]

Contemporary Mexican undocumented immigration is characterized by a significant presence of women and entire families, increasing integration into permanent settlement communities, and employment in diverse sectors of the economy. This chapter traces the legacy of the bracero program, and economic and political transformations in Mexico and the U.S. as they supported the trend toward long-term settlement of many Mexican undocumented immigrants in the U.S., especially since the late 1960s. These larger structural transformations are best understood by reviewing the historical antecedents of contemporary Mexican immigration.

HISTORICAL ANTECEDENTS

The historical movement of Mexican workers to the U.S. has been characterized by an "ebb and flow" or "revolving door" pattern of labor migration, one often calibrated by seasonal labor demands, economic recessions, and mass deportations.[2] As early as 1911, a report to the U.S. Congress issued by the Dillingham Commission lauded temporary Mexican labor migration and warned of the dangers of permanent Mexican settlement, claiming that although Mexicans "are not easily assimilated, this is of no very great importance as long as most of them return to their native land. In the case of the Mexican, he is less desirable as a citizen than as a laborer" (U.S. Congress, 1911:690–91). Although some employers encouraged the immigration of Mexican women and entire families in order to stabilize and expand an available, exploitable work force, many other employers, assisted at times by government-sponsored "bracero programs," recruited only men for an elastic, temporary labor supply, a reserve army of labor that could be discarded when redundant. Employers did not absolutely command the movement of Mexican workers, but employers' needs constructed a particular structure of opportunities that shaped migration.

Mexicans began migrating to work in U.S. agriculture, mining, and railroading during the late nineteenth century, when post–Civil War U.S. industrial expansion generated new demands for the Southwest's primary products. Previously, a predominantly male Asian immigrant labor force had provided the key to development of the West, but the 1882 Chinese Exclusion Act and the 1907 "gentlemen's agreement" with Japan curtailed this source of labor. As the railroads extended into western Mexico in the late nineteenth century, *enganchistas* (labor recruiters) sought Mexican workers to build and maintain the railroad lines, and then to work in U.S. mines and agriculture (Cardoso, 1980). Mexican migrants in the late nineteenth century were primarily men, but many Mexican women were also working in the Southwest during this period.[3] Most of these migrants appear to have stayed temporarily, as they did not significantly increase the permanent Mexican-origin population in the United States (McLemore and Romo, 1985).

Economic development in the Southwest and the extension of the railways coincided with Mexico's rapid-paced economic development based on foreign investment and export-led growth. The consolidation of the hacienda system under Porfirio Díaz's autocratic regime (1876–1911) displaced a growing peasant population from a communal system of land tenure and transformed them into landless workers who lacked sources of employment.[4] Together with inflation and U.S. labor demands, these conditions accounted for a substantial increase in the U.S. Mexican population from 1900 to 1910. Although Mexicans were concentrated in southwestern agriculture, by 1908 they worked throughout the Midwest and as far north as Chicago in numerous industries. Many of these laborers eventually returned to Mexico, but settlements emerged around isolated railway camps, and along the border in South Texas, where labor recruiters went to seek more workers (Cardoso, 1980).

The period from World War I until the Great Depression marked the first great wave of Mexican immigration, launched when wartime labor shortages in U.S. agriculture prompted a contract-labor program for male Mexican workers.[5] During 1917–21, seventy-two thousand Mexicans registered to work in the fields of the Southwest and the Midwest as temporary contract workers, and countless more migrant workers worked without official contracts or documents. Thousands of Mexicans also found work in factories, packinghouses, and restaurants in eastern and midwestern cities, and in 1918 the contract-labor program officially expanded to include nonagricultural workers (Cardoso, 1980:48). Still, until the 1920s, most of these Mexican workers were concentrated in rural areas.

The economic disruption and violence of the Mexican revolution (1910–19), and of the Cristero Rebellion in the central western area of Mexico (1926–29), motivated more northward migration during the 1920s.[6] During this period the booming U.S. economy provided both urban and rural jobs for Mexican workers, and Mexican families settled into the already growing barrios of Los Angeles, El Paso, and San Antonio. These settlement communities also served as labor-distribution centers for Mexican workers who were recruited to rural areas of the Southwest and the Midwest (Romo, 1983).[7]

By the 1920s, many employers sought a more stabilized, steady immigrant labor force. In the sugar-beet fields of Colorado and the midwestern states, growers discovered that they could encourage stabilization by hiring entire families to work (Taylor, 1929; Valdés, 1991).[8] Similarly, in the cotton fields of Texas, growers restricted labor mobility by incorporating Mexican women into a system of family tenant farming. Growers found that they could put women and children to work at lower wages, and that when accompanied by their families, men more willingly endured harsh working conditions (González, 1983).[9] Many of these families performed seasonal farmwork, and lived in cities in between harvests. Although the majority remained concentrated in the Southwest, by the 1920s Mexicans were working in many areas of the United States.

In the 1920s, family immigration made up a larger portion of Mexican immigration than it had in prior decades. Although men accounted for 65 to 70 percent of the Mexican immigrants who legally entered the U.S., it is probable that many of them were later joined by their wives and families, who entered "illegally" in order to avoid paying entry fees (Cardoso, 1980:82). During this period, the Mexican anthropologist Manuel Gamio (1971a, first published 1930) chronicled the emergence of segregated settlement communities. Based on numerous sources—including data gathered from postal money orders remitted to families in Mexico—he concluded that most Mexican migrants were intent on staying only temporarily in the United States. Paul Taylor (1929, 1983), an economist who also conducted studies of Mexican immigrant labor in the 1920s and 1930s, argued that the winter decline in remittances reflected seasonal patterns of agricultural work, and that Mexican immigrants were in fact settling permanently in the United States.[10] Other sources concur that Mexican immigration during the 1920s was characterized by family immigration and settlement into urban areas (Romo, 1983; Weber, 1989).

The Great Depression prompted the deportation to Mexico of as many as half a million people, a group that included Mexican undocumented immigrants, legal permanent residents, and U.S. citizens of Mexican descent (Hoffman, 1976:126). The deportees, reflecting the increase in family migration during the 1920s, included substantial numbers of women and children.[11] Beginning in 1931, local governments and relief agencies threatened to cut Mexican families' public relief, and sometimes paid for the families' return transportation to Mexico. Thousands of Mexican families with their accumulated possessions loaded automobiles and boarded trains bound for the border.[12] By 1940, the Mexican population in the United States had declined to about half of what it had been in 1930 (González, 1983). Deportation campaigns, seasonal agricultural work, and labor-recruitment programs sponsored by the government and employers ensured that a significant proportion of Mexican immigrants during the early twentieth century remained in the United States only temporarily (García y Griego, 1983).[13]

The Second World War brought Mexican workers back to the U.S. when the U.S. government initiated the "bracero program," a contract-labor program designed to meet wartime labor shortages in agriculture; that program continued until December 1964. Between 1942 and 1964, nearly 5 million temporary labor contracts were issued to Mexican citizens, and apprehensions of Mexican workers working without documents numbered over 5 million (Samora, 1971:57; Kiser and Kiser, 1976:67).[14] During the post–Korean War recession in 1954, the Immigration and Naturalization Service launched a deportation campaign, Operation Wetback, which apprehended over 1 million undocumented Mexican workers (Bustamante, 1975; Cornelius, 1978). Yet migration resumed during the late 1950s, when over four hundred thousand Mexican workers each year entered the United States through the bracero program (Cornelius, 1978; Samora, 1971; Galarza, 1964).

Virtually all bracero contracts went to men.[15] This gender-discriminate labor policy mandated an elastic supply of labor, one that could be synchronized with seasonal agricultural fluctuations and that would externalize labor reproduction costs to Mexico. The bracero program legally codified the recommendations made by the Dillingham Commission in the early twentieth century. What the designers of the program had not anticipated, however, was the extent to which the bracero program would stimulate more Mexican immigration, both legal and undocumented. Many of the braceros acquired permanent legal status through labor certification, while others repeatedly migrated without documents or contracts; many of them started social networks that facilitated the future migration of their friends and family. And importantly, the bracero program ultimately germinated large-scale permanent settlement of Mexican immigrants.[16]

THE CONTEMPORARY SETTLEMENT OF MEXICAN UNDOCUMENTED IMMIGRANTS

The end of the contract-labor program heralded a new era of massive legal and undocumented immigration characterized by greater representation of women and entire families, the establishment of permanent settlement communities in geographically dispersed areas, and more diversified uses of Mexican labor (Portes and Bach, 1985; Cornelius, 1990). Between 1960 and 1980, over 1 million Mexicans legally immigrated to the U.S., exceeding earlier numbers. But the biggest increments were shown in records of apprehensions of the undocumented. During the 1960s the INS recorded more than 1 million, and in the 1970s over 7 million, arrests of undocumented Mexican immigrants.[17] INS figures for apprehensions and deportations do not precisely enumerate undocumented immigration because these figures signify events, not persons, who may evade capture altogether or be arrested repeatedly before successfully making one entry. Although the apprehension figures and nativist sentiments led to wildly inaccurate, inflated "guesstimates" (6 million to 12 million) of the size of the Mexican undocumented immigrant population, most observers agree that the proportion of "illegals" in the Mexican immigrant population significantly increased during the late 1960s and the 1970s.

Using census data, demographers estimated that by 1980, approximately 1.7 to 2.2 million Mexican undocumented immigrants lived in the United States (Heer and Passel, 1985; Passel, 1985), 68 percent of them in California (Passel, 1986:191). Based on estimates of annual net flows during the early 1980s, by 1986 the figure had risen to 3.1 million (Passel and Woodrow, 1987), a figure that may be accurately reflected by the 2.3 million Mexican undocumented immigrants who applied for one of the 1986 Immigration Reform and Control Act's legalization programs (Bean et al., 1989; Durand and Massey, 1992).[18]

By the 1970s, both undocumented and legal Mexican immigrants had established a significant number of permanent settlement communities in the United States (Browning and Rodríguez, 1985), and these have been referred to as "settling-out" processes (Cornelius, 1992), as "daughter communities" (Massey et al., 1987), and by the unfortunate, but perhaps illustrative, term "sediment" communities (Portes and Bach, 1985). Women and families played a key part in building these permanent communities (Browning and Rodríguez, 1985), and research conducted during the 1970s and 1980s recorded a significant presence of women in the population of Mexican undocumented immigrants.[19] While women participate in seasonal or sojourner undocumented immigration (Guendelman and Pérez-Itriaga, 1987; Kossoudji and Ranney, 1984), they concentrate in the settler portion of the undocumented population, where they are evenly represented with men (Cárdenas and Flores, 1986; Passel, 1986).

A related development consists of the exit of many Mexican immigrant workers from agriculture and their diversification into various sectors of the economy (Cornelius, 1989b, 1992; North and Houstoun, 1976; Portes and Bach, 1985). Although this trend predates termination of the bracero program, since the late 1960s a greater proportion of Mexican immigrants than ever before have located urban employment. Currently as few as 10 or 15 percent of all legal and undocumented Mexican immigrants work in agriculture in California, Texas, and Arizona (Wallace, 1988:664–65). Undocumented as well as legal Mexican immigrants now work in "plant nurseries, construction firms, foundries, shipyards, cement companies, furniture factories, rubber factories, paper factories, restaurants, hotels and motels, car washes, and butcher shops" (Portes and Bach, 1985:81), in "toy assembly, garment sewing, and electronics production" (Cross and Sandos, 1981:55), and in housecleaning and child care (Cornelius, 1989b; Solórzano-Torres, 1987; Ruiz, 1987; Hogeland and Rosen, 1990).[20]

The late 1960s mark the transition to an increasing volume of documented and undocumented Mexican immigrants, the multiplication of permanent settlement communities, a greater participation of women and entire families in Mexican immigration, and the absorption of Mexican immigrant workers into diverse labor markets. The bracero program and the maturation of social networks certainly played a key role in stimulating these developments, but it is macrostructural transformations in both Mexico and the United States that allowed for their realization. The remainder of this chapter examines these transformations.

STRUCTURAL TRANSFORMATIONS IN THE UNITED STATES

In the United States, the growth of settled-out, urban-based Mexican immigrant communities was fostered by a changing configuration of immigration legislation and labor demand. Although political and economic transformations are intertwined, I look first at legislative measures in U.S. immigration law. In the legislative arena, the termination of the bracero program in 1964 coincided with passage of the Civil Rights Act of 1964, and was immediately followed by the 1965 amendment to the prevailing immigration law. As Bach (1978) points out, antidiscriminatory principles inspired by the civil-rights movement fueled all of these legislative actions.

The 1965 amendments to the Immigration and Nationality Act of 1952, which is still the principal U.S. immigration law, ended racist national-origin quotas, imposed for the first time an annual quota of 120,000 for the Western Hemisphere, and developed a preference system where labor certification and family reunification serve as the primary criteria for obtaining legal immigrant status.[21] Although restrictive in intent, the amendments prompted an increase in immigration and a shift of place of origin from Europe to Asia and Latin America (Keely, 1974; Massey, 1981).[22]

Before the 1965 amendments went into effect, many former braceros and *mojados* (wetbacks) began to legalize their status through their employers' labor certification. Later, the preference system based on family reunification allowed them to legalize their family members. As an attempt to curtail the rise in Mexican immigration, a national quota imposed on all Western Hemisphere countries in 1976 restricted the annual number of Mexicans, excluding close family relatives, who could be granted legal status to twenty thousand. These quota restrictions had the unanticipated effect of stimulating more undocumented immigration.[23]

The most dramatic change in immigration legislation affecting Mexican immigrants after 1965 occurred with passage of the 1986 Immigration Reform and Control Act (IRCA). IRCA, which had been debated in Congress since the 1970s, intended to curb Mexican undocumented immigration by imposing sanctions (civil and criminal penalties) on employers who knowingly hire undocumented immigrant workers. IRCA also included provisions for an amnesty-legalization program for undocumented immigrants who could prove continuous residence in the U.S. since January 1, 1982, and for those who could prove they had worked in U.S. agriculture for ninety days during specific periods.[24]

Although IRCA was restrictionist in intent, 2.3 million Mexican undocumented immigrants applied for legal status under one of IRCA's programs.[25] By granting legal status, the legislation recognized and accelerated the further integration and permanence of long-staying, previously undocumented immigrants in the U.S.[26] And in spite of IRCA's restrictionist provisions, several sources of data gathered after employer sanctions went into effect indicate a noticeable increase in the numbers of Mexican women, children, and first-time migrants crossing the border without legal authorization.[27]

Demographic analyses suggest that after IRCA, women may even compose a majority of the Mexican undocumented immigrant population (Woodrow and Passel, 1990:66). There are several reasons for this. Family members of many newly legalized men came out of fear that the "door was closing," with the hope that they too would qualify for legalization (Cornelius, 1989a, 1992). The increasing number of Mexican women participating in undocumented migration may also reflect the maturation of social networks, as these almost invariably incorporate more women over time (Massey et al., 1987; Durand and Massey, 1992). Once women migrate to the United States from Mexico, they are likely to migrate again (Donato, forthcoming). And IRCA's employer sanctions may have less detrimentally affected Mexican undocumented immigrant women's ability to find jobs, since many of them find employment in domestic work, an occupation situated in private households, which lessens the chance of detection (Bean et al., 1990).[28]

In any case, sanctions on employers who hire undocumented immigrants have had only a modest effect in deterring undocumented migration from Mexico (Bach and Brill, 1990; Donato et al., 1992; Kossoudji, 1992). Most employers comply with the letter of the law by asking for documents before hiring new employees, but employers are not required to check the documents' validity. As one California employer noted: "Blatantly fraudulent documents we don't accept—and we've had some miserable reproductions. Some of the forgeries are absolutely magnificent, however, and we don't question them." And another employer more succinctly stated that "the technology of falsification is far more advanced than the technology of detection" (Cornelius, 1989b:43–44). Employer sanctions exacerbate discrimination, but they do little to curb employers' demand for undocumented immigrant workers, institutionalized in many sectors of the economy since the late 1960s. Due to the imposition of employer sanctions, undocumented immigrants now face an added waiting period while they secure fraudulent documents before seeking employment, a step that may have prolonged the average stay of undocumented immigrants (Bach and Brill, 1990). Some undocumented migrants appear to be staying on longer in the U.S. and returning to Mexico for shorter periods of time between trips in order to compensate for IRCA (Kossoudji, 1992).

I turn now to the processes of economic restructuring that promoted this increasingly diverse labor demand for Mexican immigrants. A large literature focuses on the effects of Mexican undocumented immigrant workers on the labor market, but the discussion here focuses on identifying why there has been a major shift in the concentration of Mexican immigrant labor from seasonal, large-scale agricultural firms toward jobs in year-round, urban-based, relatively small or medium-sized firms in services, construction, and light industry.[29] The explanation involves labor-market segmentation, the global fragmentation of production processes, income polarization, and the expanding role of producer services in the economy.

Relying on a "dual-economy" thesis, Portes and Bach (1985) argue that the diversification of demand for the labor of Mexican immigrants stems from pressures faced by small competitive, labor-intensive firms. These firms face economic uncertainty, and so, to remain profitable, they create "secondary-sector jobs" characterized by relatively low pay, manual work, lack of benefits, low status, and few opportunities for occupational advancement. Portes and Bach (1985:19) indicate that the competitive sectors' reliance on undocumented immigrant labor, much of it Mexican, "accelerated in the mid-1960s and reached both numerical importance and notoriety during the 1970s." This reliance coincided with the decreasing willingness of citizens with access to protective social welfare—youth and racial-ethnic minority workers—to accept the conditions of secondary-sector jobs (Bach, 1978; Sassen-Koob, 1980; Portes and Bach, 1985). In this context, undocumented immigrant workers' "illegal" status translates into vulnerability in the workplace, a feature that enhances their attractiveness to employers in competitive firms in many industries (Thomas, 1985).[30] Since the late 1960s firms in the construction and service sectors—hotels and restaurants, convalescent homes, and building and landscape maintenance—have met competitive pressures by hiring Mexican undocumented workers in expanding suburban areas and metropolitan centers, especially in California.[31]

Foreign competition prompted the relocation, fragmentation, or elimination of many upper-tier manufacturing jobs and their restructuring into a system consisting of millions of globally dispersed, downgraded, de-skilled assembly jobs. By the mid-1970s, firms with large work forces in the garment industry had virtually disappeared, replaced by subcontracting arrangements (Bonacich, 1990; Fernández-Kelly and Garcia, forthcoming); similar patterns emerged in the automobile industry (Morales, 1983) and the electronics industry (Hossfeld, 1990).[32] In order to maintain flexibility, manufacturers in these industries and others now typically contract out labor-intensive tasks to small, nonunion, immigrant-dominated firms, which may in turn subcontract industrial homework (Bonacich, 1990; Cornelius, 1989b; Soldatenko, 1991). It is not the influx of immigrants that has created the concentration of immigrant workers in certain jobs, firms, and industries; rather, processes of national and global restructuring have transformed the occupational structure that sustains and encourages immigration (Cornelius, 1989b; Sassen-Koob, 1984; Sassen, 1988).

Sassen's (1988; 1991) research indicates that trends of economic growth in the 1970s and 1980s favored the expansion of producer services and created an increasingly polarized income and occupational structure in the United States. As manufacturing has become increasingly dispersed, major cities in the U.S. serve as global and national centers of corporate management, finance, and technical and legal services that coordinate geographically scattered production facilities. High-income professionals and managers employed in these advanced producer services have generated an entire "reorganization of the consumption structure," creating new labor demands in the informal sector for unique luxury goods, personal services, and residential and commercial gentrification. And it is largely immigrants who fill the void as janitors, gardeners, domestic workers, and producers of custom-made goods (Sassen-Koob, 1984:157).

An important outcome of these processes is the multiplication of domestic work and child-care jobs for immigrant women (Morales and Ong, 1990; Salzinger, 1991). Census and Department of Labor data underestimate the growth of domestic labor because they do not accurately capture occupations where "under the table" pay arrangements and undocumented immigrants are common. Although Mexican immigrant women have prevailed in these jobs in areas of the Southwest for many decades (Romero, 1987, 1992; Ruiz, 1987; Solórzano-Torres, 1987), income polarization and the mass entrance of women into the U.S. labor force have dramatically increased the demand for domestic services. As an elite class of educated women fill business and professional jobs, they and their families increasingly depend on personal household services, especially in areas with concentrated immigrant populations. In fact, the new "spousal egalitarianism" among high-income, dual-career corporate couples, routinely heralded in the popular media, is often predicated on the employment of immigrant women as domestic workers (Hertz, 1986).

STRUCTURAL TRANSFORMATIONS IN MEXICO

Contrary to popular stereotypes, migration originates not in stagnating, "backward" societies, but in those societies undergoing rapid-paced urbanization and industrialization. Mexico provides the classic example of this dictum.[33] A configuration of government economic policies and changing global and national markets stimulated major transformations in Mexico's agricultural and industrial structure after World War II, undermining rural subsistence economies in the mid-1960s and 1970s, and disrupting the livelihood of middle- and working-class sectors in the 1980s. These developments are perhaps best understood by examining the "Mexican miracle" of combined political stability and spectacular economic growth rates, which spans the period between 1940 and 1965; the late 1960s, which witnessed the decline of maize production and the subsequent dependency on food imports; and the period since 1982, during which Mexico has experienced a series of economic and political crises and has pursued neoliberalization policies.

The absence of imported commodities from the U.S. due to the Second World War allowed Mexico to pursue import-substitution industrialization, a development strategy fueled by modernizing agriculture (Alba, 1978).[34] The main source of government investment for the domestic production of previously imported goods came from foreign exchange earned by commercial, export-oriented agriculture.[35]

Government agricultural support became increasingly bifurcated in the 1960s, favoring large-scale, irrigated, commercial agriculture over small-scale, rain-fed, subsistence growing of food crops.[36] With the objective of keeping down food prices for urban consumption, government policies regulated the price of maize, and peasants responded by reducing production to subsistence levels (Grindle, 1986). In search of supplemental income, peasant farmers migrated as seasonal wage earners to the large, irrigated agricultural areas of northwestern and central Mexico, sought work in Mexico's growing urban centers, or worked in the U.S.— an alternative facilitated, until 1964, by the "safety valve" of the bracero program.

Both symbolically and structurally, Mexico's need to import basic foodstuffs after 1965 marks the miracle's demise. The expansion of private and public investment in commercial agriculture continued throughout the late 1960s, while cultivation of basic foodstuffs for domestic consumption declined (Warman, 1978). By the late 1960s and early 1970s, both market pressures and government incentives encouraged the cultivation of cattle-fodder crops such as sorghum and alfalfa, effectively restructuring production and use of cultivation space, and undermining previous land reforms by exacerbating the already inequitably skewed distribution of land in Mexico (Barkin, 1987).[37] Meanwhile, the "golden age" of plentiful urban jobs in industry and construction in the 1940s and 1950s no longer awaited city-bound migrants in the 1960s, as Mexico experienced the exhaustion of the import-substitution industrialization strategy (Arizpe, 1981).

These developments coincided with the termination of the bracero alternative. In 1965, in an effort to stave off rising unemployment, the Mexican government instituted the Border Industrialization Program (BIP), a program designed to generate the infrastructure and legal conditions to successfully attract foreign manufacturing investment along the border with the United States. Although the BIP was originally intended to occupy primarily male migrant workers, the plants it initiated employed predominantly young, single women. Fernández-Kelly (1983) explains that this was due to employer preferences, and to the growing population of single women without the financial support of husbands or fathers.

The growing rural population faced grim prospects: a declining peasant economy, diminishing urban job growth, *and* the restructuring of agricultural production. By the late 1970s, rural peasant communities were thoroughly integrated into international markets and increasingly unable to achieve food self-sufficiency (Barkin, 1987:292), prompting segments of the rural population to seek migration and what would eventually become permanent settlement in the U.S.

In the 1970s and 1980s, the outcomes of government policies also adversely affected the urban population. The economic crisis initiated by dual agricultural policies, growing trade imbalances and debt, government budget deficits, and the world economic recession of the mid-1970s culminated in 1976 when the International Monetary Fund pressured Mexico to enact a major devaluation of the peso. After years of maintaining a stable currency, the government devalued the peso nearly 100 percent, causing capital flight, decline in private investments, and high unemployment along the border *maquiladoras* and in the interior. Although momentarily mitigated by a brief oil boom (1977–81), the problems associated with the debt crisis were exacerbated by the dramatic increase in the number of people entering the Mexican labor force each year, and by the major population shift from rural to urban areas.[38]

Since 1982, when inflation reached nearly 100 percent, Mexico has undergone one of the world's most severe, prolonged economic crises.[39] Characterized by harsh austerity measures, unemployment, and dramatic inflation, the crisis cut into real wages of urban workers, professionals, government employees, and middle-class entrepreneurs, and so prompted a major shift in the demographic composition of U.S.-bound immigrants—what Cornelius (1988) has called "*los migrantes de la crisis.*" The Mexican population bound for the U.S. became increasingly heterogeneous, drawing from large industrial urban centers without traditions of northbound migration, such as Puebla and the Federal District, and began to include more people from the urban middle and working class (Cornelius, 1988).[40] Women, children, and the elderly also represented a greater proportion of U.S.-bound immigrants, which Cornelius (1988) attributes, in part, to the symptoms of the 1980s economic crisis that has driven more Mexican women into the labor force.

Although women's participation in the Mexican labor force increased approximately 50 percent in the 1970s, when many women assumed formal-sector jobs as teachers and office and factory workers, women's integration into the labor force accelerated in the 1980s, driven by the economic crisis and informal-sector job growth (de Oliveira, 1990; González de la Rocha, 1988). Structural-adjustment policies enacted in the 1980s propelled more women into the labor market and altered the characteristics of women workers. Until the early 1970s, most employed women in Mexico were young, single, and childless; upon marriage or the birth of their first child, they typically withdrew from the labor force. This pattern was substantially modified in the 1970s and 1980s, especially after 1982, when a greater proportion of older women, married women, and mothers entered the labor market. The crisis also modified the traditional positive correlation between schooling and women's employment, as women with little education joined the labor force in greater numbers (García and de Oliveira, 1991). Since the 1980s, increasing proportions of married and single women have found work in microbusinesses, where they manufacture shoes, clothing, and rubber products (Escobar Latapí and González de la Rocha, 1988); in industrial subcontracting and homework, where they assemble toys and electronic and plastic parts (Benería and Roldán, 1987); in agribusiness, where they pick and pack fruits and vegetables for export (Mummert, 1990); and in various informal-sector activities (de Oliveira, 1990).

Since the 1980s, the Mexican government has pursued monetarist policies—reducing public-sector spending in order to meet foreign debt service requirements—and has liberalized the regulation of trade and investment, much of it oriented to export development. This is exemplified by the Mexican government's strong push to enact the North American Free Trade Agreement.[41] Wages deteriorated throughout the 1980s, while the prices for basic foods rose and nutritional standards declined.[42]

INSIDE THE GLOBAL PARAMETERS

Since the mid-1960s, political and economic transformations in both Mexico and the United States have resulted in the settlement of large numbers of Mexican undocumented immigrants in the United States. While political and economic transformations in the United States and Mexico constantly transform the market of labor needs and opportunities, the effects on Mexican immigrants' lives are mediated by the microstructural context of family and community. In this regard, I prefer to think of these broader global processes as setting the parameters for Mexican immigration. Global processes define the parameters, but individual lives are situated and animated within families, social networks, specific communities, and local economies. In these specific social contexts, people act in consort and in conflict with friends, family, and kin, and looking at this realm complements the structural portrayal with an acknowledgment of agency. The following chapter introduces several of the Mexican immigrant families who have settled in Oakview, California, describes the evolution of the barrio, and presents a typology of gendered migration patterns. Chapter four examines the dynamics of family and social-network relations that account for the variation in this typology of migration patterns.

CHAPTER THREE

The Oakview Barrio

Mexican immigrant women and men are often referred to as "pools of immigrant labor" or as "migrant streams" or "waves" responding solely to economic currents; such phrases provide a picture which flattens the varied contexts and experiences of migration.[1] This depersonalized language says little about the primary actors and why they behave as they do in the variegated drama of migration and resettlement.

This study was designed to look more intimately at immigrants' lives, examining both the social context in which immigrants decide to migrate, and the new social environment that they encounter and help to create in the United States. While it is necessary to examine the macroeconomic and political impulses behind Mexican undocumented immigration, recent research has drawn attention to the complex social networks and family ties that support migration processes. Gender is a vital part of this social landscape, conditioning people's opportunities and responses, and enabling them to act in particular ways. Gender relations, however, are not uniform or always predictable; they interact with immigration in multiple ways.

This chapter describes how the Oakview barrio has matured from a small male immigrant outpost to a bustling, demographically diverse, settled immigrant community. A typology suggests varied patterns of family migration, and profiles of five families illustrate the multiple ways in which these immigrants organize their daily lives.

THE EVOLUTION OF THE OAKVIEW BARRIO

Today the Oakview barrio is a busy, relatively self-contained immigrant community where Mexican immigrant families can worship, cash paychecks, get medical attention, and buy groceries in Spanish. But as recently as the 1950s, Mexican immigrants were a numerical minority in this area. Most of them were men who lived together with other men, usually kin and friends, and who came from a particular *municipio* (rural county) in Michoacán, a state in western Mexico with a long tradition of U.S.-bound migration. At this point, the area surrounding Oakview was not yet a major metropolitan area, but consisted of orchards, flower nurseries, light industries, and a series of suburban towns linked to San Francisco by highway and railway. Some of the study participants recalled Oakview in the 1950s as a time when language barriers inhibited communication. Community social ties were then quite narrowly circumscribed for Mexican men who lived there.

> Back then there were about twenty people whom we knew as *paisanos* [people from the same place of origin], but we didn't all live together. When the few of us that were in this one house would get the urge to talk to someone else in Spanish, we'd say, "Well, let's go visit what's-his-name to talk a bit." (Marcelino Ávila; arrived 1957)

> There was almost no one [from Mexico] here. To communicate with store clerks, you would just have to make hand signals. It was the same at work. . . . There were people who were of Mexican descent, who were born here, and I think they came from Texas. . . . In total, there were probably ten, fifteen, maybe twenty Mexican families, but they were all born here [in the U.S.]. And in certain respects, they helped us establish ourselves. Because sometimes one had to fill out an application, take care of some business, and since we didn't know English, sometimes we'd go to them for help. An elderly Spanish woman also helped us. (Arturo Barrios; arrived 1952)

> I knew about five or six guys from Mexico, all of them from my village. If there were other Mexicans here, I didn't meet them. There were *pochos* [Mexican Americans], but they didn't want anything to do with us *mojados* [wetbacks], that is, with the exception of Fred Villedas.[2] For fun, we'd go listen to boleros on a jukebox at a Portuguese guy's bar. (Manuel Galván; arrived 1950)

By the late 1960s, the area surrounding Oakview included an expanding number of office buildings, high-technology industrial parks, and new suburban homes for middle-class and upper-income residents. Employment opportunities in the service sector expanded, and newly arrived Mexican workers took jobs in restaurants, private

Figure 1.   Percent Hispanic or Spanish-surnamed Students
in Three Neighborhood Elementary Schools, 1964–87

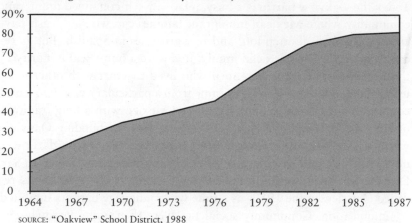

SOURCE: "Oakview" School District, 1988

households, laundries, hospitals, construction, and the Japanese-
owned flower nurseries that ranked as a key industry in Oakview
before residential property values rose. During the late 1960s and the
1970s, the immigrant community matured and grew to include
women and children from Mexico as well as men; entire families
began relocating from Mexico to the Oakview barrio. During the
period from 1964 to 1970, the percentage of "Spanish-surnamed"
children enrolled in the three local elementary schools went from 15
percent to 36 percent, and by 1987 it had more than doubled—to 81
percent.[3]

A commercial infrastructure emerged to serve the new population's needs, providing an ethnic market for both consumption and
job opportunities. Shops selling Mexican food products sprouted
along the neighborhood's main commercial street, joined by barber
shops, beauty salons, and shoe-repair services that offered services in
Spanish. Immigrants who arrived in the late 1960s and 1970s found
a more accommodating environment that offered commercial ameni-
ties and social life. Consider the impressions of these more recent
arrivals:

> I never imagined the North to be like this. It was like a little Mexico! We
> found everything that we were accustomed to having in Mexico, such as
> tortillas, chile, chorizo, and even soccer clubs. (Patricio Macías; arrived 1978)

Lots of women, practically the same as now. Plenty! Oakview was a little more, ah, the people went out more. The person who liked to drink, who liked to be liked [*que le gustaba gustar*], that person had a little more freedom with the police. People drank more at all hours, they drove at all hours of the night. It was nice, the police didn't bother you, and there weren't many problems. One earned less, there was less employment than now. Oakview was smaller then and it was very different. I'm talking about 1970. (Eudoro Ibarra; first arrived 1969)

When I first arrived, there were no hair salons where Spanish was spoken. So all of the women who had come from my town knew me, and when I arrived they sought my services. There were many women arriving here by then. (Isabel Barrios; arrived 1964)

Nearly everyone knew me. I did my church course [for confirmation] and then afterward I always helped in the church. I sang in the church choir, and I was always busy with activities at the church. (Mariana Viñas-Valenzuela; arrived 1977)

The Latino commercial establishments, the predominantly Mexican congregation at the local Catholic parish, and the local community center's various bilingual and Spanish-language programs eventually became major institutions in this emergent immigrant barrio. Although Mexican immigrants constitute the majority, Chicanos, Central Americans, Anglos, and fewer numbers of Southeast Asians, Filipinos, and Pacific Islanders now live in the area. The barrio retains a distinctively Mexican or Latino character, but there are also Anglo home owners concentrated in one neighborhood area, and Anglo outsiders enter daily for employment and commercial purposes. Located on Central Avenue, and extending eastward into a residential area, are a number of autobody and upholstery-repair shops, car-towing lots, warehouses, light-industry factories, and a large plant that fabricates plastics and chemicals. These establishments employ Mexican immigrants as well as Anglo citizens who do not necessarily live in the barrio. White, upper-income shoppers from nearby residential areas also come to the barrio. Since the early 1980s commercial gentrification gradually encroached on the area, as merchants took advantage of relatively low storefront rent to open what became a cluster of stores specializing in coffee beans, interior design, and imported antiques. A string of British and U.S. flags wave incongruously along a two-block stretch of the avenue, announcing several antique furniture shops that serve as a consumer outpost for wealthy clientele, while in their midst, low-income Mexican immigrants gather to eat tacos sold by mobile vendors.

For most of the study participants, a good deal of daily life occurs within the confines of the barrio. It is here that people conduct most of their shopping, visiting, and church and school activities, although they circulate elsewhere for work and leisure. Mexican immigrant barrio residents work in adjacent neighborhoods and cities, and visit medical offices and banks in these areas as well. On Sundays—for many of the respondents, their only day off—families enjoy relaxing with friends and kin around picnic tables in open grassy fields, the most popular of which are located in public parks immediately outside the barrio in predominantly Anglo, middle-class areas of Oakview, and some families travel by car to shop for bargains at the large outdoor flea market in San Jose that recalls memories of the outdoor *tianguis* in Mexico. Still, with these significant exceptions, the barrio area serves as the hub of daily social and commercial life.

Many of the Mexican immigrants in the Oakview barrio found employment in nearby municipalities, where they concentrated in low-end service-sector jobs. While some are working as janitors, bakers, assemblers, ditch diggers, warehouse employees, and stable hands, and others are doing child care, the men typically work as gardeners or restaurant workers and the women as paid domestic workers. This is no surprise since the Oakview barrio is surrounded by affluence and suburban opulence; three of the bordering and nearby cities rank among the top ten wealthiest cities in California, each of them surpassing the per capita income of Beverly Hills.[4]

In the section that follows, I introduce a scheme for classifying migration patterns and present profiles of individuals in five families who are representative of these migration typologies.

A TYPOLOGY AND PROFILES
OF FAMILY IMMIGRATION

Researchers have developed a number of typologies to grasp the complexity of immigration.[5] The primary usefulness of a typology is in providing a point of departure for analysis. For this study of undocumented immigrant settlement, looking at diverse patterns of migration alerts us to the varied ways in which families are formed and reconstituted in the United States. This is crucial to the study, since family formation often goes hand in hand with permanent settlement.

To pursue my interest in families and processes of migration, I have developed a typology by taking a magnifying glass and focusing on the differences found among a particular group of Mexican immigrants who entered the U.S. without legal authorization and who have performed manual labor and resided for relatively long periods of time in the U.S. In abbreviated fashion, this larger group can be referred to as undocumented immigrant workers who are long-term settlers. Within this aggregate, people's migration experiences can be classified into three "types" of family migration: *family stage migration,* where family migration occurs in stages, with husbands preceding the migration of their wives and children; *family unit migration,* where spouses and children migrate together; and *independent migration,* where single men and women migrate independently, without family members. The critical vectors in this typology are gender and generation.

Family migration which occurs in stages, with husbands migrating before their wives and children, is common in Western Europe as well as in Asia. This pattern is sometimes referred to as "associational migration" (e.g., Thadani and Todaro, 1984), but I prefer the term "stage" because it better conveys the notion of family migration occurring in sequential points in time, drawing attention to separable events of migration. Calling this pattern "associational" or "dependent" migration suggests that women become migrants only by association; this assumes patterns of dependence and subordination, which may or may not be warranted.

The twelve families who fit the pattern of stage migration had accumulated more time and experience in the United States than others within the sample, and thus were generally older. The husbands had more immigrant experience than their wives, but as a group, these people had already lived in the U.S. for many years by the time they participated in this study. When the families who migrated in stages are divided by settlement experience into two subgroups, differences in socioeconomic background are underlined. These differences in class and rural/urban origin reflect the trend of more recent Mexican immigrants coming from urban backgrounds (Cornelius, 1992). The six families where the men had begun undocumented migration prior to 1965, when the bracero program was still in effect, came from somewhat homogenous peasant backgrounds in Mexico. The six families where migration first occurred after 1965 were younger when the study occurred and had last lived in both urban and rural areas of Mexico, although many of the people who had lived in cities had been rural-urban migrants as well. I later profile Dolores and Marcelino Ávila, representing the pre-1965 group of families who experienced stage migration, and Blanca and Patricio Macías, who serve as an example of the post-1965 group.

The six families who migrated together as intact, nuclear families did so during the late 1970s and the early 1980s. Unlike the *campesino* and working-class families who migrated in stages, some of those who came as members of a family unit had enjoyed significantly higher socioeconomic status in Mexico. This suggests that class shapes family gender relations and migration patterns. The pursuit of family unit migration often requires higher levels of economic resources than are initially expended in family stage migration. Three of these six families came from modest middle-class backgrounds, having last worked as small entrepreneurs and office workers in Mexican cities, and the other three families came from backgrounds where they made a living by combining various wage-earning activities with peasant agriculture. The profile of Ausencio and María Mendoza represents an example of family unit migration.

Traditionally, migrating alone to the United States has been a relatively inaccessible option for single women, but this is changing. Eight women and five men in the study had come to the U.S. when they were single, separated, or widowed; by the time of the research in the late 1980s, many of them (eight) were married or living with a companion.[6] Like the families who migrated together as a unit, most of this group had come to the United States in the late 1970s and early 1980s, so they had already resided in the U.S., without official authorization, for an average of eight years when I met them. They came from *campesino* and urban working-class backgrounds, and with the exception of two women, aged fifty-three and seventy, these women and men were in their twenties and thirties when I met them. María Alicia Navarro, a single mother of three, who first migrated alone and then later brought her children, and Reynaldo Castrillo, who migrated as a young single man and who had begun a small family in Oakview by the late 1980s, are introduced in this chapter as examples of female and male independent migration.

DOLORES AND MARCELINO ÁVILA: AN EXAMPLE OF PRE-1965 FAMILY STAGE MIGRATION

Of all the families in this study, Marcelino and Dolores Ávila's unorthodox household division of labor best contradicted the stereotype of Mexican machismo. Fifty-two-year-old Marcelino dusted, vacuumed, washed clothes and ironed, and "most of the time," Dolores added, "he leaves dinner prepared for me and my sons before he goes to work." The spouses described these daily arrangements in a similar way; the patterns were also confirmed by my friend, their next-door neighbor and *comadre* (co-godmother), who introduced us. During one of my first visits to their house, Marcelino readily admitted that "back in Mexico, I didn't know how to prepare my food, iron a shirt, or wash clothes. All I knew was how to work, how to harvest a crop." How did he come to perform these chores, which remain, in spite of the feminist movement, frequently ignored by men both in Mexico and in the United States? Recounting his residential and job situation during his initial years in California, before his wife and family joined him, Marcelino offered: "Necessity forced me to do things I had previously ignored."

Given their origins as rural *campesinos*, the comfortable life which Dolores and Marcelino carved out in the U.S. for their family surpassed any standard of living they would have likely achieved in Mexico. With the intention of improving his family's economic circumstances in Mexico, Marcelino came north in 1957 at the behest of his father and uncles. In California he found restaurant work and lived as part of a small but growing bachelor-like community of Mexican labor migrant men. Although he worked long hours and lived Spartanly, he still fondly recalled his initial reactions to the U.S as though it were only yesterday that he was dazzled by the orderly freeways and by a particular discount store selling a wide variety of products—car tires, jewelry, clothing, pharmaceuticals, bakery goods, groceries—under one roof. "Everything," he recalled, "was so clean, so pretty."

Dolores had remained in the village with her in-laws, and although migration separated the Ávilas for only five years—a relatively short period compared with what many of their peers experienced—Dolores grew increasingly impatient with these arrangements. She understood all too well the family financial necessities prompting these circumstances, but the small remittance Marcelino sent home from his meager wages— earned at the rate of eighty cents an hour—hardly met their needs. Like many women in her situation, Dolores worried about the children's well-being: "I thought that perhaps our daughters would never love him as a father because they only saw him during his brief visits." Exhorted by her in-laws, she managed to convince Marcelino to reunite the family, and so in 1962 Dolores and their two daughters came to California.

Both of the Ávilas have since enjoyed long histories of stable employment in the U.S. In over thirty years, Marcelino had worked at only six jobs, including two—as a cook and as a pipe fitter—that had lasted for a total of twenty-one years. Dolores had cleaned houses, spent seven years packing flowers in one of the many Japanese nurseries that once dotted the area, and was a sixteen-year veteran employee at a hospital linen laundry. The Ávilas recognized that unlike many people in their immediate community, they had enjoyed more than two decades of stable employment, which had provided them with a degree of financial security that allowed them to spend leisure time together. After Mass on Sundays they sometimes went out for brunch, they had twice vacationed in Acapulco, and on special occasions they enjoyed live mariachi music. Unlike most of the families in this study, the Ávilas had also vacationed in their Michoacán village, a luxury afforded them by their salaries and by legal status, which they attained through certification from Marcelino's employer in the early 1960s.

Dolores and Marcelino purchased their home during the 1970s, just before skyrocketing real-estate prices made home ownership in the San Francisco Bay area a privilege of the well-to-do. Lavish draperies, wall-to-wall carpet, a matching dining set, and a well-protected, ornate velvet sofa adorned the main living area, but the family spent most of their time at home in the family room, a converted garage whose walls displayed their children's high school graduation photographs.

At the time of the research, the Ávilas' six children were in their teens and twenties. The two eldest daughters were born in Mexico in the late 1950s, the second while Marcelino was working in California; they had attended U.S. schools and junior college, and by the late 1980s, they were married and working as secretaries. Four sons were born in the U.S. after Dolores and the girls joined Marcelino in 1962; the eldest worked full-time as a mechanic, and the three others, who lived with their parents, combined part-time jobs with schooling. The sons contributed part of their earnings to household expenses, but Marcelino and Dolores took responsibility for mortgage payments and monthly bills.

Dolores Ávila talked and moved very slowly during our late-afternoon and evening visits, reflecting, I surmised, her employment schedule at a laundry, where she worked from five in the morning until 2:30 P.M. Her relaxed, almost lethargic stance contrasted sharply with her husband's seemingly indefatigable store of energy.[7] Marcelino worked an opposite shift, from 3:30 in the afternoon until one in the morning, as a janitor at a firm that manufactured plastic parts for aircraft. His job didn't seem to deplete the energy with which he attacked household chores, or the animation with which he always spoke.

Perhaps more than their comfortable standard of living, their nontraditional division of household labor—and the pride and satisfaction that Marcelino drew from his household chores, such as washing and ironing clothes and vacuuming—exceeded their own expectations for how life in the United States would contrast with their daily lives in Mexico. Although Marcelino's activities were different only in degree, not in kind, from those of other men who had experienced similar migration experiences, Dolores believed that her husband was different than "most Mexican men, who have that machismo, that belief that only women can do these tasks. Marcelino is different, he never orders me to do things." When I asked to what she attributed this, she paused for a moment, answered that her husband "recognizes the value of a woman," and then said somewhat inquisitively, "Could it be a blessing from God?"

BLANCA AND PATRICIO MACÍAS: AN EXAMPLE OF POST-1965 FAMILY STAGE MIGRATION

On the surface, Blanca and Patricio Macías almost resembled the Mexican immigrant version of an ideal nuclear family from a 1950s television show, sans suburban home and white picket fence. Whenever I met the Macíases and their three elementary school–aged children at church or the legalization clinic, they always appeared to be the picture-perfect happy family, carefully groomed and in good spirits, and friends and acquaintances remarked on how much the couple seemed to be in love. Blanca, a thirty-one-year-old stay-at-home mom, strongly identified with her role as wife and mother. She left special notes for the children in their sack lunches or under their pillows, and she was proud that, unlike her husband or other women she knew, she had never left her children in Mexico in order to pursue work in the U.S. Thirty-five-year-old Patricio, the responsible breadwinner, worked two full-time jobs to support his wife and three children, and he always tried to provide the best merchandise for his showcase family. He also, I learned later, used his earnings to support other people, a factor which was a major source of tension in the marriage.

Both Patricio and Blanca came from families in Guadalajara, where U.S.-bound migration had evolved into a tradition, especially for men. Patricio's father had worked in a Chicago foundry for many years, and Blanca's uncles, cousins, brothers, and sister had accumulated extensive migration experience. Still, when Patricio lost his job and breezily announced his departure in 1978, Blanca was caught by surprise. Left alone to care for three infant and toddler children, she worried that Patricio would abandon her for another woman, and she prayed for the Border Patrol to capture her husband and send him home. Her prayers were answered only momentarily, and as the months passed, she began to lobby Patricio to help her go north too. Blanca succeeded in this endeavor only because her sister who lived in Los Angeles had urged her to undertake it and lent her money to make the journey north so Blanca might check on her husband. Blanca and the three small children joined Patricio approximately one year after his departure.

The Macíases rented a spacious two-bedroom apartment perched alongside the railroad tracks, an apartment kept so orderly that it belied the presence of three rambunctious children. Blanca cooked, cleaned, shopped, frequently rearranged the living-room furniture, and chauffeured the children about, but she was not a stay-at-home mom by choice. She had been employed in Mexico when the children were babies, leaving them in the care of her mother-in-law, and after she and the children joined her husband in Oakview, she continued employment, often not returning home until 7:00 P.M. While working as a motel maid in 1985 she suffered a spinal-column injury, and a subsequent operation had left her unable to hold a job. She walked with a limp, suffered chronic headaches, worried that she was growing fat, and took steady dosages of painkillers. Still, she insisted that "it's better for the children this way," rationalizing that her physical disability allowed her to spend more time with the children.

On the side, however, and unbeknownst to Patricio, Blanca worked part-time as a house cleaner two mornings a week, while the children attended school. She stashed her earnings, building a future safety net for herself. Patricio's marital infidelities threaded the couple's relationship, and it was not uncommon for Patricio's women friends to telephone the home. When this occurred during one of my afternoon visits, Blanca limited herself to several sarcastic remarks. Patricio had first insisted the caller was a man, and when he admitted it was a woman, he defended himself by claiming she was just a friend. Blanca typically held her resentment at a simmering level, for as long as Patricio fulfilled his breadwinner responsibilities, she reasoned that it was in her best interest to keep silent on these issues: "If my husband gives me and my children everything, what more do I want? I'd only resent it if he said, 'Give me twenty dollars so I can spend it on another woman.' That, I would not stand for!"

Patricio earned a good combined income from his day job as a cook and from his second, night job as a janitor, which he took after Blanca's accident, but debts from major consumer purchases haunted the family finances. More emotional conflicts in the home centered around the presence of Patricio's brothers, who periodically arrived from Mexico to work and live with the family. Their long-term stays ignited explosive conflicts with the children and signified a major financial burden for the family. The couple also disagreed about how to best discipline their rebellious eleven-year-old daughter, Carla, whose excessively high-combed, sprayed hairdos and interest in certain boys seemed to presage a *chola* adolescence.[8]

In nearly all matters, Blanca ostensibly conceded to Patricio's author-ity: she did all of the housework, she asked his permission to go on special errands, she more or less tolerated his spendthrift habits and marital infidelities, and at home she wore her long hair in braids, a style she personally disliked, maintaining that "Patricio prefers me this way." Yet in more fundamental matters—such as employment and her secret savings—she surreptitiously defied him.

Patricio justified his role as head of household on the basis of his earnings. "I came to this country for one reason," he explained, "to give my family what I could not give them in Mexico." As evidence of his accomplishments, he could cite the Ford station wagon Blanca drove, the children's up-to-date clothing, and other acquisitions as the fruits of his hard work. In less sanguine moments, however, he wondered about the virtue of his dawn-to-midnight work schedule, as he soberly noted: "Sometimes it seems like I just came to this country to work and to work. What kind of life is this?"

AUSENCIO AND MARÍA MENDOZA: AN EXAMPLE OF FAMILY UNIT MIGRATION

"I worry about my wife," sighed an exasperated Ausencio Mendoza. "Every day," he continued, "she is on the go, leaving in the mornings to clean who knows how many different houses, and then dedicating her afternoons and evenings to these committees, these meetings, and then still more activities. No wonder she doesn't feel well! If she would just stay home a little more, her illnesses would heal fast." María Mendoza, a svelte and always stylishly dressed thirty-eight-year-old, suffered from various ailments: arthritis, digestive problems which had required sur-gery and for which she was now experimenting with herbal-tea remedies, and *nervios*—excessive anxiety and stress. Although she did in fact de-vote many of her waking hours to life in the public sphere, a small part of them with me when we helped launch a public-information campaign, her busy schedule of activities seemed paradoxically to restore her health as much as they exacerbated her symptoms. She could scarcely contain her enthusiasm for church, school, and community activities, frequently telling me, "Whenever there is a meeting in San Francisco, just let me know, because I want to go too."

In Mexico, Ausencio had operated a thriving furniture store and factory. At the pinnacle of business success, Ausencio supervised forty workers, and he belonged to the Guadalajara chapters of the Kiwanis and Lions clubs. His work took him away for several weeks at a time, as he drove to sell wholesale to shops in small towns throughout the state, leaving María to run the household and their furniture store. A family photo album testified to the middle-class standard of life which the Mendozas had enjoyed in the late 1960s and during the 1970s. The photographs chronicled family vacations in Acapulco and Disneyland, María attired in festive party dresses for birthday and baptismal celebrations, and everywhere, babies and toddlers. Gleaming tile floors, polished by their *muchacha* (their young live-in maid), displayed matching furniture sets.

Ausencio, the only son in a middle-class family who had not studied for a professional career, started his business with loans from his two brothers, a pharmacist and a physician. During the boom years in Mexico, the small firm flourished, but business faltered in the late 1970s, and the Mendozas finally declared bankruptcy in 1983. As María explained, "We could no longer endure. We no longer had any economic support. We had been robbed, and then with the economic situation, we were left only with our debts." María's parents had initially migrated to Guadalajara from a rural area, and over the years her parents and brothers migrated north, accumulating contacts and experience that would ultimately facilitate Ausencio and María's migration to the United States. The Mendozas had visited María's kin in California on three occasions, which they referred to as "shopping trips," catching a glimpse of immigrant life before finally making the big move themselves in 1982. Still, those short trips hardly prepared Ausencio and María for their respective incorporation into the U.S. as a cleaner of horse stables and a paid domestic worker.

During the initial settlement period, they lived with kin, and then on a horse ranch. Using a combination of savings brought from Mexico, loans, and cash earned in California, the Mendozas launched their current business in 1985. Daily life for María and Ausencio and their six children now revolved around their mobile produce and butcher-shop business, which they operated out of a truck equipped with refrigeration, scales, and a cash register. Forty-one-year-old Ausencio, with a large white apron tied around his thick torso, took the truck out six days a week, parking in prime sales locations around the barrio. On the job, he exercised his wit nonstop, affectionately greeting and joking with regular customers, sprinkling his steady rap with "How's your mother doing?" and "May God bless you," and even offering job referrals and informal drug counseling to youths. The Mendozas' teenaged daughter and son, one paid employee, and occasionally María, also worked in the truck.

After payments on the truck, and capital outlay for supplies, Ausencio estimated that they cleared approximately twenty-five hundred dollars a month from the mobile butcher/produce shop, and when domestic work was steady, María's earnings amounted to approximately five hundred dollars a month. Although they carried tremendous debts and paid eleven hundred dollars a month in rent, the Mendozas were among the most financially solvent within the undocumented immigrant community in Oakview, which made them feel smug. "Those who live in poverty here," announced Ausencio once when we were talking about their next-door neighbors who lived in a garage with their two children, "do so because they like to live that way."

Although the Mendozas' household division of labor did not directly challenge patriarchal orthodoxy, María's numerous public engagements reflected her nonconformity to women's traditional domestic roles. The teenage children assumed a good deal of responsibility for the household chores, and the younger ones pitched in as well. Although Ausencio did not cook, clean, or do the laundry, he resented María's frequent absences from the home. An ongoing point of contention centered not on María's employment, but on what Ausencio perceived as her competing dedication to, on the one hand, home and family and, on the other, community and church activities. For María, these activities were an important escape from the domestic sphere: "He wants me to stay home, to be with the children all day. I love my children, but just staying home, closed within those four walls, well, I find that boring. I want to give what I can to improve the community." At least on one occasion, their argument became violent, and one of their six-year-old twins demonstrated for me how his father had hit his mother, and how she had responded with her arms flailing. These arguments were also played out verbally in public settings, and once during a social event at the church, when friends and kin were present, Ausencio had drawn attention to María by exclaiming, "Seems like staying with the family at home makes her itch! She must be allergic to it!" As time passed, Ausencio could not force her to stay home; María eventually recruited him to some of her groups.

MARÍA ALICIA NAVARRO: A WOMAN'S EXPERIENCES
WITH INDEPENDENT MIGRATION

In the large Mexican city of Monterrey, María Alicia Navarro, a single
mother of three, had maintained a middle-class lifestyle for her children
by sheer ingenuity and by working multiple jobs from dawn to late at
night. She held two formal-sector jobs, one as a secretary at a government ministry office, and another as secretary and bookkeeper at an elite
private school, which provided not only another salary but free tuition
for her two eldest children. Additionally, she operated, at different times,
a number of small enterprises—a fast-food stand, a school-cafeteria con-
cession, and a small grocery—and by piecing together earnings she had
even purchased a second house for rental income. Her industrious activities had enabled her to send her two eldest children to Disney World,
purchase dance lessons for her daughter, own a car, provide a home
where each child enjoyed a separate bedroom, and employ a maid to
clean and cook. For María Alicia and her children, this life crumbled
with Mexico's inflationary crisis.

By 1984, making ends meet became impossible, and the school principal who had allowed her to keep flexible hours was departing. María
Alicia had heard that in California a woman could earn up to one hundred dollars a day cleaning houses. "I had to see if it was true," she
recalled, although the thought of going north had never before crossed
her mind. She left her children with her mother, and cautiously took a
six-month leave of absence from her two office jobs. With the help of her
brother's former mother-in-law, who worked as a live-in domestic in
northern California, María Alicia came north "without papers" to take
a low-paying live-in domestic job with the understanding that the employer would help her find day housecleaning jobs. When this did not
occur, she moved in with a Mexican immigrant woman. After several
months María Alicia started to build her own domestic-work clientele,
and eventually she brought her children to California.

When the children arrived, they were shocked to find themselves living first in a garage, and then in a house infested with rats and cock-
roaches. When I met them in 1987, they were living in a one-room studio
apartment, and Amador, a coworker at the government ministry whom
María Alicia had dated in Monterrey, had joined them as well. The
downward class mobility affected no one more acutely than seventeen-
year-old Magali, who felt especially ashamed for potential boyfriends to
see her home: "What will they think when they learn that all five of us

sleep on the couches and the floor?" María Alicia tried to accommodate her children as best she could, eventually moving to a larger, two-bedroom apartment when her sister and brother joined them, but she also frequently reminded the children that "this is not Mexico. Here what matters is not appearances, but work and what you can earn."

Thirty-eight-year-old María Alicia served as the main source of financial support for a household that came to include, in addition to her, her three children, her two siblings, and Amador; everyone but her youngest son, aged ten, worked and contributed to expenses. She worked long hours six days a week, trying hard to increase her earnings, and she was proud that she had always been *muy luchona*, a real struggler, always innovating income-earning activities so that she had never asked for or received financial assistance from either of the fathers of her children.

Yet at the same time, she resented Amador because he didn't help support her or her children. "People from his state, from Durango," she once whispered to me, tapping her elbow, "are like that, they're very stingy." Amador contributed three hundred dollars a month toward his rent, utilities, and food expenses, and out of that money, María Alicia bought special food items and cooked separate stews without chile so Amador's ulcer would not become inflamed. This economic exchange seemed unfair to her, and Amador's lack of interest in, or at best ambivalent commitment to, the relationship also bothered María Alicia. He often spoke of returning permanently to Mexico, and he once went there for several months after he gained legal status.[9]

Although the instability of the relationship troubled her, María Alicia relied on Amador for emotional support, intimacy, and affection. Several women friends advised María Alicia on various personal and employment issues, but she never fully relied on these friends, claiming that "it's better to be alone," that friends were ultimately untrustworthy. Her real anchor seemed to be her family of origin, with whom she kept in contact through phone calls and cassette-recorded "letters," and the satisfaction she drew from developing a thriving route of domestic-work clients.

Of all the immigrant women I met who cleaned houses, María Alicia maintained the most ambitious number of *casas,* cleaning anywhere from ten to eighteen different houses each week. Her ability to drive, her relative youth and ability to work fast, and her meager but apparently sufficient English-language skills helped her in this regard. María Alicia's responsibility as the principal source of household support left her no alternative but to maximize her earnings by accumulating as many domestic jobs as possible. She approached work in the U.S. with the same sense of urgency and inventiveness as she had in Mexico. "When I have an idea to do something," she explained breathlessly, "I can't rest until I've done it."

REYNALDO CASTRILLO: A MAN'S EXPERIENCES WITH INDEPENDENT MIGRATION

"Ever since I was a kid, when I was nine, ten years old, I always knew I was going north. My uncle Gustavo would tell me stories about the railroads, the fields. . . . I always knew I would be going to seek out my own adventures, but what I didn't know then," he added, momentarily dropping his usually upbeat, jovial demeanor, "is that I would pass half my life here in this land." Reynaldo, the eldest of eleven children in a poor *campesino* family, had first left home at age seventeen to try his hand in the big city of Guadalajara. He had returned home after several months of selling candy on the street, but cultivating the land with this father offered little promise, and so he left once again at age twenty-one, this time bound for the United States with two cousins and a brother-in-law.

In the early 1970s he worked a steady job at a water-bed factory in Los Angeles, and when he was laid off in 1975, he joined kin in central California, where he harvested vegetables and grapes, and began living with a young Mexican immigrant woman, Soledad, and her three children. When he returned to take a job in another Los Angeles–based water-bed factory in 1978, Soledad and her children accompanied him. During this period Reynaldo's U.S. earnings peaked, as he derived income from both his factory job and his activities helping *coyotes*—those who smuggle undocumented migrants into the U.S. Eventually he brought his parents and younger siblings to Los Angeles, but his relations with them and with Soledad soon soured. Reynaldo drank heavily, he was arrested for numerous traffic violations, and his parents returned to Mexico. Soledad packed up all of the household belongings and left him after she saw an incriminating photo of Reynaldo with another woman.

In 1981 Reynaldo came to Oakview and joined kin members, including several of the men with whom he had initially departed from Mexico. By day he worked as a gardener, and in the evenings he dulled his pain by drinking in bars. At one of these bars he became enamored of Anabel, a very appealing seventeen-year-old waitress newly arrived in the United States "without papers" and without the support of kin. Initially Anabel would have nothing to do with him, but Reynaldo's persistent charm and offer to help her find paid domestic work won her over, and they soon started living together.

When I met Reynaldo and Anabel in 1987, they lived with their four-year-old daughter in the garage of a large but somewhat run-down estate. They lived in a residential area where homes easily cost a million dollars, but a five-minute car ride took them to the barrio, where they shopped for Mexican pastries and tortillas, cashed the small checks Reynaldo earned, and visited Reynaldo's relatives. They furnished the garage with a sofa, a bed, a color television, and a VCR, and they stored their clothes in large suitcases; a small refrigerator, a toaster oven, and a hot plate clustered around a table and chairs served as the kitchen; and they walked to the estate home to use the bathroom. Their domestic surroundings were improvised, but their domestic division of labor tenaciously clung to orthodoxy, with Anabel cooking and looking after their child. Chickens wandered in and out of the garage, and as winter approached, Reynaldo nailed plasterboard on the ceiling and walls nearest the bed so as to deter the cold drafts and rain from seeping into their abode.

The owner of the estate, a middle-aged Chicana whom they referred to disparagingly as *la pocha* (a derogatory term for a U.S.-born person of Mexican descent), allowed Anabel and Reynaldo to live in her garage in exchange for Reynaldo's yard maintenance and Anabel's weekly cleaning services. Anabel had not looked for steady work since the birth of their daughter, although she occasionally cleaned a house or two, and Reynaldo was permanently underemployed, working two or three days a week with his cousin, a gardener with established clients. Although they always needed more cash, they managed to keep their food expenses low by raising chickens and rabbits, and by cultivating a sizable vegetable plot behind the garage, and Reynaldo had given up his costly drinking since the birth of their daughter, to whom he was extremely devoted.

Although they joked around, Reynaldo and Anabel rarely expressed much respect or appreciation for one another. During our first meeting, at a Sunday-afternoon birthday party, Reynaldo had exclaimed: "When I first met her, Anabel couldn't even write her name. She was a *burra* [donkey]!" Although he boasted that she had progressed, thanks to his tutelage and his urging her to attend school, Anabel had agreed that yes, she was still a *burra*. Her lack of self-esteem did not, however, restrain her own criticisms of Reynaldo's poor performance as a family provider, a recurrent theme she voiced when friends and kin were present.

At social gatherings, friends and relatives joined Anabel in ridiculing Reynaldo's lack of employment and poor living conditions, labeling him lazy and unmotivated. Reynaldo repelled their remarks well enough, generally with one of two responses: either he would defend himself by listing his future aspirations, claiming that once he cleared his police record, he would obtain legal status, find a better job, and send Anabel and his daughter to school full-time; or he would simply cite the futility of it all. After seventeen years of what he described as treachery, dead-end jobs, and bouts with alcoholism in California, he felt *gastado*—worn out. Recalling his days with Soledad in Los Angeles, he once said: "I was responsible, I paid the rent, I bought the kids shoes, food, everything, and where did it leave me? Nowhere. So, why should I want those problems?"

These profiles of some of the people I got to know in Oakview suggest diverse routes leading to migration and settlement. They show people in different stages of the settlement process, from the long-established Ávila family to more recent newcomers like María Alicia Navarro and her family. The experiences are representative insofar as they reflect patterns of decision making about migration, and the ways in which daily work and family life are typically organized, but each family approached these issues in a unique fashion. I next turn to the theme of gender relations and how they shape the different patterns of migration. As the portraits show, these families have established a multitude of arrangements for work and family life, reflecting not only personal choices and idiosyncracies, but also social patterns.

CHAPTER FOUR

Gendered Transitions

"No, I did not want him to leave," a wife recalls of her husband's departure to go north. "I feared he would leave me and the children for another woman, but what could I do?" A young man who left his parents and siblings to seek adventure and dollars in California admits that "my parents would have liked to keep me for as long as possible on the ranch, so that I could work for their benefit. But I had to leave, and they understood." And a young woman with similar inclinations threatened to marry an alcoholic unless her father allowed her to go north. Instances such as these suggest that, contrary to the orthodox view of migration, Mexican immigrants do not always pursue migration as part of a unified household strategy. Although feminist scholarship has drawn attention to gender and generational conflicts in family and household units (Benería and Roldán, 1987; Hartmann, 1981; Thorne, 1982; Wolf, 1990), assumptions of household unity still prevail in much of the migration literature. This chapter evaluates these assumptions in light of the study and begins to develop an alternative migration theory, one that acknowledges the place of gender in shaping migration. It analyzes the politics of gender in families and social networks as these relations mediate between macrostructural transformations of a political-economic nature and specific patterns of migration.

NOTE: Some of the materials and ideas presented in Chapters 4, 5, and 6 initially appeared in articles written for *Gender & Society* and *Social Problems*.

THE HOUSEHOLD STRATEGIES MODEL

From the late 1970s through the 1980s, variations of the "household strategies" model served as a dominant paradigm in the migration literature, and guided much of migration research.[1] This model was explicitly used in those projects where investigators self-consciously used "household strategies" (Pessar, 1982; Selby and Murphy, 1982; Dinerman, 1982; Arizpe, 1978, 1981), and implicitly used in studies that adopted the household as a unit of analysis (Mines, 1981; Massey et al., 1987; Reichert, 1981).[2] In recent years, the household model has been challenged by research on international migration (Rouse, 1987; Grasmuck and Pessar, 1991) and on women's labor-force participation in third-world countries (Benería and Roldán, 1987; Wolf, 1990). These critiques, informed and driven by feminist insights, have countered the image of a unitary household undivided by gender and generational hierarchies; in some cases, critics have offered more sophisticated conceptualizations of the household as a contested arena (Grasmuck and Pessar, 1991; Selby et al., 1990).[3] In spite of these advances, however, a casual glance at the recent migration literature testifies to the currency which the unmodified household model still enjoys. For this reason, it is useful to begin by identifying the basic tenets embedded in this perspective.

First, proponents of the household model generally agree that the household is a clearly and relentlessly bounded *unit* which shares a set amount of land, labor, capital, and social resources. Social solidarity, altruism, and a sharing ethic characterize household social relations, creating a "moral economy" very much unlike what occurs in the market and in forms of capitalist production (Folbre, 1988). Rather than conflict and competition, the model presumes the existence of not only shared income and resources, but also a collective ethos of shared interests and goals. Accordingly, all individuals have an equal stake in the household.

When the household model is used in studies of intranational or international population movements, migration is seen as an adaptive or *reactive* response, one pursued when household economic necessities outstrip locally available income and resources. According to this scheme, "immigration to the United States is an adaptive response on the part of enterprising households to the regional political economy" (Dinerman, 1978:485), or, in the words of another proponent, "migration is an option that is contingent on the relationship between the household's consumption needs and its productive capacity" (Wood, 1982:314).[4]

Finally, this model assumes that *strategies* based on deliberate house-hold-wide calculation drive migration, regardless of whether people migrate as individuals or as family units. The claim that "migration is not an individual decision, but one taken by the whole household" (Selby and Murphy, 1982:9) typifies this perspective. Migration is assumed to be one of many choices available to households. Yet the attribution of individuals' actions to household strategies has generally been assumed, not investigated. Wolf suggests that proponents of the household strategies model typically dispense with inquiries into the subjects' viewpoints because they assume that people—especially poor people—cannot explain their own behavior (1990). Once we actually listen to the voices of Mexican immigrants, however, the notion that migration is driven by collective calculations or household-wide strategies becomes increasingly difficult to sustain.

An exclusive focus on the household suggests that households are insulated from social connections with people outside the household. This view, fortunately, has not characterized the literature on Mexican migration, which has indeed emphasized the importance of extra-household social relations, particularly social networks. Immigrants are experts at developing social networks which reduce migration's financial and social costs and risks by providing the new migrant with valuable information, cash loans, job contacts, and other resources. Many studies of Mexican immigration highlight the importance of these social infrastructures in facilitating and maintaining migration flows (Mines, 1981; Massey et al., 1987; Portes and Bach, 1985).

While research has correctly identified the male origins of social networks central to migration, indicating men's role as the "pioneers" of these networks (Mines, 1981), many studies continue to operate under the implicit assumption of the household model—and so assume that all resources, including social networks, are shared equally among household and family members. These studies either ignore women's place in these social relations altogether or erroneously assume that women are simply inserted into their male kin's networks and therefore automatically benefit from men's social resources and expertise (Mines, 1981; Massey et al., 1987). Kossoudji and Ranney (1984) analyzed Mexican survey data and found that by the 1970s young single women involved in U.S.-bound migration had developed networks. This chapter shows how gender, together with age, intervenes in immigrant networks in ways that both facilitate and constrain migration opportunities for Mexican women and men. These networks are significant in both migration processes and settlement outcomes, and their gender dynamics further undermine the homogeneity of the household model.

The case-study material that follows suggests how family stage, family unit, and independent migration are each shaped by a particular configuration of gender politics. Family decision-making processes precede migration and enter into the dynamics of the migrants' social networks. I asked respondents, "Who decided you would migrate?" But I was more interested in probing the contexts in which these decisions were situated. These decision-making processes often involved contention, long-term negotiation, and persuasion, as well as dominance and acquiescence. Although I did not observe the decision making as it occurred, I attempt to reconstruct these processes by relying on information gathered through interviews and through conversations in informal social settings. It is also important to remember that these decision-making processes occurred in the broader context of social change in gender relations in Mexico.

FAMILY STAGE MIGRATION

Like the classic Mexican migrants portrayed in the literature, the men in this study who migrated before their wives and children said that they did so in order to fulfill a target goal: to earn enough money to buy land, build a house, or pay off past debts in Mexico.

> I came here so that I could build a house, because I didn't have one. We were there living in my father's house, we were very crowded there. . . . So I decided to come here until I had enough for my house.(Rubén Sánchez)

> I wanted to earn enough money to buy my own rancho. I was tired of always renting someone else's land in order to work. (Manuel Galván)

> In Mexico if one is contracted for work, well, there it's called *el jornal*, when they pay you daily wages for each day. Well, if they paid you that way, you could earn twenty-five Mexican pesos. That was about enough to buy a kilo of meat, and I had many debts. . . . So one is left in the circumstances of having to raise the courage to come here and search for a different life. (Eudoro Ibarra)

These men identified themselves as family breadwinners, migrating north to resolve economic difficulties, and it is easy to see their migration incentives deriving from collective family or household needs. Their migration, however, reveals a gender dimension not only with respect to breadwinner obligations, but also with regard to who had the authority and power to make such an assessment and carry out migration.

In those families where men migrated before their wives and children, women were not included as active participants in the decision to migrate. Rather, the husbands unilaterally decided to migrate north with little regard for their wives' concerns and opinions; migration was not the outcome of conjugal or household decision-making processes. Husbands either announced their imminent departure, or sought their wives' tacit approval by justifying their actions on the basis of family economic need. This pattern reflected both the legitimacy of husbands' and fathers' authority to act autonomously, and the context of the immediate opportunities in which they acted.

Many of these men did not plan their migration months in advance, nor did they necessarily take the initiative to seek out a contact, a social link in the network chain to the U.S. Typically, a letter arrived one day, or a return migrant uncle or brother appeared, and an opportunity—an invitation or a proposition to migrate—suddenly materialized. These men decided to migrate in this context of seemingly reduced risk, a context that encouraged them to act quickly, almost impulsively. Héctor Valenzuela, for example, who at the time was married and the father of three children, recalled that he promptly departed after receiving a letter from his brother in Oakview. He borrowed money for his trip to the border, and once there, he telephoned to ask his brother to arrange for *coyote* (smuggler) assistance.

> My brother had come around 1965, he came before he had married. He came here to Oakview, to the house of one of my aunts, who is my father's sister. In 1966 he sent me a letter to see if I wanted to come. I told him yes, because I didn't have a house or anything back there. He asked if I was willing to work, then I should write to say if I would come. He only told me that. But me, with the desire [*ganas*] I had, well, I didn't even answer his letter. I just came to Tijuana, and from Tijuana I telephoned him. I said, "Here I am."

Similarly, in 1973, Luis Bonilla, then the father of six children ranging in age from one to sixteen, told his wife he was departing for California. His father had written and offered to help pay for his trip north.

> We had just left the rancho and moved to the city [Guadalajara] so that the children could attend schools, and that is when my father told me there was work in California. I told him I was ready to go and he sent me money for my passage.

The men were typically invited to accompany brothers, uncles, or friends who were already veteran migrants journeying back to California. Patricio Macías, the father of three infants and toddlers, was laid off from his job as a restaurant cook in Guadalajara in 1978, and although he had already secured a new job in a brewery, where he was scheduled to begin the following week, he opted to migrate when a concrete opportunity arose.

> Two of my cousins had been here [the U.S.] many years and they were going again. They were from families that lived in a small town, but they stopped in Guadalajara to see us, and they asked me if I wanted to go too. Well, I thought, what do I have to lose? So I went with them.

Similarly, in 1950, when two of Manuel Galván's friends from nearby ranchos were headed for California, he readily departed with them. "I went with them, we were good friends. I had already gone to Texas as a *mojado* [wetback], so I just changed from being a *mojado* to an *alambrista* [fence crosser]." The invitation to migrate rarely went to a wife, but was presented to the husband.

All of the men who preceded their family's migration, with the exception of one, reported that they were the ones to make the decision to migrate. The one exception was Marcelino Ávila, a young man of twenty at the time of migration, who, although married and the father of an infant, worked and lived with his wife and infant in his parents' home. He was still under the authority of his father, and it was his father who decided that he and Marcelino would go north in 1957. As Marcelino's wife, Dolores, put it:

> He was like the son of the family, not very responsible. So we were living with his parents and then his father decided to go to the U.S. My father-in-law had a brother here and that brother was always saying, "Why don't you come to the U.S. and you'll earn more money and won't have to work as hard as you do on the ranch?" It was his father who decided that the two of them should come here. My father-in-law got up the enthusiasm for the two of them to go take a spin.

When I asked the men to recall if their wives agreed with their initial migration decision, they generally sketched a scenario in which their wives accepted their husbands' migration because of economic need. Their wives had fundamentally agreed, they said, or at worst, they were resigned to this situation. Men typically stated that their wives' ambivalence was tempered by economic incentives. Héctor Valenzuela, for example, whose first wife is now deceased, recalled:

It gratified her very much to know that my brother remembered us. Oh, she was very happy! I read her the letter and everything. But at the same time she was sad, right? She cried because I was going to come here, but she also wanted me to, because back then people talked a lot about the North. . . . And my wife remained sad. She stayed back there with three children.

Other men stated that their wives had responded similarly.

She had to say sure. How could she disagree? My brother was here, and things were going well for him. And so she said yes. [*Was your wife in agreement that only you should come?*] No, well, no. Well, she wasn't, but in a certain way, she got up the enthusiasm, to see if this way our situation might improve. Separating, especially when one is young, is not very appealing, but we always had an interest in progressing in our lives, one way or another. (Arturo Barrios)

She was sad, but she also supported me in my decision to go north so that I might advance. (Marcelino Ávila)

Well, she felt very bad, as we were recently married. But I explained it to her and so she also understood why I was coming here. She also didn't like being there [his parents' house], she could see that we needed something, that we needed our own house. (Rubén Sánchez)

She had to get up the enthusiasm to see if that way we could improve the circumstances in which we lived. We were newly arrived in the city [Guadalajara], and it wasn't easy with so many children to feed and educate. (Luis Bonilla)

Eudoro Ibarra responded more bluntly: "In those days, wives obeyed whatever their husbands said, whether they wanted to or not."

When I asked the women how they had responded to their husbands' migration, they gave various responses. They recalled feelings of ambivalence, principally because they feared becoming a *mujer abandonada* (abandoned woman) if their husbands deserted them. One woman, speaking of her hometown in Mexico, estimated that "out of ten men who come here [the U.S.], six return home. The others who come here just marry another woman and stay here, forgetting their wives and children in Mexico." Women feared that their husbands' migration would signal not a search for a better means of supporting the family but an escape from supporting the family. Their husbands' migration promised an uncertain future for themselves and for the children who would remain behind.[5]

Women objected to their husbands' migration and prolonged absences for family reasons. Isabel Barrios told a story full of resentment and bitterness:

I was never in agreement that he should be apart from us, I never agreed. Because in the first place he had his profession as a teacher, and when I married, I married with, well, how should I say, eh, not with the intention that he would make lots of money, but that he was a man prepared for home life. So when he decided that [to migrate], I never agreed. The entire time he was away, from the time we were newlyweds until we [she and the children] arrived here in 1964 . . . the entire time, it was always against my will.

Few of the women were as vehement as Isabel Barrios in expressing either to me or to their husbands their dissenting views. In retrospect, many of them recognized that as young brides, they could not easily disagree with their husbands' decisions or question their judgment because they were accustomed to obeying men, either their fathers or their husbands. When their husbands first departed, many of these women were teenagers with infants. Dolores Ávila's statement summarizes the sense of powerlessness that several of these women expressed:

Once Marcelino asked me how I would feel if he came to the United States with his father and I told him, "Do whatever you think is best." This is because I was so young. I never thought he could fall for another woman here. I had to believe that he knew what was best for us, that he knew how to advance our situation.

Women who did oppose their husbands' migration rarely voiced their opposition, but sometimes expressed it in silence, through the form of prayer. Blanca Macías had three small children, including a one-month-old infant, when her husband abruptly decided to migrate in 1978. Blanca felt that she must accept her husband's impending migration, but at the same time she secretly prayed that the INS would apprehend him and send him back to Mexico. She told me that, when informed of his plans to go north with relatives and casually asked, "What do you think?" she had responded to his rhetorical question with an equally rhetorical answer, one that reflected her powerless position:

I said to him, "I can't tell you to go, and I can't tell you to stay. If I tell you to go, and things don't work out well for you, then you'll blame me, and if I tell you to stay, and the new job [in the brewery] doesn't work out, you'll say that it was my fault too, and that things would have worked out better in the north."

Blanca Macías feared that her husband would leave her for another woman in the U.S., yet she contained her strong reservations, and instead told her husband, "You have to decide."

Other women reported that while their husbands autonomously decided to migrate, they initially supported their migration in hopes that
U.S. remittances and savings would solve urgent financial problems.
Later, they changed their minds. The remittances were not always forthcoming, and some women, like Tola Bonilla, heard rumors of their husbands' extramarital liaisons:

> In 1972 he said to me, "Look, I'm going to go to the U.S. I will send you
> money every eight days." So I told him, fine, if he wanted to stay and work
> as long as five years, okay. I had hope that he would return soon. But after
> about a year I began to hear rumors about my husband, rumors that he had
> another woman and a little daughter. So then I did not want him to stay. I
> would ask God in my prayers to have the *migra* [Border Patrol] throw him
> out [of the U.S.].

Only one woman fully supported her husband's long-term sojourns.
Although Griselia Morales and her eight children endured many hardships during her husband's absences, the remittances he sent allowed her
to endure this arrangement. She reported that if the children fell ill, she
did not send word of it to her husband until after they had recuperated,
and if they lacked food, she spared telling him so as not to distract him
from his employment. She deliberately never sent word to him of the
adversity she experienced in his absence. Griselia Morales recognized
that this tacit approval set her apart from most women, and she took
pride in acknowledging that she was unique among her peers in this
respect:

> A lot of women do not allow their husbands to work in peace in the U.S. But
> I did make an effort [to do so] because if I hadn't, I wouldn't have escaped
> my [financial] urgencies. . . . I did not like to discourage him, because without
> him, we couldn't have supported ourselves.

When a husband announced his plan to go north, often the only realm
in which his wife exercised decision-making power was choosing where
she would reside in his absence. Blanca Macías recalled: "He told me his
intentions [to go north]. When he asked, 'Well, if I go, where would you
prefer to stay, here, with my parents, or with your parents?' I knew then
that he had made up his mind." In some cases, the women lived on their
own with their children; in others, they lived with in-laws or their own
family of origin. Given these limited options, most young women opted
to stay with their own parents, but in those cases where returning to their
families of origin was never an option, or in cases where their husbands'

sojourns continued for many years, the women eventually moved out on their own with their children.

The husbands' departures initiated lengthy spousal separations, and in many of the families, these separations induced significant transformations in the gender ideologies and practices governing spousal relations. These transformations played a key role in fomenting the women's migration. In the following sections, I explore how women in these circumstances achieved migration by challenging patriarchal family authority and by overcoming the obstacles of male-dominated networks. To understand these women's migration, we need to examine rearrangements in the domestic realm of family and household, rearrangements set in motion by their husbands' departures.

THE LIVES OF WOMEN WHO STAY BEHIND

The women who stayed in Mexico, especially the wives of the pre-1965 sojourners, experienced relatively long marital separations. In the absence of their husbands, women's work routines and responsibilities expanded. Studies conducted in Mexico confirm that in these circumstances women assume new tasks previously performed primarily by men, such as administering resources, making decisions about children's education and disciplining youth, doing work associated with the care of agriculture and livestock, and participating in other income-earning activities (Ahern et al., 1985; Alarcon, 1988; González de la Rocha, 1989; Mummert, 1988, 1991, forthcoming).

For the women in this study, remittances sent by their migrant husbands arrived sporadically and in smaller amounts than expected, and while store credit, loans, and assistance from kin and trusted friends provided emergency relief, these sources could not be relied upon indefinitely. In response to extreme financial urgency, women devised ways to earn money to meet basic needs.

Not all areas of Mexico offer women opportunities for agricultural wage labor and craft work. But in Copandro and Las Ciénagas de Chapala, as in migrant-sending communities surrounding Zamora, all located in the state of Michoacán, women enter agricultural labor (Mummert, 1988), and in areas of Michoacán near Patzcuaro, women engage in commerce and artisanal crafts (Dinerman, 1982). In rural communities in the states of Jalisco and Aguascalientes, women embroider tablecloths, sew, and participate in networks of *maquila*—doing piecework in their homes (Crummet, 1987; González de la Rocha,

1989). And in northern Mexico, in the state of Chihuahua, the women who stay behind earn income through agricultural work, by raising livestock, and by selling goods and services (Moreno, 1986).

In many small Mexican towns and in big cities, few formal-sector or steady employment opportunities are available for women, and fewer still for those women not formally schooled. Women in this case study typically engaged in informal-sector employment, usually vending or the provision of personal services, such as washing and ironing, which they could perform in their homes. They devised income-earning activities compatible with their child-rearing responsibilities, and children provided significant help when they could. Griselia Morales recalled that during her husband's migrant sojourns:

> There were times when we didn't have as much as a tortilla in the house. I had to mobilize myself with my neighbors to get some [food] for my children. I worked for my neighbors, I ironed, I washed clothes. Emelio helped when he was only eight, ten years old. He earned a few cents guarding cars at the men's club in town, and this helped us to buy beans, corn, wood for fuel.

In exchange for food, Griselia Morales washed and ironed her neighbors' clothes, and when her children were older, they helped her sell fruit and beverages. Illiterate and unable to count change, Griselia prepared slices of seasoned cucumber and flavored beverages at home, where she could watch over the younger children, and the eldest children sold the products from tables and trays which they set up in the vicinity of the plaza, the bus terminal, and the school.

In Guadalajara, Tola Bonilla initially tried to find work by going to stores, food markets, and factories. Everywhere employers requested an elementary school diploma, but Tola barely knew how to write her name. She was even excluded from working as a domestic maid, because employers, she explained, preferred to hire young, attractive, childless women, who were generally referred to as *gatitas* (kittens). After exhausting nearly all other income-earning possibilities, she discovered that washing and ironing clothes was the only alternative open to her. Teresa Ibarra, in her small town in Michoacán, also reported doing this type of work:

> When he came here [to the U.S.], I started to work. . . . This woman came to my house and said, "Why don't you work with me?" and thereafter, I went to wash clothes every day. And I stayed at that job until I came here. . . . I also took a second job where I cleaned the house, washed the clothes, and changed the bed sheets for an engineer, a German. That man paid me one thousand pesos a month. At that time, that amount stretched quite a ways. The woman paid me five hundred pesos a week, but that was a much harder job.

Even as these women searched for employment and engaged in various income-generating activities, they remained primarily responsible for the care of their children. A field study in a migrant-sending area in the state of Nayarit revealed that in these circumstances women's responsibilities as wives diminish while women's parenting and income-earning responsibilities increase. Women assume breadwinner responsibilities and activities normally assigned to fathers, such as disciplining and advising adolescent boys (Ahern et al., 1988). For the women in this case study, taking on these multiple activities did not always go smoothly.

Women did their best to meld child-rearing responsibilities with income-generating activities. Rebecca Carbajal did not initially seek wage work once her husband departed, but busied herself with raising small children and stretching savings and remittances. She also assumed some of the work her husband had performed, such as tending the *milpa* [small plot of maize] and livestock. As she explained, "When he went, I did men's work and women's work." Initially, her only income-earning activities consisted of selling a few small animals and eggs, but after nearly five years passed, she moved to town, where she opened and operated a small shoe store from her home, a small business that allowed her to earn income while looking after her seven children.

Isabel Barrios did not initially seek employment, but over the years, she learned hairstyling techniques from her sister, and then acquired a cosmetology credential that she parlayed into a successful salon of her own. Eventually she employed two other women in her salon.

> I didn't work in the beginning, as I was with my mother. But later I did and when it was party season, well, things went very well for me as there was a lot of business. There were parties for the Virgin of Guadalupe, Palm Sunday, so people from the little villages would come, and during that time, I would work all day and sometimes into the night as there were so many people coming from the ranchos. And then later I moved to the capital, and I tried opening my own salon. I obtained a certificate, and then I had my salon and my furniture, and two graduates of the program came to work with me. . . . The *colonia* [neighborhood] was new, business was good.

Although few women earned as much as Isabel Barrios, women's earnings in these circumstances of scarce remittances can represent a significant portion of family income. Indeed, in the absence of remittances or savings, their earnings became crucial to family sustenance.

These new responsibilities proved to be rewarding for some women. For Teresa Ibarra, who began wage work together with her two eldest sons, the new arrangements offered the immediate satisfaction of receiving and administering a steady income. For her, this marked the transition from agrarian domestic production to participation in what Tilly and Scott (1987) have called the "family wage economy," where wages are earned and pooled.

> We left ranch work where you only earn money when you sell the harvest. In other jobs, it's different, because you're paid every eight days. We had more money in the home. And we all agreed. On Fridays we'd get paid, we'd put all the money together, and at that time, I'd give them [her sons] their part and the rest we'd spend on necessities. . . . When he came here [to the U.S.], everything changed. It was different. It was me who took the responsibility for putting food on the table, for keeping the children clothed, for tending the animals. I did all of these things alone, and in this way, I discovered my capacities. And do you know, these accomplishments gave me satisfaction.

In this case, hard work and the anxiety of ensuring family sustenance were tempered by Teresa Ibarra's children's help, by the newfound autonomy of earning and administering household income, and by the absence of a "womanizing," heavy-drinking husband with whom she'd had many conflicts. Although she worked very hard, both in her home and at her jobs washing clothes and housecleaning for a local merchant and for an engineer, she was freed from some of the daily services that she had previously performed for her husband. Teresa Ibarra added that with her husband's departure, her life changed in unexpected ways: "When he [her husband] went to the United States, I stopped grinding corn by hand for tortillas. I bought tortillas then."

Over time, these women became increasingly competent at performing an expanded number of tasks in order to secure family sustenance. Initially, their husbands instructed them in how much money to spend and save, but gradually the women learned to make these administrative budgetary decisions without counsel. Before, they had always obeyed their parents or husbands, but their husbands' migration enabled them, indeed required them, to act decisively and autonomously. This interpretation of the findings echoes conclusions reached by investigations conducted in migrant-sending communities in Mexico (Hernandez, 1985, cited in Mummert, 1988; Ahern et al., 1988; Baca and Bryan, 1985; González de la Rocha, 1989). One commentator refers to this situation as one in which "thousands of wives in the absence of their husbands must 'take the reigns'" (Mummert, 1988:283), and another observer suggests the creation of "matrifocal" families (Alarcon, 1988). In a field study conducted in a village in Nayarit, this process is explained as one in which a woman increases her sense of self-esteem as a good wife and eventually identifies as a *mujer fuerte* [strong woman] (Ahern et al., 1985:18). Wives of veteran migrants experience "a freedom where women command" (*una libertad donde mujeres mandan*) (Baca and Bryan, 1985). As women expand their activities and skills, they develop identities that are both enabling and increasingly independent of their husbands' patriarchal control.[6]

The studies mentioned above focus on the wives of migrants who stay behind, and on how women's activities and esteem sustain male migration. These processes, however, are also key to understanding the stay-at-home wives who eventually migrate north, as it is the newfound autonomy that enables these women to exercise their own will with respect to migration. This interpretation concurs with Curry-Rodríguez's analysis of fourteen Mexican immigrant women who migrated after their spouses. Curry-Rodríguez finds that the ability of such women to act decisively in migration hinges on their "*de facto* family headship," which itself is a result of their husbands' migration (1988:61). Without this transformative process it is unlikely that the women in my case study would have developed and actively pursued their own migration objectives.

Earning and administering an autonomous income without the added burden of having to tend to their husbands' daily needs did not automatically translate into a better life for these women. For the women that I interviewed, male sojourner migration exacerbated a situation where women performed a disproportionate share of household reproductive tasks and men controlled the greatest share of income. While men migrated in order to better support their families, they were less accountable to their families while in the U.S. than were the women who stayed behind. In addition to being in charge of cooking, cleaning, and washing, these women had the responsibility of securing money to purchase food, shoes, and other basic necessities, and typically they were solely responsible for the discipline and guidance of children. As one woman remarked, "The entire burden falls on one, and that isn't fair."

In some cases, departing migrant husbands leave behind a series of "wife-helpers"—male kin, compadres, and trusted friends who provide assistance to their wives and families, especially during the early stages (Ahern et al., 1985). While some of the male respondents reported securing help in this manner, their wives did not always agree with them on the degree of help this strategy provided. Some of the women acknowledged receiving assistance from their own parents or siblings, but most of them saw themselves as struggling alone with their children. When I asked Teresa Ibarra if relatives or neighbors had provided assistance, she said no and described a situation in which mutual assistance existed only among her and her children:

> No, they [relatives and neighbors] never helped me with anything. Just me and my children. My children have always been responsible, they have always helped me, more or less. At five in the morning I would make my sons' lunches so they could take them to work, and the other children, the three youngest, made the beds and Estanislao and Paco swept the floors for me, and I would quickly clean the kitchen. When they left for school, I left for work. And that's how it was. They would be running to help me with the chores and me too.

Living arrangements with in-laws may form part of this support system (Ahern et al., 1985), yet in some cases, the wives in my study reported that the delegated "helpers" who lived with them represented more of a drain on their resources than a source of assistance:

> I never had any help from his family, never, nothing. . . . To the contrary, one or two of them often stayed with us and the thing was to support them. If it wasn't his mother, it was his youngest brother, and he stayed for a long time. They came from their ranch, and they would stay there [at her house], and so I was supporting them too. And then his mother fell ill, she was very sick with cancer. I tell you, she stayed with us for a year and a half, and her family would come visit, and I couldn't find anything to feed them. . . . You can't imagine the sacrifice when the visitors would be there [at her house] for four or five days and they wouldn't go out to buy anything, and me with my little creatures, not knowing what to feed them. (Rebecca Carbajal)

Over time, many of these women developed a sense of indignation toward their husband's prolonged sojourns, and this anger shaped their own migration motives. Some women believed their husbands were shirking their responsibilities as fathers, and for women such as Isabel Barrios, this belief served as an impetus for migration:

> Every time that he returned home to visit I became pregnant. I had children, and more children—as they say, "fatherless children." The check that he sent was very different from being a father. As the priest at San Cristobal says, such men are fathers only by check [son padres de cheque no más]. They are fathers who in reality have not helped raise the children until they [the children] arrive here [in the U.S.]. I fought hard for him [her husband] to return or to bring us here. In reality, I didn't want to keep raising them all by myself. I had to work to earn money, and I had to raise the children alone. It was exhausting.

SCARCE REMITTANCES, SCARCE INFORMATION

The men went to the U.S. in order to better fulfill their responsibilities as breadwinners and to save money to purchase a house or land in

Mexico. But, paradoxically, the low wages, the extraordinarily high cost of living in the San Francisco Bay area, and the constant INS apprehensions and expulsions made problematic the accumulation of U.S. earnings and remittances. Arturo Barrios complained that especially during the 1950s, "they [the INS] would hardly let me work sometimes, they were always sending me to jail." Eudoro Ibarra, when asked how much he sent home, said:

> Not much. Why should I lie about this? When I started working in Oakview I earned more than I did when I was in Los Angeles. . . . I can't precisely recall, but the paychecks back then were very small. I earned very little. . . . I hardly kept any for myself, just a small amount for my necessities. . . . I'm not sure, but I think I sent her twenty dollars, no forty dollars, maybe it was eighty dollars.

While absentee fathers were condemned as "fathers only by check," the sober reality was that even this one obligation was difficult to accomplish. The women I interviewed said that the money their husbands sent home from the U.S. was not enough to cover basic family needs. Even if the men's migration did not result in family desertion, the small amount of money sent home, and women's ignorance over where the men's U.S. income was spent, fueled women's discontent. Some women suspected that their husbands frivolously squandered the money elsewhere.

> One can't always be watching over them because when men are alone, there is not much certainty they are saving all of the money. . . . In any case, they don't have the same thoughts that mothers have to care for their children. (Isabel Barrios)

> He would send me money and then all of a sudden, nothing. Who knows where that money was spent? Only he does. My children needed shoes, I had to buy medicine, but I never knew when I would be able to do so. (Delia Duarte)

> I don't know how much money he earned when he was here by himself, but Luis would send me money each month. He would send, oh, about one hundred dollars a month for the payments on the house in Guadalajara, and a smaller amount for our expenses. And then, sometimes nothing at all. (Tola Bonilla)

Several of the men remained deeply opposed to bringing their wives and children to the U.S. Without admitting these motives as his own, Luis Bonilla explained to me some of the reasons he believes men wish to defer bringing their families:

> For many husbands it's just not convenient for their wives to come here. Sometime they don't want their families to come here because they feel more liberated alone here. When a man is by himself, he can go anywhere he pleases, do anything he chooses. He can spend money as he wants. Instead of sending them four hundred dollars, he can send them three hundred and spend the other hundred on what he wants. He's much freer when the family is in Mexico.

In this manner, men's absence from the home increased their ability to withhold information on the exact amount of their earnings—a practice already not uncommon in Mexico—and this increased men's ability to spend their earnings on personal pleasures, if they were so inclined.[7] In informal conversations, many immigrant women and men insinuated that some men prefer the life of an independent migrant, free of the constraints and daily responsibilities imposed by a wife and children.

> Many times they become accustomed to being without their families and many times they are much happier that way because they don't have to put up with children's annoyances. And perhaps when there are a lot of children in the family this is even more true. (Rebecca Carbajal)

CREATING MIGRATION INCENTIVES

Women's incentives for migration are created in the ambivalent context of increasing self-esteem and burdensome family and work responsibilities. In Curry-Rodríguez's study of fourteen Mexican immigrant women who migrated after their husbands, all of the women reported coming to the United States in order to relieve the burden of being the sole head of household and to make their husbands economically and socially responsible to their families (1988). The Mexican immigrant women in Curry-Rodríguez's study expressed motives virtually identical to those of the women in Oakview: they no longer wanted to deprive their children and themselves of their husbands' financial and social support.

As time passed, most of the women I interviewed wished to join their husbands in the U.S. The women listed a series of gender-specific migration motives: they desired to reunite the family so that their children would no longer be deprived of their father, they sought a better standard of life for their children, and they wanted relief from their overworked lives as effective single-parent, working women in Mexico. Motives, however, are often ex post facto rationalizations. More telling is the decision-making scenario which preceded these women's migration.[8]

Women's desire to migrate rarely coincided with their migrant husbands' wishes. During their brief visits home, or in letters sent from the U.S., the men discouraged their wives from migrating. More than half of the sojourning husbands remained deeply opposed to their wives' desire to migrate. These men told their wives that no one would rent to a large family in the U.S., that the jobs and life in the U.S. were too hard, and that adolescent children would be corrupted by drugs, gangs, and other bad influences in the U.S. Migrant husbands who had not yet obtained legal status told their wives that surreptitiously crossing the border was too dangerous for women.

Many of the men who migrated before 1965 managed to legalize their status during their long solo sojourning careers, yet they did not automatically use their legal status as a resource to facilitate their families' migration. In fact, most of the men remained steadfastly opposed to their wives' and families' migration, and they had to be pressured to share their legal status. How, then, did the women challenge their husbands' authority to achieve family reunification and migration? These women developed a variety of strategies to counter their husbands' opposition.

PERSUADING THE MEN

The wives of the pre-1965 migrants pursued their goal of migration by persuading and urging their husbands to help them go north. Until the mid-1970s, when a larger pool of migrant women were already in Oakview and other areas of the U.S., the support of family members in Mexico and reliance on resources such as jobs and, in one case, literacy skills gave women leverage in these negotiations. The long separations fostered by the men's sojourner years diminished the hegemony of patriarchal authority in the family, and these women had grown more independent and accustomed to carrying out a wide repertoire of activities. Most of the pre-1965 migrant men had obtained legal status, and in order for their wives to do so, the women needed the men's cooperation and formal assistance. Thus in order for these women to migrate, they had to first coax their husbands into helping them.

Isabel Barrios, the outspoken woman who operated a successful beauty salon throughout most of her husband's twelve-year absence, gave her husband an ultimatum. She was determined that their seven sons would live with their father, and whether that occurred in Mexico or the United States was irrelevant to her. To her mind all the conditions for family reunification in Mexico were set; the principal at her children's school had even assured her that a teaching job was available for her husband should he return.

> So I said there is no longer a reason for us to be separated. This year we'll see if we stay together or what. A lot of time had passed, and he had given a lot of excuses—that he didn't have enough money for this, for that, for the house and so on. But our house was paid for, the salon was open, he had work waiting for him, so there was no excuse at all. (Isabel Barrios)

For Dolores Ávila and Rebecca Carbajal, family members in Mexico helped convince their husbands to bring their families to the United States. For years Raymundo Carbajal resisted the migration of his wife and children, yet he finally conceded when their eldest daughter joined forces with her mother. The daughter pointed out that she and her siblings were approaching twenty-one, and that after that age they would not be eligible to receive legal status through their father. Raymundo finally consented to the family's migration, but he made it clear that more than one income would be necessary to support the family in the U.S. In retrospect, the Carbajals portray the family migration decision as a trade-off negotiation whereby Raymundo allowed for his wife's and family's migration on the condition that Rebecca and the teenage children seek employment in the U.S.

In Dolores Ávila's case, her husband's grandparents, with whom she stayed during her husband's migration to the U.S., helped to persuade her husband to let her migrate. The grandparents-in-law, like Dolores, did not want Marcelino Ávila to remain an absentee father, a stranger to his young children. In contrast, Sidra Galván, now seventy-three, did not have children, but she stubbornly persisted in convincing her husband that she would accompany him on his next trek north:

> A lot of time had passed, and he always gave excuses. But after he came back that time [after deportation], I saw no good reason why I shouldn't go too. . . . He always said it was too dangerous for women to cross, but his boss was going to fix his papers, so now he had not one pretext.

Since Manuel Galván could not pass the literacy requirement to obtain a U.S. visa, Sidra took the test for her husband on the condition that she, too, would go with him to work in California.

SUBVERTING THE MEN'S AUTHORITY
THROUGH WOMEN'S NETWORKS

By the 1970s and 1980s, women who wanted to migrate to the U.S. after their husbands were more likely to rely on the direct assistance of other migrant women to subvert or challenge their husbands' resistance. Migrant women's networks functioned much the same as the migrant men's networks, with one difference: they provided prospective migrant women assistance either in persuading husbands to allow them to go north or in achieving migration without their husbands' knowledge. Return migrant women and sisters and friends in the U.S. encouraged women to go north and helped write letters imploring their husbands for permission to migrate; when this strategy didn't yield results, they lent money for travel costs and *coyote* assistance, sometimes unbeknownst to the men. In some cases, separate income funds covered spouses' migration costs, and sometimes husbands, much to their chagrin, did not learn of their wives' and children's migration until after the fact.

Teresa Ibarra's experience is a case in point. She followed her husband to the U.S. in 1970 and again in 1981, and each time it was the assistance of other women that enabled her to overcome her husband's resistance. While she ultimately depended on her husband's consent, the support of one of her friends and her eldest daughter proved to be decisive in gaining his approval. The first time she came north, a friend who was a return migrant helped her, as she recalled:

> Well, I came with this friend, because for years I had suffered from that illness in the eyes [migraine headaches]. My friend said to me, "They'll cure you in the United States, they'll cure you over there," and in that way, she encouraged me to go. And she told me to write to him so I could go. She stayed in Mexico for three months and during those three months I kept writing him, to see if I could go, until finally he gave in.

The second time she migrated, it was her eldest daughter, Consuelo, married and living in Los Angeles, who encouraged Teresa and who pressured her father into funding her mother's migration trip. Teresa recalled her daughter saying: "Come, come, here we can see each other more often even if one of us lives in Los Angeles and the other in San Francisco." After Consuelo lobbied her father over the phone, he finally agreed that Teresa and only their eldest son should make the trip north. But Teresa did not wish to be apart from her youngest daughter, and so she used money borrowed from her daughter in Los

Angeles to bring her youngest daughter north, too. Her husband, Eudoro, did not discover that she had gone against his wishes until they arrived in California.

When husbands resisted, women's dyads and networks made available material forms of assistance to circumvent men's power. A case in point is Tola Bonilla. In 1974, Tola, an illiterate woman, managed with the help of a friend to write letters to her husband in the U.S. asking that he either return home or bring her and the children to the United States. Luis ignored her pleas, yet he unexpectedly arrived home for a brief visit after an INS expulsion. She pleaded with him to allow her to migrate, but he said no. Just as he was about to depart once again, she insisted, telling him, "If you go again, I'm going too." Tola reported that Luis had smugly laughed at her: how could she possibly go without money? And so Tola produced the money she had secretly borrowed from her mother and sister who worked in California. Tola and Luis migrated northward together, yet separate income funds covered their migration costs. Tola was pregnant at the time, and at her insistence they took their eldest son and youngest daughter with them and left their remaining four children at home, where their teenage daughter and a next-door neighbor looked after the younger children. Once in the U.S., Tola saved part of her earnings as a baby-sitter and borrowed money from a friend to bring the remaining four children. She arranged for their passage secretly: "Luis didn't know they were coming. He became very angry when they called from Tijuana, but by then it was too late. They were practically here."

Similarly, Blanca Macías pleaded for her husband to return when she heard rumors that he had established a relationship with another immigrant woman in California. Although she had anticipated a degree of marital infidelity on his part, she feared that he would abandon her and the children for the other woman:

> When he left I told him, "I know you'll need another woman there, and I understand that, but all I ask is that you don't move in with another woman, or bring one to stay in your place. Once you've done that, you've buried your wife and your children. Don't forget what you are leaving behind."

When Blanca began hearing the same types of rumors about her husband that Tola Bonilla did, she confided her problems to her sister in Los Angeles. Through letters and phone calls her sister urged her to go north and authorized Blanca to borrow money she had sent to their mother in Mexico. For these women, their husbands' philandering was tolerable so long as it did not threaten financial support of the family.[9] When it appeared that their husbands' new relationships might supplant the family, these women migrated to remedy the situation.[10]

Women acted decisively in these matters. In Curry-Rodríguez's study, eleven of the fourteen women reported that "they themselves procured the money necessary for documentation, as well as made travel arrangements for themselves and their children" (1988:52). Women did not expect or depend on their husbands to secure documents, purchase tickets, or contact *coyotes* for themselves and their children.

The experiences of the women reported in this chapter point to the importance of women's social-network resources, resources that were not generally widely available to women in the 1950s and 1960s, when, as one woman recalled, "it wasn't customary for women to cross without papers." By the 1970s, women were migrating "illegally" to join undocumented migrant husbands. Unlike the wives of the bracero-era men, who had obtained legal status, they did not require their husband's formal cooperation and assistance. In a sense, their husbands' illegal status helped to erode patriarchal authority in the family. And since more migrant women had settled in communities like Oakview by then, a greater pool of social resources was available to women.

COERCION

Not all "stay-at-home" women were eager to go north. In fact, Delia Duarte and María Gándara, the women separated from their husbands for the shortest period of time (one to three years), were coerced into migration by their husbands. During their husbands' sojourns, these young women lived with their parents and were not anxious to migrate. In particular, María Gándara did not want to leave behind her middle-class status and comforts. When I asked these women why they came to the U.S., they responded with blank, terse statements, such as "I don't know why" or "Because he [the husband] said so." On the surface, their experiences would seem to support the view of women as passive migrants and nonparticipating household strategists, but this view masks the power relations involved in the migration process.

In these families, the husbands continued to exercise patriarchal authority in family migration matters, and the women submitted, perhaps because they had endured relatively short separations and stayed with their parents. The women had not been separated from their migrant husbands long enough to develop the autonomy necessary to directly challenge their husbands' demands. These two women in particular did not experience long periods where they were overburdened with work and solitary child rearing. Instead, they were relatively content living with their children and with the support of their parents and siblings.

Between the two extremes of women who wanted to migrate in spite of their husbands' opposition and women who were coerced into migration was the case of Griselia Morales. She was the only woman who did not report dissatisfaction with her husband's long-term sojourning, and when her husband asked her to join him, she happily did so.

FAMILY UNIT MIGRATION

Intact nuclear families and heterosexual couples also migrate without documents to the U.S. I examined this pattern of migration by trying to identify what allowed women in my sample to avoid the "stay-at-home" scenario while their husbands migrated. The experiences of five of the six families who migrated as a unit suggest that family unit migration is shaped by access to social networks composed of the wife's kin, and by shared and negotiated conjugal power in the family. In five of the six couples, the wives had either siblings, cousins, and/or parents in the settlement community who facilitated family migration, and a few of the women themselves had migration experience.[11] These couples also exhibited relatively egalitarian patterns of decision making, a factor that may be attributable to the women's income-earning work.

Of the various migration alternatives, migrating as a family entails the greatest risks and monetary costs, especially for those families traveling with young children. *Coyote* and transportation fees have to be covered, as do the basic necessities to maintain daily sustenance in transit for a number of people. Some of the more middle-class respondents who migrated as a family unit did so by flying to U.S. ports of entry and entering with official passports and tourist visas with the intention of staying past the visa expiration date. Securing those official documents and purchasing airline tickets required a major capital outlay. Typically they sold their property or depleted their savings, a factor that testifies to their relative class privilege.

Spontaneity in migration was not typical of the families who went north with children. With the greater risks and costs involved, planning was necessary. Unlike the people who undertook family stage and independent migrations, these families conceived of migration as a probable long-term arrangement, an outcome of hardships and uncertainty they endured during Mexico's economic crises of the 1970s and early 1980s. When they departed for California, most of them intended to remain there for at least several years, and some intended to remain indefinitely.

SEEKING REFUGE FROM THE CRISIS

All six of these families migrated during the late 1970s and the early 1980s, years during which Mexico's economic crisis intensified. Bankruptcies, peso devaluations, and inflation in Mexico encouraged long-term settlement in the U.S. Overnight, these families' customary sources of livelihood in Mexico disappeared. Firms which had provided years of steady employment suddenly declared bankruptcy, and small entrepreneurs could no longer operate profitably. The timber company where Ignacio Cerritos had worked shut down. Jesús and Filomina Oseguera had accumulated many debts with their apartment building and were having a hard time extracting back rent from their tenants. Both Roberto and Francisca Melchor were unemployed, and the Mendoza family's previously prosperous furniture business faced bankruptcy.

With nationwide hyperinflation and rising rates of unemployment, new alternatives for making a living in Mexico did not readily materialize. María Mendoza's description of her family's situation summarizes the conceivable finality which migration takes on under these circumstances:

> With the peso devaluations [in 1976 and 1982], we had many losses. And we lost a very good business due to a bad investment my husband made when he added a shoe store to our furniture factory and store. That was the beginning of our failure. That was in 1980. We were left with many debts. . . . We paid off most of our debts and we came here. We sold our things, and that was a big sacrifice. . . . I gave a lot of it away and we came here. We came here by plane with tourist visas. I brought my clothes in one suitcase, that's it! That's all we brought. When we came in 1982, we said, "Okay, its final, now we'll take whatever comes our way."

Class privileges differentiated people's experiences with family unit migration. For middle-class families like the Osegueras and Mendozas, the long-term risks of undocumented migration and settlement were mitigated because they had visited the wives' kin in the United States on several occasions before making the final decision to sell their businesses and belongings in Mexico and migrate. Filomina Oseguera, accompanied by her eldest son and later her husband, had visited kin in Oakview three times before the entire family of six sold their property and household belongings in Mexico in order to migrate. Similarly, the Mendozas' "shopping and vacation" trips—as they characterized them—to California in 1979, 1980, and 1981 no doubt facilitated the final plunge of long-term family migration in 1982.

WOMEN'S KIN TIES

The men who migrated along with their wives and children may have never migrated at all had it not been for their spouses' family ties. Ausencio and María Mendoza migrated after María's brothers offered help in finding jobs and residence. Trinidad Ochoa and Felipe Palacios came when Trini's brother sent for her, and the Oseguera family migrated to Oakview because they knew they could count on the help of Filomina Oseguera's siblings. Francisca and Roberto Melchor migrated with the help of Francisca's parents, who made the migration arrangements and also paid for the *coyotes*' fees. Neither Felipe Palacios nor Roberto Melchor had kin in the United States, and although Jesús Oseguera did have cousins in California, he had no contact with them, not even after he arrived here. Jovita Cerritos's experienced sojourner brother invited her husband, Nacho, to go north along with him, and while Nacho considered this option, Jovita successfully thwarted this alternative.

But access to migrant networks through the wife's kin does not entirely explain this pattern of family migration. While these kinship networks can be viewed as a resource favoring women's participation in migration, the women in my sample still needed to negotiate migration with their husbands. As we have seen, migration is seldom a decision which is arrived at through harmonious consensus. In all of these families, with the exception of the newly married Ramírez couple, the wives and husbands collaborated to various degrees on the decision to migrate. This contrasts starkly with families where the men unilaterally decided they would migrate north, leaving behind their wives and children.

In two of these families, the Osegueras and the Melchors, it was the women who wanted the family to migrate and then worked hard to convince their husbands. Filomina Oseguera spent five years trying to convince her husband that they should go north, and she reported being motivated as much by the desire to reunite with her mother and siblings as by financial problems in Mexico. She recalled that her husband, now deceased, had initially resisted migration:

The apartment building [that we owned and operated] became a living hell for me. It was impossible to live in Mexico City any longer. . . . I was thirsty for the support of my family. I couldn't count on my husband for anything, we were always so distant. There was no other solution except this one [to migrate], but even so, it took years to convince him to sell the building and for us to leave. Together with my eldest son, Carlos, we spent many hours talking to him, until finally he saw the light.

Francisca Melchor also reported that it was she who proposed migration to her husband, who was initially reluctant to migrate:

He was a little timid about going north. We didn't have anything there [in Mexico], we didn't have a house, we didn't have steady jobs, we had nothing! Still, he had to be coaxed.

Roberto Melchor agreed that the uncertainty of what awaited them made him hesitant, but his more realistic view of immigrant life in the United States also explains his reluctance:

It's not that I didn't want to come here, but I knew that life here is not always as they [return migrants] say it is. They say there is plenty of work, that one earns a lot of money here, that dollars fall from trees. But that is not always true. She insisted, "We must go, we must go," and we did.

In other instances, husbands and wives approached migration more collaboratively. For Trini Ochoa and Felipe Palacios, who had lived together as a couple for only one week before they came to the U.S., neither precisely initiated the decision to migrate. For months, Trini had intended to go to the U.S. so that she could earn money to better support three sons from her first marriage. She left her village in Michoacán, accompanied by an aunt, a legalized immigrant, but when they arrived at the border, Trini could not easily cross, so she stayed in a border town and worked as a live-in domestic for two years. When her brother unexpectedly sent a *coyote*, she was able to go to the U.S., but by then she was living with Felipe. Felipe negotiated the right to go along as well, as he recalled:

In 1979 I finally won her over, that's when we got together [as a couple]. We rented a house, really two rooms behind the pharmacy, and my idea was to furnish it. . . . After eight days, her brother who was here in Oakview sent a *coyote* to take Trini. When I arrived home one day, there was the *coyote*. "I've come for you on behalf of your brother" [he said to Trini]. I don't know what came over her, I didn't understand the way she acted: she started packing her bags! That's when I interrupted. "What are you doing? You are not going, and you are certainly not going by yourself. You know you are no longer alone, you are with me now." . . . So we went to a public telephone [to call her brother], he accepted us, paid the *coyote*, and we left that evening on a bus headed for Tijuana.

Even though Felipe and Trini had lived together for only a short time, Felipe already believed he wielded the authority to stop Trini from going to the U.S. Yet with or without him, she was determined to go. Felipe said he gave up a good job so that he might accompany her:

I was happy living there [in the border town in Mexico]. I had a job [as a police officer], doctors, medical insurance, medicine, access to loans, what more did I want? But sometimes love takes you where you hadn't planned on going. . . . What I most wanted was not to be separated from her. But I didn't know how long we would last together.

The case of the Cerritos family also contrasts with the decision-making processes in those families where men decided to migrate alone. In one of the taped interviews conducted with both spouses present, the following emerged:

NACHO: We both decided [to migrate]. The company went broke; there was no other alternative there.

JOVITA: My brother Manuel went to the house to talk to Nacho. He said he was coming here, and that Nacho could go with him, and we [she and the children] could stay there with my mother—but no. [*Why not?*] Because Joel was about to be born. . . . So I told him, "If you go, we're all going. Or you don't go. Its all or nothing!" Not once did he repeat that he was going alone. My brother Manuel insisted, but he [her husband] didn't say anything. He said, "Well, you know we will suffer." And I told him, "Well, if you go, the one who will suffer is me!"

As the previous section on family stage migration indicates, the women who had quietly, however unwillingly, watched their husbands depart for California did not act with the same sense of assertiveness or indignation that Jovita Cerritos did. What accounts for Jovita's assertiveness? Or Trini Ochoa's willfulness in continuing to pack her bags, regardless of what Felipe said? Or Filomina Oseguera's stubbornness in convincing her husband to sell the apartment house and migrate? Access to immigrant networks composed of one's kin cannot entirely explain the dynamics of conjugal power. The assertiveness of these women in promoting family migration suggests the absence of strict relations of patriarchal authority and the presence of some degree of shared, or at least contested, conjugal power.

These five women, like the wives of the long-term sojourners, were accustomed to a certain amount of decision-making power, either because of marital separations and/or because they were participant breadwinners in the family. In the Mendoza and Cerritos families, both conditions obtained. In these families, the husbands were regularly away from home even when they were still in Mexico, so in many ways, their family situations resembled arrangements under family stage migration. Nacho Cerritos worked for a timber company, on a schedule that allowed him to return home for only thirty-six hours each week. Jovita, his wife, spent most of the week alone with the children and tending small animals and their garden plot. Ausencio Mendoza, a prosperous entrepreneur, regularly spent two to three weeks at a time as a traveling furniture salesman in Jalisco and nearby states, while his wife, María, administered their furniture store and looked after the household and the children as well. As María recalls:

> My husband went around as a traveling sales agent and so I went and started to work too. At that time I had two children—Rosalia was five and Tito was four years old—and I was also pregnant with him [*motions to a child*], and I would open the store at nine in the morning and I would leave at eight at night, and Ausencio was out selling furniture on his routes, or he was there with me too.

Francisca Melchor was also accustomed to a certain amount of independence, as she had once separated from her husband for nearly two years. During that time, she had left her rural village in Michoacán to work as a domestic in Mexico City, and then with the help of her migrant father she had gone to California. Although her father and other kin assisted her, her description suggests that she lived the life of a fairly independent young woman:

> I lasted a year [in the U.S.]. I lived with the family I worked for, a Mexican family. I made tortillas by hand, took the children to school, cleaned, and cooked. They paid me twenty-five dollars a week, but if I baby-sat their relatives' kids, I could earn fifty dollars. On weekends I would stay at my aunt's house and visit my father. . . . When he [her father] came to see me at work one day, he saw me bathing the dog, and he became very angry and told me to leave that job immediately. But I wouldn't, not until I had something else lined up, as I needed the money. I left there only after I found a job at a factory where they made Christmas wrapping paper and ribbons.

Nor was Trinidad Ochoa a stranger to earning an independent livelihood. After she separated from her first husband, whom she described as a "drunkard who beat me," Trini supported herself and her three sons by taking in washing and ironing and by cleaning a butcher shop in her town. In response to her aunt's invitation, she went north in search of better employment, but she initially only got as far as the border, where she met Felipe. Even though they moved in together, Trini did not feel particularly inclined to heed his commands. And since Felipe was more deeply in love with Trini than she was with him, he was more willing to accommodate to her plans.

Filomina Oseguera described her employment as a hairstylist and nurse's aide during the early years of marriage as "helping" her husband, but later, when her husband retired from his job in a government office, the major breadwinning responsibility fell on her shoulders:

> The children were growing and they needed an education, and he [her hus-band] was bringing very little money into the house. That's when we decided to build that apartment building. We borrowed money from my brother, who was here [in the U.S.], and we bought a piece of land. But it was me who supervised everything. That's when that purgatory began.

Over the course of fifteen years, they built a twelve-story apartment building, adding a floor each year, renting out the units on each floor as they were completed, and then with that income, purchasing the materi-als and labor for the next floor. Filomina Oseguera bitterly complained about how her husband, who is now deceased, offered very little support during these years when she served as wife/mother, construction super-visor, and apartment manager. She cried as she recounted how his irre-sponsibility burdened her with multiple roles:

> It was a marriage without communication, with many disappointments. I always felt disappointed by him. . . . All of the decisions that had to do with the household, the children, work—all of this he just left up to me.

These women were accustomed to responsibilities ranging well be-yond the domestic sphere. Middle-class women like María Mendoza and Filomina Oseguera managed family businesses, and poor women from rural villages, like Francisca Melchor, Trini Ochoa, and Jovita Cerritos, had innovated income-earning activities on their own as well. The auton-omy and the responsibility they shouldered for earning a substantial portion of household resources acted as leverage, giving these women a rightful say in the negotiation of migration.

As the preceding stories indicate, some of these women also had direct experience with migration. Three of the women had migrated when they were single, or separated from their husbands, so in the Mendoza, Melchor, and Palacio families, it was the wives, not the husbands, who had migration experience. In addition to their kin in the U.S., this proved to be a migration resource for the families.

The one exception where spouses did not negotiate migration together, and where the wife's kin did not play a role in facilitating migration, was the newly married Ramírez couple. Jorge Ramírez had worked in the U.S. and returned to the village to marry. Unlike the five couples who collaboratively negotiated the decision to migrate, he alone decided that the two of them would go north:

> We were recently married, we were young. When we were courting I had been working here [in the U.S.] for so many years to save money, and once we were able to marry, I wanted her by my side. It is never easy to be apart, but one feels this more when one is recently wed.

Josefa Ramírez, then seventeen years old, was unenthusiastic about the entire plan, as she recalls:

> He decided that we should come here. He said it was easier to work and earn a living here, and he already had a job waiting for him here. In Mexico, you only earn once a year, when you harvest, but not here. Even so, I didn't have any desire to come here.

Josefa Ramírez's parents and siblings did not want her to go north either, but because she was married, they expected and approved of her move to follow her husband. In this respect, Josefa's migration circumstances were similar to the powerlessness experienced by the two women discussed in the previous section who experienced relatively short spousal separations due to their husbands' sojourns. Throughout their lives, these young women had been accustomed to following orders imposed by their parents, in-laws, or husbands, and for them, migration to the U.S. was not a personal achievement but an expected family obligation, a response to others' commands.

In summary, shared or negotiated conjugal power, and access to social networks composed of the wife's kin, characterized five of the six families and couples who migrated together. Unlike the men involved in family stage migration, the men in these families did not enjoy unilateral or uncontested authority in the home, and women participated in the decision to migrate. In some instances, the women had prior migration experience. Unlike other migrants, most of these families conceived of migration as a probable long-term strategy, one neccssitated by Mexico's severe economic crisis of the 1970s and 1980s.

INDEPENDENT MIGRATION

> "There are many other families where the parents do not want their children to come to the U.S., especially their daughters. They fear for the safety of their daughters. I came without any protection, just with my aunt." (Anabel Castrillo)

> "One's parents, well, they never really want one to leave. They would like for one to remain there by their sides on the rancho, working there forever. But by being here, I can help them more. I can send them money. With fifty dollars, they have fifty thousand pesos." (Carlos Hernández)

The literature portrays the migration of young, unmarried men and women as part of a strategy whereby households "send" sons and daughters to urban centers or to the U.S. in search of monetary remittances (Arizpe, 1981; Dinerman, 1982; Selby and Murphy, 1982). Yet not one of the thirteen respondents in my study who migrated while single reported that they had been sponsored or sent to the U.S. as part of a family or household strategy. While many of them *did* send remittances home to their families, and while they rationalized their migration in terms of the money they sent back, they reported that their families' collective interests were not a motivating force in their own migration. In fact, their families generally disapproved of their migration. Interviews with these eight women and five men do, however, indicate that gender is an important factor in shaping migration, as different types of family organization facilitate or constrain migration options for unmarried men and women. Patriarchal families hinder young women's migration, while for the men, they facilitate migration.

SINGLE MEN: MIGRATION AS A
PATRIARCHAL RITE OF PASSAGE

Young, single men are the heroes of the mainstream immigration literature. Portrayed as the classic "target earners," they presumably migrate to the U.S. in order to supply their families in Mexico with monetary remittances. Yet the men I interviewed reported that their primary incentive was not to seek money for their families in Mexico, but a desire for adventure and to see new sights. The remittances they sent home were more of an afterthought or a rationalization for migration. Fidencio

Flores's comments are typical: "I came north out of curiosity, to see what it was like. I had heard so many stories from my uncles, cousins, other guys. So I came for a spin." Gerónimo López echoed this longing for newness and adventure: "If you live on a rancho, everything seems more curious to you. I was curious. . . . I wanted to see what life was like here, I wanted to see another place, what might happen."

The autobiographical accounts of Mexican migrant men collected by the anthropologist Manuel Gamio indicated that the desire to leave one's home and see new sights was already prevalent in the 1920s (1971a). These same incentives, combined with economic ones, continue today. Return migrants reproduce a folklore so that eventually a migration culture takes root, and migration becomes an expectation among young, single men (Davis, 1990; Escobar et al., 1987).

This culture of migration is sustained through return migrants' stories and through concrete ties of assistance. Many researchers have documented the highly developed ties of migration assistance among male kin and friends, between fathers and sons, brothers, cousins, uncles and nephews, and *paisanos*—friends and acquaintances from the same place of origin (Massey et al., 1987; Mines, 1981). These networks also partially account for the spontaneity in migration, as Reynaldo Castrillo, the young man who lived with his family in the garage, suggests in his recollection of his first trip north:

> I always knew I was going north. My uncle Gustavo would tell me stories of the fields, of the money one could make. So then one day my cousins from the village arrived in town and they invited me to go to California with them. Well, before nightfall, my bag was packed. I didn't have money, but they said that was no problem. What a lie that was! They left me at the border.

But while migration certainly assumes its own momentum, aided and abetted by information provided by return migrants, it is also shaped and informed by gender. The notion of migration as a young man's rite of passage underscores this dimension. Gender expectations in the family and tolerance of young men's impulses help explain these migrants' behavior.

When I examined patterns of authority and organization in the families of origin, I began to see the ways in which gender shapes the migration of these men. A hierarchically organized, patriarchal, cohesive family does not constrain a young man's migration, but neither does it necessarily delegate him as a "target earner" emissary for the family.

Four of the five young, single male migrants in this study came from tightly knit, rural-based nuclear families where they had well-defined roles to help support the family. Fidencio Flores, who came from this type of background in the state of Jalisco, had for many years told his family of his desire to go north. He reported that his parents discouraged him from doing so, but once his mind was made up, they could not effectively stop him.

It is expected that young Mexican men will eventually act autonomously and independently of their families, but family conflict over the desire of sons to migrate is not uncommon. In some cases, the young men migrated in defiance of their fathers' wishes. For example, Reynaldo Castrillo and Felix Flores, both of whom migrated in their youth, told me that they did so without consulting their fathers. These young men departed by sneaking away at night while their families slept. Each confided his secret migration plan to his mother but not to his father, who as *el jefe*, the boss or patriarchal figurehead, held the authority to veto it. Both of the fathers later forgave the actions of their insubordinate sons. In fact, after these young men had established a semblance of stability in the U.S., they helped their fathers migrate. The familial circumstances of Gerónimo López's departure were slightly different, as he migrated several years after his father was murdered in a land dispute. He recalled that his mother did not want him to go north, yet she too "got up the enthusiasm" (*hizo el ánimo*) to accept his departure. Carlos Hernández reported that his father saw the futility of trying to stop him from going north:

> My father knew that either way, if he said yes or no, I was going to go. And so he saw that he didn't have reason to stop me. Perhaps if he had opposed me, I would have become more distant from them.

For these young men, asserting their own autonomy through migration, against the will of their fathers and families, signified a first step toward independence and establishing their own authority. Carlos Hernández, who worked a small plot of land with his parents and ten siblings in the state of Mexico until he came north in 1978, suggested that he had approached migration as a way to achieve manhood:

> I knew it was time, that I had to become independent [*tenía que independizarme*], so when my uncle asked me if I wanted to come, I didn't have to think it through. I knew that as a man I had to take this action. If not, I would remain there on the ranch with my parents.

Carlos Hernández did in fact send substantial quantities of U.S. dollars
to his parents over the years, as I witnessed when I saw the carefully
collected money-order receipts that helped him obtain amnesty legalization, but he insisted that his migration was not undertaken on behalf of
his parents and siblings.

These young men had first to shun their well-established responsibilities in their family of origin before they could assert their rights to the
privileges of patriarchy. In this context, migration appears to be less of a
household or family strategy, and more of a step toward staking independence from their families. Striking out on one's own and going to the
U.S. were seen as part of a maturation process for these men.

Like the married men who left behind their wives and families, most
of the unmarried men departed when an opportunity arose in the form
of a concrete invitation to go north; generally they did not initiate migration. They were drawn into well-developed migrant networks, especially
in rural areas located in the traditional migrant "sending" states, such as
Michoacán, Jalisco, and Zacatecas. By virtue of these networks, as well
as the freedom accorded by gender, young men are prime candidates for
informal migrant recruitment.

Friends, older brothers, uncles, fathers, and cousins proposed migration to these men. Gerónimo López, at the invitation of his uncle in San
Jose, California, came north with his cousin, but he had to wait until his
uncle thought he was old enough, nineteen or twenty. Both Reynaldo
Castrillo's cousin and his brother-in-law asked him to go north with
them, but due to a lack of funds, he only got as far as the border, while
they went ahead. He worked in the border area for a year before he was
able to join them. Carlos Hernández's uncle, an established legal permanent resident in the U.S., invited him and paid his way.

Just as their married peers migrated north with the idea of a short-
term sojourn, and then decided to stay indefinitely, these men also became increasingly anchored to their daily lives in Oakview. All of them
had come north in the 1970s and early 1980s, and by the late 1980s,
when I conducted the study, returning home seemed a remote possibility.

SINGLE WOMEN: PIONEERING NEW PATHS

Like their male peers, unmarried women generally did not instigate migration but acted once an immediate opportunity arose in the form of a
proposition, invitation, or promise of a job. They were not "sent" to the
U.S. to seek money for household reproduction in Mexico, although

several of them did send money home. Two factors distinguish them from the men: the direct migration assistance they received came principally from other migrant women, further substantiating the significance of migrant women's networks; and most of the single women came from weakly bounded families that provided little economic support and lacked patriarchal rules of authority.

Like the men, the women reported wanting to migrate "to know other places" and to earn a target amount of money. In this case, there were similarities of age across gender. Even though they had not grown up immersed in a culture that oriented them to northward migration, these women were easily convinced to migrate and take a chance at increasing their earnings in the U.S. While most of them worked as cooks, secretaries, or vendors in Mexico, their jobs were not sufficiently attractive to stave off migration, and by the 1970s, they, like their male peers, were saturated with many stories of how much one might earn in the U.S.

Eight women in the sample migrated when they were single, and two were single mothers. As they were primarily responsible for supporting their families, the single mothers with young children *did* take the initiative to seek out migration possibilities. Single women with dependent children experienced economic urgency, so they actively sought out contacts to help them migrate. They did so cautiously, however, in order to minimize the risk to which they might expose themselves and their children.

María Alicia Navarro, for example, migrated in 1984 when the effects of Mexico's worst economic crisis threatened the middle-class standard of life she tenuously maintained by working two jobs and occasionally running various small businesses. She had heard rumors that in the U.S. a woman could earn as much as one hundred dollars a day by cleaning several houses, and so she contacted several women who had gone to the U.S., and eventually her brother's ex–mother-in-law helped her go north. She temporarily left her three children in the care of her mother, and she prudently took a six-month leave of absence from her jobs as a secretary at a government ministry and as a school secretary/accountant. Another single mother, Rosario Quiñones, took her two children with her when she departed in 1976, fleeing her small town where the police and neighbors had accused her of prostitution. Faced with the tremendous uncertainty of migration, she left behind as equity insurance, in case migration didn't yield the expected benefits, both her small house and money in the bank from the sale of her deceased parents' house. She reasoned that if things did not go well for her in the North, the house and savings would provide a cushion for her return to Mexico.

How do family authority and decision making affect single women's opportunities for migration? I found that tightly knit, patriarchally organized families constrain unmarried women's migration options in ways that they do not constrain those of men. The single, childless women who migrated often lacked both family economic support and patriarchal family constraints on their behavior. This echoes Fernández-Kelly's (1983) finding that most of the women who had migrated from the interior of Mexico to work in the northern border *maquiladora* industry were young, single, childless, and without the support of parents or spouse. The findings presented here and elsewhere confirm that, beginning in the late 1970s, unmarried, childless Mexican women migrated beyond the northern border states (Kossoudji and Ranney, 1984; Cárdenas and Flores, 1986).

Although the women in my sample had resided with family members in Mexico, and contributed their earnings to family sustenance, most of these women's family residential arrangements were relatively fluid. This facilitated their migration, allowing them to skirt the direct patriarchal constraints typically imposed on young, unmarried women. With the exception of two women, the single women I interviewed were not confined to the domestic sphere by a domineering father or other male figure. Moreover, most of them were wage earners in Mexico.

A case in point is Marisela Ramírez de Hernández, who came north in 1981 at the age of fifteen when her cousin, who was also her best friend, suggested she accompany her, her brother-in-law, and her aunt. In Mexico City, where she grew up, Marisela had begun working at age twelve, first as a seamstress, then as a street vendor and in a crystal-figurine workshop. She reported that she was always "in the street," as opposed to cooking and cleaning in the domestic sphere. While neither her mother nor her father (who lived with and had children with another woman) enthusiastically supported her plan to go north, they did consent and they contributed toward her two-hundred-dollar passage. As Marisela put it:

> Well, they didn't want me to leave, but as I was already a person with a certain amount of time working, they saw me as an adult [*una persona grande*] who could make such a decision. And after all, as they were not together, they let me go [to the U.S.].

Marisela's earning power gave her leverage in these negotiations, and because her immediate family was not tightly knit or ruled by a patriarch, she was less stringently tethered. In fact, she believes that this explains why she wanted to prolong her stay in the U.S. while her young cousin quickly returned to Mexico:

> Well, she [her cousin] was not here for very long. She missed her family more than I did. I was more accustomed to not being with one or the other [parent], because I didn't spend the entire day with my mother or with my father, and my family situation was more irregular than hers. She was more integrated with her family than I was. It was harder for her than for me.

The parents of another single woman I interviewed, María del Carmen Ochoa, were deceased. Immediately prior to migration, María del Carmen lived in the state capital of Morelia, Michoacán, with two of her sisters. Although her eldest brother disapproved of her plans to go north, he had no legitimate basis for controlling her behavior. He did not financially support María del Carmen, who worked as a cook in a home-operated *comedor* [dining hall] for college students, nor did he live with her. Thus, she had no obligation to do as he wished. As she explained:

> No one tried to stop me. Of course they [her siblings] did not want me to go, as I didn't know much. But I didn't have to consult with him [her brother]. He couldn't boss me.

Lack of familial support also contextualized migration for the only woman in the study who was senior and widowed when she left Mexico for the United States. When Milagros Aguilar's children married, she felt betrayed by her sons because they transferred their emotional allegiance and economic support to their spouses. She came north in 1978 at age sixty-one when her recently married daughter came to visit her new Cuban mother-in-law in Oakview. Her daughter soon returned to Mexico, but Milagros overstayed her visa and worked. Other senior and widowed women I met in various households came north with their children's families or were "imported" to look after the young children of kin.[12]

Another young woman who migrated while still a teen came from a rather fluidly composed household. Anabel Castrillo was raised in rural areas of Michoacán with her mother, siblings, and a series of abusive stepfathers. At age seventeen, Anabel found herself more or less coerced into accompanying her aunt, a return migrant who was trafficking contraband drugs to the U.S. Although neither Anabel, her mother, nor her employer wished for Anabel to go north, her willful and self-interested aunt ultimately won. As Anabel tells it:

> I had worked almost a year at the seafood place. And she [her aunt] just arrived one day and said she was coming to the U.S. and she took me from my job, and she invited me to come along. I didn't really want to and neither did the woman for whom I worked. It seemed so far away. . . . She [her aunt] is one of those people who support themselves selling drugs, drugs and that's all. She was bringing drugs to sell here, and for that reason, she brought me. For that reason. It was so they wouldn't suspect she was bringing that stuff.

Anabel Castrillo's experiences are exceptional, since nearly all of the single women reported they wanted to migrate. But her case is typical in that even though, as she said, her mother "was sad because she didn't want me to come here," her mother's opposition was not a deterrent. For those women who encountered effective resistance from their family members, it was more often their fathers who imposed barriers.

Among the eight single women I interviewed, two did come from families organized along traditional, patriarchal lines of authority, where their fathers wielded power over their daily behavior and all major decisions, such as whether they would be allowed to work, attend school, or have boyfriends. Daughters in these families encountered their fathers' opposition to their migration. Yet these willful daughters worked hard to persuade their fathers to let them migrate and ultimately transcended these seemingly unyielding familial constraints. For example, when Margarita Cervantes's sister invited her to join her and a brother in California, Margarita obtained her father's consent by offering to travel north with the protection of another brother, and by promising to send money home. She thereby convinced her father that her migration and anticipated remittances were in the family's best economic interest. In her case, family economic interest did not foment migration, but it served instead as a way for Margarita to justify her own migration and obtain parental permission.

> My father was so strict that I did not dare go out anywhere. Many times, for example, I had asked for permission to go study in Hermosillo with a friend of ours, in schools that were free, but he had not let me go because if I were to study, I would stop contributing the small amount of money to the house. . . . I thought he would be even less likely to let me go north to work, because then he would think that I would just work for myself. . . . So when I finally decided to tell him that yes I wanted to come, I told him that perhaps this way we would send him more money. But this was in order to get him enthused, because it was money that interested him.

Margarita Cervantes believed that economic interests like her father's explained why parents wanted to prevent their daughters from migrating north. After all, she reasoned, both marriage and migration signified transfer of their labor from the family of origin:

> I was twenty-four years old and he still did not allow us to have boyfriends, and this happens to many people in Mexico. . . . Parents in Mexico don't want their daughters to marry because they want them to help support the home. . . . I'm sorry to say this, but I'm saying this because I think this is what happens: many parents, for whatever mistake or error, they just sacrifice one [child]. The truth is, they especially sacrifice women, their daughters.

A more unusual case is that of Mariana Viñas-Valenzuela, who creatively manipulated permission to migrate from her father. The eldest daughter in a large rural family, she was relegated to the domestic sphere, where her responsibilities were to cook, clean, and care for younger siblings. Her father had forbidden her to seek wage work in town, and when her city-dwelling aunts offered to sponsor further schooling in a nearby city, her father said no. He was even more vehemently opposed when Mariana's cousins wrote from the U.S. and suggested that she join them, yet Mariana contested patriarchal confinement of her mobility by threatening to marry a suitor despised by her father, and her father finally relented:

> I didn't love him, but I wanted to marry because I felt disappointed by life because my father never let us go anywhere, nor did he allow me to have friends or go to a dance. I felt like a prisoner. I thought that by marrying, I would escape. . . . So when he [her suitor] asked for me [to marry him], my father became angry. . . . So I said, "Well, there is only one way I won't marry, and that is only if you let me go to the United States." Because for a long time my cousin had been telling me that I should come, but he wouldn't let me. "Yes, any day that you wish," he said. "I won't stop you. I no longer boss you. If you want to go, go."

Mariana effectively used the chips of patriarchal control—whom she should or should not marry—as leverage for migration. Rather than transfer control over her labor and sexuality to this man, her father preferred that she migrate. Still, when Mariana migrated north and joined her female relatives, she was allowed to do so only on the condition that she be accompanied on the border crossing by her brother. Her female cousin lent her money and first suggested the idea that she join them, but her brother physically accompanied her on the journey north. In these cases, the brother was there to offer physical protection.

The experiences of these two women suggest that family patriarchy is not an insurmountable obstacle, but rather a malleable one. As the culture of migration gains more influence among young, single women, it seems likely that there will be more international migration for daughters from closely bounded, intact families guided by patriarchal rules of authority. A fundamental reason for this is the growth of women's networks, a subject to which I now turn.

Single Women's Networks   The experiences of the women in this case study suggest that the unmarried, undocumented women who migrated during the late 1970s and 1980s were able to do so precisely because of the assistance they received from other women like themselves. Kossoudji and Ranney (1984) analyze the formation of new network ties among single women from previously nontraditional sending areas in Mexico. Looked at from the vantage of the Oakview settlement area, network ties among single women appear to now lead out of both traditional and nontraditional migrant-sending areas.

This is a fairly recent development, since the women in this study who migrated during the 1960s and the early 1970s were more likely to migrate with the assistance of male kin who preceded them, usually a migrant brother or father who was contracted as a bracero, or who migrated north without a contract. This pattern reflected a gender bias built into the bracero program, which recruited only male Mexican workers for temporary contract labor in the U.S. In effect, this bias became institutionalized in the informal networks of migrant recruitment and assistance.

Migrant networks, however, are dynamic and open-ended, and over time they make available opportunities to a wider audience, so that as these networks mature, evolve, and extend themselves, more women, children, and the elderly participate in migration (Mines, 1981; Massey et al., 1987; Reichert, 1979). By the mid-1970s, as Kossoudji and Ranney (1984) suggest, women-to-women networks were common. Typically, a woman's sister, cousin, or friend proposed migration or urged her to go north, and supplied the valued social connections and job contacts. In this manner, undocumented single women are forming links in chain migration among themselves.

Single women regularly received assistance from other migrant women. With the exception of one woman, Rosario Quiñones, a single mother of two who traveled north with her children and joined her brother—albeit unsolicited by him—all the unmarried women in this study received direct assistance and information from other women. Women offered advice and described job opportunities, directly proposed or suggested northward migration to one another, provided encouragement and job contacts, lent money, and accompanied first timers on the journey.

Women also encouraged other women, sometimes explicitly by urging them to migrate, and at other times simply by setting an example through their own migration, in effect serving as role models. For example, before Mariana Viñas-Valenzuela migrated, she favorably compared herself with her female cousins who had gone north, seeing herself as generally more competent than they. She reasoned, "If they can do it, why can't I?"

> I wanted to come here [to the U.S.]. People said the work here was really hard. But I said to myself, how can it be so hard if I've seen so many people go there? I had seen my cousins [go], whom I had taught to read and write their name because they were raised in the mountains. I saw that when they returned from here, they dressed very elegantly, and they spoke English and had nice cars. They were raised way up in the mountains, they practically couldn't write even their names, and I thought, well, why not me? Why shouldn't I go?

The extension of migration assistance, however, was not always altruistically motivated, as in the case of Anabel Castrillo and her aunt. Yet the important pattern that emerges from these various women's stories is that it was female friends, cousins, sisters, and aunts who provided key information and resources for migration. For example, María del Carmen Ochoa related that concrete assistance from a friend, in the form of a job and a place to stay, was critical in her ability and her decision to go north:

> For several years I had that dream of coming here, but I felt timid to do so alone, as I knew nothing. . . . Once one of my friends who had married here [in the U.S.] came back and she recounted all of the things they had here, cars, a big house, and she returned in a big truck. She said I could go north with her, but even so, I didn't have enough confidence because I had to get a passport, and I was fearful of going to the police to get a permit. . . . Then another one of my friends [a return migrant woman] told me of a restaurant [in Oakview] where they needed someone to cook. She told me it would suit me better than working with the students [in the dining hall], that I would earn more, that they would pay me $160 a week, and also room and board. . . . Once I had somewhere to work, a home and work lined up, well, that's when I got up the courage to come, because to come as many people do, to look for work and a place to live, I would not have done that.

As is true of migrant networks everywhere, migration of one individual opens up opportunities for others. María del Carmen, for example, departed Morelia with another prospective first-time migrant, her thirty-year-old niece, but the niece only got as far as Tijuana before returning to her government office job in Morelia.

As seen in the case of family stage migration, social ties of migration assistance among women work in much the same fashion as do men's social-network ties, but they also help women discover ways to negotiate patriarchal barriers. Margarita Cervantes's sister, who initially proposed migration to her in 1975, also suggested to Margarita how she might persuade their father to let her go:

> My sister sent me a letter to invite me, saying, "Margarita, if you also want to come, ask my father permission, and I've already saved three hundred dollars for your [migration] expenses [by taking care of their aunt's children]. And also, maybe if Armelando [their brother] comes with you, my father will allow you to come. So ask permission for the both of you. If Armelando comes too, we could get together another three hundred dollars. Write to say if you are coming—yes or no, and when." That's what she said. And so I said to my father, "I accept what she is offering and perhaps with four of us [siblings—another brother was already in the U.S.] being over there, I think that in that way we can send a little more money to you. Let me go with Armelando, and that way I won't be going alone."

Like the men, most of these women went north intending to earn a quantity of money during a fixed period of time, and then to return to Mexico. Margarita Cervantes hoped to start a small business upon her return, but thirteen years elapsed. Eventually she did open a small business, selling flowers on the street and to restaurants, but it was in Oakview, not Mexico. María del Carmen Ochoa aspired to, and actually purchased, a house for herself and her sister in Mexico, yet she never returned to live in it as she had initially planned. María Alicia Navarro planned to return to Mexico after several years, yet once she brought her children to the U.S. and developed a large housecleaning clientele, this goal became more remote. Regardless of whether their initial goals were met, as time passed they accumulated social ties, job experience, and often a spouse and children, and the women became increasingly anchored to life in the U.S.

After looking at dynamic relations inside the household to see how various types of migration are formed, it is virtually impossible to retain the image of a unified household planning and enacting a particular migration strategy in calculated reaction to capitalist market forces. Opening the household "black box" exposes a highly charged political arena where husbands and wives and parents and children may simultaneously express and pursue divergent interests and competing agendas. How these agendas become enacted draws attention to the place of patriarchal authority in shaping migration. The case of migrant men who depart for the U.S. without regard for their spouses' views directly challenges the assumption that households act in a uniform fashion. The women who urge their husbands to allow them to come north, or failing that, women who come north against their husbands' wishes, or the women who pray for the Border Patrol to capture their husbands—all counter the image of conjugal solidarity in migration "strategies" and instead demonstrate asymmetrical power within families. Similarly, the young men who said their parents commanded and implored them to stay, only to find their sons gone in the morning, also temper the image of automatic solidarity among members of migratory households. Generational authority also shapes, but does not necessarily constrain, migration. Perhaps family unit migration best approaches the strategies model, but even when respondents collectively decided to come north, their actions were frequently preceded by a period of negotiation, with some family members expressing hesitation and others eagerness.

Evidence also dispels the notion that resources are necessarily equally shared and automatically pooled within the household or family unit. We have seen that the social resources most crucial for migration—social networks—are not equally accessible to all household members. Traditionally these social infrastructures were made available to men, and husbands, sons, and brothers have not always automatically shared them with their female kin. As more women migrated to the U.S., they developed female networks of their own, so that it is now not uncommon for family and household members to use different social networks. Similarly, immigrants do not always share their income with their families in Mexico; husbands, wives, sons, and daughters may retain money for their own individual purposes. Hierarchies of power help organize income allocation, but within these arrangements, individual immigrants may retain income from their families out of defiance, rebellion, or selfishness, although they may express regret or develop elaborate and convincing rationalizations for doing so.

The materials presented in this chapter also suggest an empirically grounded critique of the notion that migration is the outcome of household strategies and calculations. As has been pointed out elsewhere, a household cannot think, decide, or plan, but certain people *in* households do engage in these activities (Wolf, 1990). Quite aside from the issue that it is human and not household agency behind these actions, we find very few immigrants who report being delegated, sponsored, or sent as a household emissary. The parents and husbands I studied rarely took the initiative to order or delegate a household member to go north.[13]

One finding I found particularly striking was the number of people who reported that they did not plan, plot, or carefully strategize migration. Rather, albeit with some significant exceptions, mostly among those who migrated as a family unit, the majority of respondents said that they migrated after an opportunity became available. Others have noted the prevalence of this type of spontaneity among young, unmarried men (Davis, 1990; Escobar et al., 1987; Gamio, 1971), but the materials assembled here suggest that women, when they can, also respond quickly to these opportunities. In these cases, women and men acted after a concrete proposition or invitation to go north was extended from a friend or a kin member. Instead of careful household calculation, it appears that often migration is the result of a social opportunity which must be grasped and acted upon immediately, before it vanishes, and gender relations shape both these opportunities and people's ability to respond to them.

The rapidity with which people respond to migration "invitations" indicates the extent to which the social networks linking Mexican migrants to the United States have matured, expanded, and intensified a culture of migration. As many observers have noted, the participation of each new migrant opens migration opportunities for still more people. In this regard, Massey et al. (1992) observe that in the later stages of network maturation, migration becomes a "generalized social and economic practice" and includes a more demographically diverse population. This chapter has underlined how gender governs the manner in which this occurs. Traditionally, gender relations in the networks have facilitated men's and constrained women's migration, but this is changing. While patriarchal practices and rules in families and social networks have persisted, through migration women and men reinterpret normative standards and creatively manipulate the rules of gender. As they do so, understandings about proper gendered behavior are reformulated and new paths to migration are created. When exclusionary practices persist in the networks, Mexican women have devised their own systems and networks of support.

Households do not pursue migration as an adaptation or reaction to externally induced forces. I propose an alternative framework for understanding migration, one that acknowledges the significance of gender in social life and cultural understandings. This perspective highlights and draws attention to the gendered and generational interactions within families and social networks that shape migration patterns.

In this regard, we can delineate at least three different levels of analysis, which can be approximated by a figure consisting of three concentric circles.[14] The nucleus consists of individual economic calculations that have to do with the way in which individuals perceive economic incentives and disincentives of labor migration. The middle circle encompasses generational and gender relations as they play out in families and social networks. This chapter has focused on this intermediary dimension of migration, highlighting the ways in which changing gender relations facilitate or constrain people's abilities to migrate. The larger circle in this figure represents broader economic and political transformations. It is these macrostructural transformations that provide pressures for migration, but families and social networks shape specific responses. People formulate their actions in social contexts that are fluid and dynamic, and in this context, gender and generational relations play an important role in constraining and facilitating action. Migration may be conceived of as an individual project or event with origins in macropolitical and economic transformations, but at an intermediary level of explanation, its causes are preeminently social.

CHAPTER FIVE

Reconstructing Gender through Immigration and Settlement

After immigration, marriage patterns that once seemed set in stone may shift as spousal separations, conflicts, and negotiations and new living and working arrangements change the rules that organize daily life. Compared with patterns prior to migration, many of the immigrant families in this study exhibited more egalitarian gender relations in household divisions of labor, family decision-making processes, and women's spatial mobility. I now discuss these transformations by examining how gender relations are both reconstructed and selectively reproduced through migration and resettlement.

Listening to what people actually say about staying in the United States provides some insight into the meaning that settlement assumes for immigrant women and men. I discovered that, regardless of the years or even decades of continuous residence in the U.S., men are more apt than women to say they wish to return to Mexico, while women are more likely to say they wish to remain in the U.S. These stated preferences are not necessarily indicative of what people will do, but they provide some clues to differential feelings and perceptions about life in the U.S., and I will use these as a prelude to examining the reconfiguration of gender relations through the process of migration and settlement.

THE MEN: "AS SOON AS I WIN THE LOTTERY, I'M GOING BACK TO MEXICO."

Most of the men I interviewed said they longed to return to Mexico with enough U.S. dollars to invest in a ranch or small business that would provide a livelihood less degrading than their jobs in the U.S. Marcelino Ávila, an energetic man who did the bulk of housework in his family, reported that he maintained the dream of retiring in Mexico:

> I've passed more of my life here than in Mexico. I've been here for thirty-one years. I'm not putting down or rejecting this country, but my intentions have always been to return to Mexico. . . . I'd like to retire there, perhaps open a little business. Maybe I could buy and sell animals, or open a restaurant. Here I work for a big company, like a slave, always watching the clock. Well, I'm bored with that.

Marcelino's well-established position in the U.S.—he enjoyed permanent legal status and had lived in Oakview for thirty-one years—makes him atypical among my respondents, but the preference he voiced was characteristic of the men I got to know. Gerónimo López, unmarried, undocumented, without property, and tenuously employed, said he hoped to escape the exploitation of his nine-to-five jobs in the U.S. and to return to a life characterized by greater autonomy, where periods of intense work would be interspersed with periods of idleness and rest, and where he would assume the family role that his deceased father previously held:

> I don't want to stay in the U.S. anymore. [*Why not?*] Because here I can no longer find a good job. Here, even if one is sick, you must report for work. They don't care. I'm fed up with it. I'm tired of working here too. Here one must work daily, and over there with my mother, I'll work for four, maybe five months, and then I'll have a four- or five-month break without working. My mother is old and I want to be with the family. I need to take care of the rancho. Here I have nothing, I don't have my own house, I even share the rent! What am I doing here? The rancho is now in my name and I have to take care of it. And I'm not that well. I broke my hand and my foot, and being here I must be on my feet eight hours a day. Over there, I'll go take care of the cows when I feel like it. I take life easier there. Money isn't worth as much in Mexico, but one lives easier. We have livestock, we manage to live.

Many of the men expressed a desire for individual autonomy and independence, and a wish to get away from bosses and the cycle where their hard-earned monthly wages were turned over as payment toward exorbitant rent. Research conducted in Mexico and the United States by Roger Rouse (1992) and Luin Goldring (forthcoming) revealed similar findings.[1] Regardless of whether two or twenty years had elapsed, many of the Mexican men in Oakview cited conditions of U.S. production as an argument against settlement and in favor of return migration.

THE WOMEN: "I SAY WE'RE HERE, AND THIS IS WHERE WE ARE GOING TO SPEND WHAT IS EARNED."

In contrast to the men, the women were more likely to say they wished to remain permanently in the U.S. because staying in this country promised the best opportunities for them and their children. Like the men, they too experienced daily life and work in the U.S. as difficult, but in spite of this, most of the women agreed that they would suffer greater hardship in Mexico than in the U.S. Isabel Barrios succinctly summed up many women's evaluation of the two alternatives with her declaration that "life has been plenty hard, but I don't regret coming to this country because it's been easier than if we had stayed there [in Mexico]." And Jovita Cerritos remarked: "Here with two [spouses] working, we come out ahead. This way, supporting a family is not as hard as it is for one person, and this way, we earn more and we make a better life for our children."

The women said their children enjoyed better education and nutrition in the U.S. than would be possible in Mexico, and this belief fueled their desire to stay. When I asked Marisela Ramírez de Hernández, a young mother of three small boys, if she ever thought about returning to Mexico permanently, she explained that her children's welfare mandated against such a move:

> Of course we would like to, on the one hand, as it is our country, and our roots are there, *but* I only have to think if we were to go to Mexico, there we don't have what we have here. Here, with one week's pay we can buy shoes for all three children, clothes, pants, or whatever we need, and being there [in Mexico], no, we can't. With what he earns here in one day we can eat for an entire week, and we can always have the refrigerator full of milk. Also, the milk over there is not as good as it is here. If you are going to take your children from a place where they are better off to take them elsewhere, where they will suffer more, where they will have few opportunities to study for a career, it's difficult, it's very difficult.

In most families, men's desire to return and women's desire to stay in the U.S. remained simply that: an expressed preference. Yet in some of the families, these divergent preferences went beyond rhetoric and became fodder for spousal feuds; some of these disagreements occasionally flared up, and some of them simmered over the years. Since mine was not a longitudinal study, I cannot assess which families will eventually return or permanently settle, but examining these dynamic conflicts and the newly reconstructed gender relations suggests the underlying causes of these divergent preferences.

The stated preferences are virtually identical to those that Patricia Pessar (1986) discovered in a study of Dominican immigrants in New York City. Dominican men prefer to return to their country of origin, but Dominican women prefer to stay in the U.S. because their wage income allows them to better care for their children and simultaneously empowers them with more authority in decision making over such family issues as budgeting, contraception, and discipline and education of children. According to Pessar, "Work enhances women's self-esteem as wives and mothers, affords them income to actualize these roles more fully, and provides them with a heightened leverage to participate equally with men in household decision-making" (1986:281).

Pessar's explanation for such gendered preferences complements a model of marital decision making based on relative control over resources and contributions to the family economy (Blood and Wolfe, 1960; Blumstein and Schwartz, 1983; Blumberg, 1991). Research conducted in Vietnamese, Dominican, Mexican, and Portuguese immigrant communities in the U.S. suggests that the increase in immigrant women's economic contribution to the family economy, concomitant with immigrant men's declining economic resources, accounts for the diminution of male dominance in immigrant families (Kibria, 1993; Guendelman and Pérez-Itriaga, 1987; Lamphere, 1987; Pessar, 1984, 1986). These new economic arrangements signify a vast change, especially in those cases where prior to migration, women did not earn an income, or earned only a supplementary income.

Employment does make a difference, but in this case study, paid work did not alone account for transformations of gender relations in the course of settlement, since some of the women in the study were previously employed in Mexico while others, generally mothers of young children, were not employed after settling in the U.S. A broader explanation focuses on the social context in which an individual is immersed during resettlement, and this requires an examination of the changing community of incorporation and whom one depends on for assistance. Reconstructed gender relations emerge out of resettlement experiences, and these are shaped by the migration patterns analyzed in the previous chapter.

FAMILY STAGE MIGRATION AND SETTLEMENT

MEN AND THE TRANSITION FROM CYCLICAL MIGRATION TO SETTLEMENT

Family stage migration has particular consequences for the reconstruction of gender relations during the process of settlement in the U.S. All of the men who left their families behind in Mexico had intended to work in the U.S. for a short period of time, but gradually, their stays in the U.S. became lengthier and their trips to Mexico became shorter and more infrequent. Almost imperceptibly to themselves, they became anchored to their jobs and life in the U.S. Arturo Barrios, one of the early settlers in Oakview, aptly summarized his own experiences, and those of many other men like him:

> When they first come, everyone is thinking, "I'm going to go earn some capital, or buy a ranch," or whatever, but practically without exception, they don't accomplish this. Because you come here, and later you like it, and later you are always saying that you're going [back to Mexico], but you never leave. . . . So in reality, it's a big illusion that you must come work in order to earn a little capital and better your situation there [in Mexico]. Many times the truth is that this doesn't occur. They always stay here, with papers or without papers.

Not all sojourner migration culminates in settlement, but Arturo Barrio's assessment captures the discrepancy between what these men initially intend and what they eventually do. Even after many years of working in the U.S., several of the men passed up opportunities to legalize their status because they still intended their stay in the United States to be temporary. While they began their long migration careers as temporary sojourners guided by the promise of achieving a goal such as earning a given amount of money, they became increasingly caught up in a pattern of long-term cyclical migration, and eventually settlement. This process, among other things, affects gender relations in families and communities.

For those men who initially migrated to the U.S. without legal documents while their wives and children remained in Mexico, the route to undocumented settlement and the consequences for gender relations is qualitatively different depending on whether the men began migrating before or after 1965. Historical factors and the evolution of the Oakview immigrant community created very different social contexts for settlement, and this shaped the length of male sojourning careers, and initial residential quarters.

LENGTH OF MALE SOJOURNING CAREERS
AND MARITAL SEPARATION

The men in this study who began their migration careers before 1965 entered and left the United States many times and experienced relatively longer sojourning careers, an average of twelve and a half years, before being joined by their wives and families. These families experienced lengthy marital separations. In contrast, men who first migrated after 1965 entered and left a fewer number of times, often only once or twice, and they remained in the U.S. for an average of three years before their wives migrated. The following list indicates the number of years that elapsed between each husband's initial departure and his wife's migration:[2]

pre-1965 departure	post-1965 departure
Ávila 5	Bonilla 2
Barrios 14	Macías 1
Carbajal 12	Gándara 1
Morales 8	Valenzuela 8
Sánchez 31	Ibarra 4
Galván 5	Duarte 3

The men who began migrating before 1965 experienced not only a longer but also a more circuitous route to family settlement than the men who migrated later. All of the men in the study who migrated before 1965 came from rural agricultural areas in Michoacán where they worked as peasants. As migrant workers in the U.S., they initially worked in large-scale agriculture, where they remained sometimes for many years before they moved to Oakview. Their sojourn migration can be conceptualized as geographical and occupational step migration from rent or sharecrop farming on rain-fed, small-plot land in rural Mexico to harvesting in large-scale rural California agribusiness, and finally to service-sector employment in a major metropolitan area. Men like Arturo Barrios reasoned that compared with farm work, city jobs were steadier and less backbreaking, and that the urban environment afforded greater anonymity and protection from INS raids:

> I had worked in Salinas and near Fresno, but Immigration [the INS] wouldn't let us illegals stay. And so they would come around and we would hide in the irrigation canals. That's the reason we came to Oakview. It's because Immi-

gration would come around every day to the fields. And being there all day, crouching down in the fields, is hard work.

In contrast, the post-1965 group of men originated in both urban and rural areas. Some had worked as peasant farmers, and others as urban employees, and they migrated directly to an urban area in California, forgoing the detour of a lengthy work stint in U.S. agribusiness. Contrary to findings reported elsewhere (Massey et al., 1987), rural origin did not necessarily correlate with working in a rural, farmwork occupation in the U.S. More significantly, however, these men followed a less tentative route to permanent settlement than the pre-1965 cohort of men. Since a settlement community was already well established in Oakview, social contacts guided their direct route to the city, and their wives and families joined them before long. For these families, undocumented status did not hinder settlement.

RESIDENTIAL QUARTERS

The pre-1965 migrant husbands lived in "bachelor communities." These consisted of all-male residences, usually small apartments, shared by as few as two or three men, and sometimes as many as fifteen or twenty men.

> About five or six of us lived in one house, including my brother and other friends. When so many guys get together, what a disorder! [*laughs*] They were all men, there wasn't one guy with his family here at that time. One person would buy food, and prepare it together with everyone sometimes, or sometimes just alone. At that time most of us worked in restaurants. . . . We lived in collectives of five or six, three or four. It depended on the house. We had one which we called "the depot" because was there ever a lot of people there! [*laughs*] In every corner, there was an individual. There were fifteen or twenty people in that house! You can't live with so many people like that because sometimes when one guy is going to bed, another is coming from work, and still another person is coming home drunk, another is leaving for work. And at that time, most of us worked two jobs. (Arturo Barrios)

In these all-male housing arrangements, the men learned to do domestic tasks that traditionally, in U.S. or Mexican culture, men do not typically do. Men learned to cook, iron, and frugally shop for groceries. Even if they ate some meals at their restaurant jobs, most of them still learned to prepare their own food, and in some cases, restaurant work expanded their culinary skills. Marcelino Ávila, for example, worked in a family-style restaurant, first as a dishwasher, then as a pantryman, and finally as a cook, and he still proudly maintains a little book of recipes that he gathered during those years. Reflecting back on this experience, he recited his cooking repertoire:

> I learned a lot when I worked in restaurants. I worked in restaurants eight years and I learned how to prepare steaks, hamburgers, french fries, shrimp Louis, sandwiches, and many other things. I now know how to prepare American food and Mexican food, whereas before in Mexico, I didn't know how to cook anything. Necessity forced me to do things that I had previously ignored.

Symbolically, tortillas perhaps best represent Mexican food, and their preparation is traditionally women's work. Yet in their bachelors' residence quarters during the 1950s and 1960s, many of the men learned to make tortillas.

> What we'd do is go to the market with my father and with some uncles to buy flour to make tortillas because it was more economical. We'd come home late from work and then make tortillas to eat. . . . Flour tortillas are heavier [than corn tortillas]. When I returned to Mexico, my wife commented that I had returned fatter! . . . During the second time I came, there was a little store owned by Italians at the shopping center and what a surprise when we found that they had brought in corn tortillas, which came from San Francisco or San Jose. They were a little too yellow, and they smelled of lime. But nevertheless, for us it was a big deal; we were very happy about the arrival of corn tortillas. Then later they began bringing corn flour. When they began, we bought this and made our own, because it was cheaper than buying ready-made tortillas. We earned very little in those days. (Marcelino Ávila)

Rubén Sánchez recounted a similar story about his early migrant experiences in southern California:

> Here [in the United States] is where I learned how to cook because at that time, the first time I came in 1952, I learned how to make tortillas. There were no tortillas for sale then like there are now. So I learned to make tortillas and to cook food too.

Without the presence and care of their wives and mothers, the men were also placed in a position where they had to launder and iron their clothes. Manuel Galván recalled that in the house where he lived, the men took turns doing their laundry and ironing. Laundering and ironing clothes had until then been foreign terrain to these men.

> Back in Mexico, I didn't know how to prepare my food, iron a shirt, or wash clothes. I only knew how to work, how to harvest a crop. But when I found myself with certain urgencies here [*cuando me hacía en los apuros*], I learned

how to cook, iron my clothes, and everything. I learned how to do everything that a woman can to make a man comfortable. (Marcelino Ávila)

The men who arrived in Oakview in the late 1960s and in later years were not exclusively limited to all-male living quarters. Typically they lived with their brother's family, with aunts and uncles, or with a friend's family. These men still formed all-male "bachelor residences," as new immigrants continue to do today, but they did not necessarily remain confined to these arrangements. For example, Héctor Valenzuela, who arrived in response to his brother's invitation in 1966, lived in three different residential arrangements before his wife and children joined him in 1974. His description of various residential situations reveals that he lived in an all-male household only briefly:

> First I lived about a block away from the restaurant, next to the railroad tracks, in front of where the chapel is now. That's where I lived with my brother and a friend named Alonzo Cruz, he's married to a cousin of mine. At that time, we paid sixty dollars a month in rent; each of us paid twenty dollars. So I worked at the restaurant for about two or three weeks, just until the absent person came back, and then I worked at the Pepper Tree Ranch for about three months. And when my brother returned to Mexico to marry, then I took over his job at the Park Country Club. At that time, they gave you a place to stay there. They gave me my room, they gave me food and everything. So I stayed there, but I didn't go out much. I didn't get around town as much as other guys did because I didn't drive. But on Mondays, when the club restaurant was closed, then I'd go visit my aunt and get something to eat. On Mondays, they would come for me and take me to their house. Later, the next time [after a trip to Mexico to visit his family], I came back to work in a flower nursery and then I went to live with my brother, who had brought his family here.

As the immigrant community developed and diversified to include more women and entire families, the long-term sojourning men typically found housing arrangements where the residents replicated a traditional gender division of labor. When Rubén Sánchez, who had been working in southern California since 1952, first came to Oakview in 1978, he moved in with the family of his nephew's *compadre* (co-godparent), who had recruited Rubén to work in an Oakview flower nursery. Rubén paid room and board, but he no longer cooked, cleaned, or made his own tortillas, as he had previously. "I would help him [his *compadre*] with the yard work," he recalled, "and his wife and daughter did the work in the house."

Despite the absence of their wives, these men were not impelled to learn traditional "women's work" because other women, usually kin, were present to do these chores. Traditional expectations that delegate domestic tasks to women were reinforced by kinship obligations, and this ensured that men need not perform these household chores. When Alberto Gándara came to Oakview in 1983, he moved in with his uncle's family, and his aunt and female cousins prepared his meals and laundered his clothes. Luis Bonilla told me he lived intermittently with his parents, and with his brother's family, and in all of these arrangements, women kin performed the daily chores of household maintenance.

Patriarchal kinship obligations ensured that women did the domestic chores, and in residences not organized by kin ties, patriarchal arrangements still prevailed, although men's privileges were somewhat attenuated. Eudoro Ibarra, for example, described the following arrangements in one of these households:

> First, we all cooperated to buy fifty-five dollars' worth of food, or one person would buy the food, bring back the receipt, and someone would grab a pencil and paper, and then, well, this person owes this much, the other person owes that much. We all purchased the food. There was one woman who didn't work, so she cooked, but without a commitment [sin compromiso]. If I was hungry and she was lying down resting, I wasn't supposed to bother her if she wasn't my wife or anything to me [no era nada conmigo]. I would take care of myself. So that's the way I lived there. . . . And the cook was the wife of my brother's friend. She would cook for the both of us, for me, for him, for the rest of the people.

WOMEN'S RESPONSES TO THE SHARED RESIDENCES

These residential arrangements created new burdens for the women kin with whom these men stayed, and the women responded variously, as I learned firsthand from women in families who were hosting male visitors while I conducted the study. Blanca Macías unwillingly played hostess to her two brothers-in-law during a six-month period, and she complained that these visitors created more housework for her: "He [her husband] invited them, he opened the doors to them, but it's me who waits on them."

During their prolonged stay, Blanca was saddled with more grocery shopping, cooking, and laundering. Daily she found herself wiping urine drippings around the toilet, and she even chauffeured one of the men to and from work in her large station wagon. Her husband allowed his younger brothers to stay in their home free of charge because he felt responsible for their well-being, yet she deeply resented their stay: they created more work for her, they drained family finances, crowded the apartment and invaded family privacy, and they were potentially bad influences on the children. The men teased her eleven-year-old daughter, causing Blanca to worry about the threat of incest, and they told her nine- and eleven-year-old sons not to bother with hanging up their clothes, making their beds, or clearing dishes off the table, as this was women's work. "Everything that I've worked so hard to teach the boys," she sighed in exasperation, "they are erasing by showing them bad examples and making fun of them."

Not all women felt as oppressed by long-term male houseguests, especially if the men contributed toward food and rent. Jorge Ramírez had two of his brothers living with his family on a permanent basis, and his wife, Josefa, a mother of three young children who did not work outside of the home, appreciated the money these men paid for room and board. While Josefa took primary responsibility for their meals and cleaning, she did not resent their stay; she realized that their financial contributions were critical, since Jorge's salary alone would not cover the monthly mortgage payments on their house. Similarly, Teresa Ibarra acknowledged that although the boarders and lodgers at her house created more housework for her, their monetary contributions allowed her to pay the rent and utilities bills on time. As she was primarily responsible for collecting money from household members in order to pay the bills, she saw the incorporation of boarders and their monetary contributions as an important asset. The women who hosted male boarders responded variously to their new burdens, but what is important here is that in most of the housing arrangements which included women kin, the men were not placed in a position where they had to learn to perform their own household chores.

EXTRAMARITAL LIAISONS AND THE
THREAT OF ABANDONMENT

As the Mexican immigrant community grew to include more women by the late 1960s and 1970s, the sojourner husbands sometimes discovered opportunities to pursue extramarital sexual adventures and live-in relationships. Most respondents did not discuss their own extramarital relationships, but the topic frequently emerged without any prodding. Many cited numerous cases of "this uncle" or "that acquaintance" who had left his family in Mexico in order to come to the U.S., and had then taken up with another woman, sometimes completely deserting the family in Mexico.

Only two persons in two families in my sample told me that the husband had established a household with another woman while in the U.S. Eudoro Ibarra reported that when he migrated to the U.S., he lived first in Los Angeles with a woman lover he had known in Mexico, then with his brother's friend's family in Oakview, and still later with a young woman with whom he had a child. He admitted to similar affairs in his small town in Mexico too, but he said that by comparison, the growing immigrant community and the metropolitan environment facilitated these involvements by offering anonymity:

> Here one just gets hold of a car, and you race off and nobody knows anything. Back there, no, it's different, there are fewer possibilities and those who want to do bad things don't care if everyone knows, because everyone does. Everyone knows everything, easily, even if one tries hard to hide it. Not here. Here, no one knows anything. All it takes is a phone call: "I'll wait for you at the so-and-so hill, at so-and-so motel, in San Francisco, in San Jose, wherever." Here, you cross over the freeways, and there is something secret, something forbidden.

Tola Bonilla told me that she believed her husband had lived with another woman with whom he fathered a child, but Luis Bonilla did not confide this to me. He did, however, offer elaborate rationalizations for this type of behavior, citing many examples where men's sexual infidelity served as an instrumental means to achieve legal status. He described in great detail cases of male kin who had either temporarily or permanently "abandoned" their wives and children in Mexico in order to marry a naturalized U.S. citizen or legalized immigrant woman, and thereby obtained legal permanent residency. According to these scenarios, undocumented immigrant men are best able to realize familial responsibilities and obligations to their families in Mexico through bigamy, or temporary divorce and remarriage to another woman in the United States. Luis Bonilla admitted that men often forget their first family—he claimed that half of the women in his village of origin were "abandoned women"— but he suggested that women in the U.S. were to blame:

> One of those men, a man who leaves [Mexico] in search of providing a better life for his family, well, there is no other alternative for him to grab except marrying a woman who has legal papers. . . . But then, that family ties him down, and this second wife wants everything. . . . She obligates him to take care of her.

I visited a Latina women's co-dependency support group three times, and on one occasion I taped a group interview with fourteen women, most of whom were Mexican immigrants.[3] Among their biggest complaints were *mujeriegos* [womanizing men] who come to the United States and then neglect their familial responsibilities in Mexico. When this topic came up in the group, the women became very animated, and they offered many stories which emphasized that this phenomenon was relatively recent. As one woman said, "Years ago, it was not like this. The men did not abandon their families with the ease with which they do now."

Although I did not witness these arrangements firsthand, it seems probable that many married men who lived with other immigrant women in the United States found women who cared for their daily household needs and conveniences. One woman in the co-dependency group suggested this when she said, "Men learn to make their own tortillas [in the U.S.], or they find someone else, a sweetheart, to make tortillas for them."

FAMILY STAGE MIGRATION AND SETTLEMENT: THE WOMEN

Women who migrated after their husbands did entered with some advantages. Since their husbands had already lived and worked in the U.S. for some years, the men had accumulated job experience, social contacts, and a general orientation to living in the United States, and the women benefited from their husbands' migration experience. Evidence from survey research suggests that Mexican immigrant women's access to their husbands' labor-market contacts may help them to find better jobs than those available to single Mexican immigrant women in the United States (Kossoudji and Ranney, 1984).[4] Yet even when this occurs, the women's initial settlement period is by no means easy, especially for those women who arrive without legal status. Adjusting to a foreign language, a different culture, and new surroundings is not easy, and some women, like most of the men, were initially tentative about settlement. The uncertainty of what awaited her and her family in the U.S. made Dolores Ávila skeptical:

> When we first arrived, I remember that we got off the bus and I looked around, we took down our suitcases and I thought, "What are we going to do here? We don't even have a house." . . . I wanted to return because it [being in the U.S.] was making me very sad. I'd think, "Well, I don't know the language, and then how am I going to find a job, and where will I leave my daughters?" I felt very anxious.

In spite of initial ambivalence, women perceived their new circumstances in the U.S. to be more desirable than the poverty and hardships that they had endured in Mexico during their husbands' sojourns. Griselia Morales, who migrated at the age of forty-five, cited only one regret: "I just wish I had come here when I was young enough to study, work hard, and advance."

The two women who were coerced by their husbands into coming to the United States remained at best tentatively committed to staying, and at worst, they were deeply bitter and resentful. Delia Duarte's husband returned to Mexico due to legal problems over child abuse and incest, and although Delia remained ambivalent about staying in the U.S., she did not wish to return with him to Mexico. María Gándara, who was pressured by her husband into coming to the United States, deeply regretted having migrated, as she lost her furniture and the middle-class status that she had once enjoyed in Guadalajara. She perceived her acquiescence in coming to the U.S. as a defeat, and three years after the event, she told me she was still angry at and distrusted her husband: "I've never told this to anyone, not even my husband, but when I saw him [upon arriving], I felt different. I felt suspicious, distrustful towards him. From that day on, it's been different."

"HE WANTED TO SEND US BACK!":
STRUGGLES OVER FAMILY SETTLEMENT

With the exception of these two women, after the first traumatic months of adjustment, the women wished to remain in the U.S. Yet several of the men, notably those husbands who had most vehemently opposed their families' migration, remained ambivalent about their families' prolonged stay. Some of these men worked hard to convince their wives and children to return to Mexico. In these scenarios, the long spousal struggles over the wife's and children's migration were replaced by new conflicts over whether the wife and children would remain in the United States.

> Finally he brought us [to the U.S.] and then he would sometimes say to me, "Look, here it's such a sacrifice to be burdened with so many children." In reality, this was true: the small amount he earned made it very difficult to pay the rent and all our bills. Since we still had our home in Mexico rented out, I'd say, "Well, lets go back, whenever you want." But he didn't want that. He wanted to send *us* back! He wanted me and the children to leave. But for me, all of my life, my dream was to have a home, and since we have so many children, I wanted the best for them, not to destroy them. You see, so much time passes and older kids need their father, right? And I was tired of living

alone. So I said, "Okay, let's go. A job is available for you and I left my beauty salon rented out [in Mexico]." But no, he wanted to send just us. I said no: "We all go, or we all stay, but all of us together." . . . From the moment I arrived, I liked the environment and everything. I said, "I prefer to stay here even though either way, on either side of the border, I have to struggle. Here it's easier," so for this reason I decided to stay. (Isabel Barrios)

Through her tenacity, and because she soon began working two part-time jobs which enabled her to contribute to family household expenses, Isabel avoided returning to Mexico with her children.

Not all women were as tenacious, and women's success in resisting return migration derived from their ability to help financially support family members. On her first trip to the U.S. to join her husband, Eudoro, Teresa Ibarra was not successful in standing up to him when he urged her to return to Mexico. She returned, as she had left behind the children, including an infant daughter, and she lacked the money to bring them north. Rebecca Carbajal did manage to remain with her children in the U.S., largely because she had negotiated this arrangement with her husband, using as leverage the fact that she and the eldest daughter would earn wages and contribute to supporting the family.

Tola Bonilla faced a similar struggle with her husband, who wanted to send her and and the children back to Mexico, yet she managed to remain in the U.S. with the two children who accompanied her. Later, against her husband's wishes and behind his back, she brought the other five children north too. Tola credits Magdalena, one of the residents in the house they initially shared with twenty-five other people, with helping to bring her children from Mexico:

I would cry for my children. Secretly, she would console me. . . . Luis didn't want the children to come here. Bringing the children here was my idea, and my wish. . . . I wanted them to be here so they could eat better food. In those days we'd go shopping at the Carlyle Supermarket, and we'd buy baskets loaded with food: meat, vegetables, milk, and fruit. My children were hungry in Mexico, eating just tortillas and potatoes, and here there was so much for them to eat. I desperately wanted them to eat this food too.

Magdalena urged Tola to go ahead and bring the children without Luis's knowledge or permission. With the money she had saved from baby-sitting Magdalena's three children (for which she was paid thirty dollars a week), and with Magdalena's help in making out the money order, Tola sent one hundred sixty dollars to her eldest daughter with instructions to board all of the children on a bus headed for Tijuana. She did this secretly: "Luis didn't know they were coming. He became very angry when they called from Tijuana, but by then it was too late. They were practically here." Tola arranged for a nephew to guide the children across the border illegally, and later she paid him a five-hundred-dollar fee for this service: "I paid him in ten-dollar, twenty-dollar, or fifty-dollar payments, because I continued paying out of my earnings." Just as separate sources of income had funded each spouse's migration, only Tola's earnings went toward the children's passage north.

Although I did not interview the children about their migration experiences, most of them sided with their mothers on these issues.[5] Sojourning fathers helped their adolescent and working-age sons to go north, a fairly typical occurrence (Ahern et al., 1985; Massey et al., 1987), and a few of the men in this study also helped their adolescent daughters to come north. In general, however, the men remained ambivalent about their children's migration and settlement.

The following section contrasts the differences between the resettlement experiences of the wives of men who had migrated before 1965 and the experiences of the wives of men who came after 1965. The length of spousal separation and the maturity of the Oakview immigrant community helped shape gender relations in the process of settlement.

WOMEN IN FAMILIES WHERE
MEN MIGRATED BEFORE 1965

Once the spouses were reunited in the United States, a slightly more egalitarian, less orthodox gender division of labor emerged in those families where the husbands had begun migrating before 1965. Based on what I observed during my visits to their homes, what these couples told me, and, in some cases, what I heard from neighbors, these families appear to maintain a more egalitarian division of household labor than the other Mexican immigrant families I visited.

In most of these families, the domestic skills which men were forced to learn in their wives' absence are still put to use. When I spoke with Rebecca Carbajal on a Sunday afternoon in 1983, she and I sat at the dining table while Raymundo made soup and flour tortillas from scratch. When the soup and tortillas were prepared, he joined us, and, commenting on the role reversal of traditional gender tasks, he said, without a touch of sarcasm, "This is exactly how we are, this is how we live, just as you see us." He even boasted that he, in fact, was a more talented and skilled cook than his wife.

Later, when I returned to their home in 1987 and 1988, I witnessed similar scenarios. Raymundo Carbajal still made tortillas by hand on weekends. After working as a janitor, on weekday afternoons he stretched out comfortably on the sofa, but he always rose to fetch his own beer, never beckoning for his wife, and he always took responsibility as the "host" to offer me beverages and food. When I visited Arturo and Isabel Barrios's home, Arturo was also very attentive in this manner, not only serving food, but cleaning up in the kitchen as well. His wife, however, reported that during the early years of settlement, her husband did not participate in domestic chores much since he worked two jobs, and she complained that by comparison with her grown sons, her husband was "too macho" to have ever changed dirty diapers. Isabel Barrios's comments indicate her dissatisfaction with modest changes, and the new higher expectations she now held for her husband's housework duties.

Unique circumstances precluded this more egalitarian pattern in two of the families where the men began migrating during the bracero years. Pedro Morales was incapacitated by a stroke and diabetes, and his wife, Griselia, served as his round-the-clock caretaker: "He's like a baby. I have to bathe him, dress him, feed him. He forgets where the bathroom is and urinates on the floor." Yet she recalled how surprised she and her daughters had been when she first arrived in California to see Pedro preparing a meal for them: "I had never seen him do such a thing in Mexico." In the Sánchez family, Isa Sánchez had migrated to Oakview, but had returned with the younger children, while some of the adolescent and young-adult children stayed on with Rubén. Although Rubén did some of the routine cleaning and cooking in the apartment he shared with two of his sons and another man, I sometimes saw his twenty-eight-year-old daughter, who lived nearby, sweeping and cooking for him.

Marcelino Ávila was most outspoken in boasting about the the household chores that he currently performs. Referring to the domestic skills he learned in the absence of his wife or mother in the United States, he proclaimed, "And the habit stayed with me. If my wife isn't here, I don't wait for her to do the chores." Their next-door neighbor, a friend of mine who introduced me to the Ávilas, also observed that Marcelino performed the bulk of household chores. When I interviewed his wife separately, she confirmed this. In fact, on the day I interviewed her, she had returned home from work around 3:00 P.M., and while Marcelino had departed for his janitor job shortly before then, he had cleaned the house and prepared the evening meal for her and their teenage children. Dolores Ávila also recalled that during the early years of settlement, when the children were young and she started working outside of the home, Marcelino had taken an active role in the home, and had even changed the babies' dirty diapers.

These transformations are modest if we judge them by feminist ideals of equality, but they are significant when compared with normative patriarchal practices. Most of these men did not participate equally in housework with their wives. The men generally avoided the dirty and invisible work (e.g., cleaning the toilet bowl) and took on instead part of the skilled and visible labor (e.g., cooking), where there is immediate recognition. Yet it would be a mistake to belittle these transformations as insignificant, since the new arrangements depart from status quo patriarchal practices in both Mexico and the United States. These men's repertoires of domestic duties have indeed expanded. Not only are the men assuming responsibility for tasks previously considered the precinct of women, but they are doing so in ways that obviate any sense of emasculation.

Several factors allowed for the emergence of this more egalitarian division of labor in the families where the men began their migrant sojourns before 1965. These husbands lived for several years in small, isolated immigrant outposts, where there were few women to perform domestic household chores. Moreover, the wives, as we saw in the last chapter, had grown more independent and assertive during the long spousal separations. They simultaneously learned to act in more autonomous and less subservient ways, and they placed new demands on their husbands to participate in household chores.

One final factor which distinguishes the initial settlement experience of wives of men who migrated prior to 1965 is legal status. Four of these women entered the settlement community legally, as their husbands had initially migrated without papers and subsequently attained legal status. Legal status facilitated spatial mobility, social integration, and employment, since the women did not fear INS apprehensions. Initial settlement did not produce as much anxiety for these women as it did for undocumented immigrant women, and this in turn strengthened their position in family affairs.

THE POST-1965 FAMILIES: REINSTITUTING DOMESTIC INEQUITIES

Wives of the men who migrated after 1965 initially lived in constant fear because of their legal status. This was exacerbated by the many negative stories of INS apprehensions that their husbands had used to dissuade them from coming north. Fear and trepidation translated into greater vulnerability and isolation, as many of these women reported that when they first arrived, they did not venture beyond the boundaries of their home. Women perceived their homes and apartments as the safest places.

> I was really scared. Every time I saw a police officer I thought they were the *migra* [INS agents] and that they would send us back to Mexico. I stayed home, where I took care of children. Practically the only place I'd go was to buy food at the supermarket or to attend Mass. (Tola Bonilla)

> I stayed in the house, where I felt safe. He [her husband] had told me about how the *migra* could take parents away, how children would come home from school and not find anyone home. I prayed that would never happen to me. . . . I was afraid to go to English classes. (Blanca Macías)

Many of these women reported feeling lonely and isolated during their initial months in Oakview.[6] Loneliness was compounded if they worked at home caring for the children of other immigrant women, a common first job for newly arrived undocumented immigrant women in this study. Yet this isolation, and the fear of moving beyond the domestic sphere, were tempered by the pockets of women's networks. The companionship of even one or two other women—often neighbors, kin, or housemates—lessened the feelings of loneliness, and women became more secure as they learned what activities were safe to pursue in their new surroundings. Just as women's helping networks had been useful in the process of migration, these lines of assistance proved to be instrumental in facilitating women's settlement. This was especially true for those women who arrived in Oakview in the 1970s or later.

These women initially resided in houses shared by numerous families, placing them in constant proximity with housemates, an arrangement with negative as well as positive features. Conflicts arose, for example, over issues such as shared payment of rent and utilities, kitchen privileges, and differences in child rearing and disciplining. Yet in these residential arrangements, the more experienced immigrant women offered newly arrived immigrant women a general orientation to living in the U.S.: where to shop, how to enroll children in school, where to obtain emergency medical services, and how to obtain in-home child care or paid domestic work. These orientations occurred between women in shared residences and neighborhoods.

The content of much of the transmitted information and advice centered on issues exclusive to women. For example, when María Gándara expressed concern about how she and her husband would support so many children in the U.S., a next-door neighbor told her about the local

Planned Parenthood clinic, where she could obtain information about contraception. The women transmitted information and knowledge that was crucial to the early stages of family settlement and about which their husbands remained ignorant, such as where to seek medical attention for the children and how to enroll them in school and church activities.

Women's social ties also helped them in both minor and more elaborate struggles with their husbands. Newly arrived women received advice, know-how, and skills from other immigrant women. In response to her husband's spendthrift habits, and unbeknownst to him, Blanca Macías opened a separate savings account at a bank. She was able to do so only after her friend Pilar advised her and accompanied her to the bank to assist in the procedure. Teresa Ibarra wanted to learn to drive so that she would be less dependent on public transportation and on her less-than-reliable sons for rides to her housecleaning jobs. Teresa reasoned that if she could drive, she could increase her earnings by cleaning more houses, but neither her husband nor her sons were willing to teach her. A young woman companion and boarder who lived in her garage finally taught her how to drive.

Women's helping networks were also important in solidifying family settlement by helping women to bring their children from Mexico. Recall Tola Bonilla's accomplishment in bringing her children north against her husband's wishes. Without her friend Magdalena's advice and help, as well as her teenage daughter's complicity in the plan, the five children probably would have remained in Mexico, and in their absence, Tola might have ultimately given in to Luis's demands that she too return to Mexico.

Women also offered unsolicited help. Female kin and acquaintances tried to convince Delia Duarte to leave her abusive husband, who beat her and sexually molested their daughters. Delia feared losing the little economic support he provided, but finally an anonymous person—she believes it was a woman in their trailer-park community—reported the activities of Delia's husband to the authorities, and he fled the country.

These women's networks did not, however, challenge domestic divisions of labor. In contrast to the families where the men had migrated before 1965, these families conformed to more conventional rules about who does what in the home. When these families were reconstituted in the United States, they reestablished an orthodox division of labor in the home. Even though most of the wives held jobs outside of the home, the men still expected their wives to wait on them, and to take primary responsibility for the cooking and cleaning, and most of the women did so.

The Bonilla family arrangements illustrate this pattern. In the late afternoon when Tola Bonilla returned home from cleaning other people's houses, she set about cleaning her own home, laundering, and cooking. On two occasions when I was invited for dinner, Tola cooked and served the meals, but did not eat, and she sat down with a glass of juice only after she had served us, claiming that eating heavy food at night made her ill. I felt awkward discussing community organizational tactics with Luis while Tola assumed a subordinate position on the sidelines. Although both Luis and Tola adopted the rhetoric of gender equality—part of the curricula they learned in church-sponsored weekend marriage encounters—in practice, their household division of labor did not challenge women's subordination. Similar inequities were apparent in the Ibarra, Macías, Gándara, and Duarte families, all of whom migrated after the mid-1960s.

Due to a back injury she suffered while working as a motel maid, Blanca Macías was not employed, although she did work cleaning "just a few houses" on the sly, without her husband's knowledge. Patricio Macías had worked two jobs since Blanca's accident. Early in the morning he departed for his job as a restaurant cook, and he stopped at home only for a few moments in the afternoon before leaving for his evening job as a janitor. In spite of her back problems, Blanca did all of the household work, cleaned those "few houses," and looked after three children. For six months she unwillingly played hostess to Patricio's brothers, who taxed her already significant cooking, laundering, chauffeuring and cleaning responsibilities, "because that's what Patricio wants." Yet during this time, she argued with her husband over the long-term guests, and eventually the brothers were asked to leave.

The Ibarra family represented the most extreme example of a traditional division of labor in spite of diminished patriarchal authority. Their household included anywhere from ten to thirteen people: Eudoro, Teresa, six of their children, and, at different times, from two to five other kin members or boarders. Teresa did the bulk of the very substantial housework, assisted at one point by an elderly aunt she had brought from Mexico to help care for the youngest child, then later by one of the female boarders, who lived in the garage, and occasionally by her teenage daughter. A typical day for Teresa began at five o'clock in the morning, when she cooked a stew, beans, and rice that each person took to work

or ate upon returning; next, she did a few loads of laundry and then hung
the clothes to dry behind the small two-bedroom house. With the cooking and laundry completed, she departed to clean other people's houses,
and on days for which she hadn't mustered sufficient employment, she
ran errands, taking the elderly aunt to the county hospital on the bus or
perhaps paying the utility bills in person. In the afternoons she returned
home to do a few hours of baby-sitting for neighbors, clean house, or
iron and fold clothes. With the help of her eldest son, Teresa was responsible for collecting money from each household member to pay the bills,
and when expenses outstripped cash resources, as was usually the case,
it was she who prioritized the payments by innovating ways to stretch
the limited funds and by deciding which bills might be postponed or
where corners could be cut. Her husband, Eudoro, contributed little in
the way of money, influence, or household labor, and Teresa often dis-
paraged him for not being *obligado* [dutiful], calling him *muy canalla* [a
scoundrel]:

> He sometimes gives me something, sometimes nothing. Sometimes he will
> give me thirty dollars [a week], sometimes forty, from which to buy his food,
> and sometimes nothing. I don't know. One woman asked me how I manage
> to pay all of the bills since I earn so little, and I say that I don't know, I think
> it's God who helps us. . . . He [her husband] does nothing in the house. Mario
> [her eldest son], yes, he likes to help me outside, to clean, to put in little plants,
> but not one of the other sons does, nor does he [her husband]. He just helps
> with those thirty dollars. He doesn't know how to do anything either. If
> Mario is not working [as a gardener] on a particular Saturday he helps me
> rake things up or clean, but always outside, not inside.

Eudoro did not deny his marginal position in the household. He was
barely on speaking terms with his children and his wife, and in some
ways, the boarders who lived in the garage seemed more integrated in
family affairs than he. I visited the Ibarra household for over a year and
during that time, my interactions with Eudoro were limited to a few
questions he gruffly asked me. During the spring of 1988, as the amnesty-
legalization deadline approached, he offered me twenty dollars to help
him fill out the papers his lawyer had requested, but instead, I negotiated
for taped interviews in exchange for my services. When I asked him,
"Who is the boss of the house [*quien manda la casa*]?" he somewhat
resignedly said, "Well, each person orders oneself here, something like
that. . . . Back there [in Mexico], no. It was still whatever I said that was.
I decided matters." Intertwined with Eudoro's migration and resettlement experiences was his penchant for affairs with other women, drink-

ing, and carousing, and he explained that it was this behavior that accounted for his downfall in the family:

> I met a woman who I desired after my wife, and then there were problems. I
> didn't want to leave my sweetheart, and I didn't want to leave my wife and
> children. I loved my children very much. I loved my wife too, but sometimes
> everything turns out bad. That's why I decided to come north [in 1969]. And
> I had economic problems, and I didn't know how to resolve them. . . . And so
> this is how it's always been. I would make an effort to stop, and I would say
> to myself, "Why am I doing this? I should not be doing this. I won't do it."
> But those refrains never stopped me. I could never control myself. Nobody
> can do anything that's not in their destiny, that's what I think. . . . I made
> some serious mistakes, but what can I do now?

In the Ibarra household, Teresa wielded considerable authority. She
allocated financial resources, she successfully resisted Eudoro's attempts to permanently remove their juvenile-delinquent son from the
home, and it was she who would ultimately decide to incorporate
boarders and what to charge them for their stay. The five older children, in their teens and early twenties, virtually ignored their father,
and Eudoro rationalized their treatment and lack of respect for him
by saying, "Back there [in Mexico], she suffered more with the children than I did. So of course she is going to have authority with
them." In spite of his marginalized status, Eudoro continued to reap
the benefits of Teresa's unpaid domestic labor, but he no longer had a
voice in family affairs. Neither was he able to control her where-
abouts, as she moved to and from her jobs and errands on her own,
eventually doing so in her own automobile.

The wives of the men who migrated after 1965 took primary responsibility for domestic chores, regardless of whether they were employed
or not. The continuation of a traditional gender division of labor among
this group is, I believe, rooted in the conditions of migration. The post-
1965 men migrated a fewer number of times and for shorter periods
before their families joined them. In Oakview, they encountered and lived
in a flourishing Mexican immigrant community that included both men
and women, as well as entire families, and they were more likely to live
with kin or, in some instances, in amorous relationships with other
women than in an all-male dwelling. In these residential labor arrangements, the men were taken care of, and once reunited with their wives,
they were unprepared to expect anything which strayed too far away
from traditional household arrangements where women are subordinate
and subservient to men.

When husbands and wives were reunited, they generally reinstated an orthodox gender division of household labor. Yet traditional forms of patriarchy were not reconstituted in precisely the same form as prior to migration. Women did not relinquish the decision-making power and authority they had established during their husbands' sojourns, and they enhanced their leverage through access to women's networks that provided job leads and important information. Women often participated fully in major family decisions regarding the disciplining and rearing of teenage children, whether or not to take in boarders and when to demand their departure, and how to spend hard-earned savings. And men no longer mandated their wives' relegation to the domestic sphere, as the women traversed local streets moving to and from their jobs, often unaccompanied by their husbands and children.[7]

FAMILY UNIT SETTLEMENT

Six families in this study came to the U.S. as intact nuclear families or as couples. As discussed in the last chapter, in five out of six cases it was the wives' kin that provided the important social-network assistance for migration. Initially, these families were extremely dependent on the wives' kin, usually the wives' parents or siblings, for help with their migration and resettlement, and this promoted particular rearrangements in family gender relations.[8]

Illegally migrating to the U.S. with several dependents was an expensive proposition. The Mendozas migrated with six children, the Cerritoses with three children, and the Osegueras with four, albeit grown, children; Jovita Cerritos, Josefa Ramírez, and Francisca Melchor were all pregnant when they arrived. Most of these families had borrowed money or used scarce savings to fund their travel costs, so when they arrived in the U.S., renting their own place was out of the question. Even the previously middle-class families could not afford to initially rent their own home in the United States.

With the exception of the Ramírezes, who lived in a trailer, upon arrival all the families shared a residence with the wife's kin in what were generally very crowded accommodations for periods lasting from several months to several years. Jovita Cerritos's recollection of these residential arrangements was typical:

> Let's see—me, him, and the four children, my *comadre* [co-godmother] and her husband and son, that's nine people. Then Miguel, his wife, and three children, that's fourteen. And El Huero, fifteen, El Chino, and the short guy?

That's seventeen. And Chuey? And then Crespo and Mauricio? I told you it was twenty! [*laughter from both Ignacio and Jovita*]. Yes, there were twenty people [living there]!

Ignacio Cerritos added his recollection:

We slept with my sister. She slept with her husband and their children up there [*motions to the kitchen table, simulating bunk beds*], and then we slept underneath [*motions to the floor*] with our children. She slept up there, and we slept down here. The other couple slept over here [*motions to one side*], and the other guys out in the living room.

Orthodox household divisions of labor were generally reproduced in the early phase of resettlement, as women continued to take major responsibilities for domestic tasks. In some instances, women performed routine household duties only for their own nuclear family, but when women were not employed, or when they did in-home child care for others, they sometimes assumed household duties of cooking, laundering, and cleaning for other kin members as well. In both cases, traditional ideas about gender division of labor were not challenged.

In the bewildering process of orientation and adjustment to the new society, the men in these families relied on the wives' kin for advice, general information, and, importantly, for job leads. Listening to what some of the husbands had to say about this stage illustrates the extreme dependence on the wives' kin:

I'd go out, but I couldn't go alone because I'd get lost within two or three blocks. Her father showed me the town. (Roberto Melchor)

In the beginning, we arrived in the country, in Santa Paula. María's brother-in-law helped me get my first job there working in a taco truck, but the hours were so long—I worked from six in the morning until one in the morning, and María complained that I never saw the children, which was true. After three months we left [Santa Paula] when María's brother, Luis, called from here [Oakview] to see how we were. . . . We went to live with his family, and he helped me to find work in the gardens, and then in a small factory where they made plastic parts. The factory, in reality, didn't pay much at all, and working as a gardener's helper was not steady. . . . When María's cousin left his job cleaning horse stables, he passed the job on to me, and that's when things starting looking up for us. (Ausencio Mendoza)

Since I came here, I've only had two jobs. First, I began with Mr. Larry, an old Italian guy who employs many *Mexicanos* as gardeners. . . . Trini's brother worked as a janitor during the day and in a bar at night, and he helped me find the job I have now [as a restaurant dishwasher]. (Felipe Palacios)

These families and couples migrated and resettled in the context of larger family networks. The wives' kin provided a launching pad for the newly arrived families until they could find jobs, and earn and save the large lump sum required for an apartment deposit and rent.

As a consequence of dependency on their wives' kin, and shared living quarters, some of the husbands grew resentful toward their wives' family of origin. Some of these men resented the inflated promises their wives' kin had made to them. Ausencio Mendoza, for example, felt that he had been deceived by his wife's brothers, who, he claimed, had exaggerated how easy it would be to attain affluence in the U.S. One day when he was feeling especially frustrated with the quality of his life and with police harassment in running his mobile produce and meat business, Ausencio blamed María's brothers for not warning him of how high the cost of living would be for a family of eight in California:

> María's relatives painted a very pretty picture of life in the United States. They bragged about how much better their life was here, how they had late-model cars, and they encouraged us to come here. They said they had carpeted floors. María's brothers told me that you earn a lot of money, a lot of dollars here. But so what? It all works out to be the same. If you earn in dollars here, then you must spend in dollars. If you earn in pesos, then you spend in pesos, it's all the same.

Ausencio had visited María's family in the U.S. on several occasions before he migrated, so he had already caught a glimpse of the daily reality that awaited undocumented Mexican immigrants:

> When I first came here on one of those tourist trips, Ramon, María's brother, came to me one day and said, "Listen, brother-in-law, I found a gas-station job for you, let's go." I said no! In Mexico I wore a tie at work, I carried around a briefcase, and I drove a nice car. I told Ramon I would never do that kind of work unless my business went bankrupt in Mexico, and well, that is precisely what happened. And I wound up cleaning horse shit!

Although Ausencio expressed anger toward his brothers-in-law for causing his downward class mobility, his anger and disillusionment stemmed as much, I believe, from his dependence on his in-laws, and his diminished authority in both the family and the public world.

Though Roberto Melchor never spoke to me about conflicts with his in-laws, his wife, Francisca, complained that he had mistreated her parents and behaved as an ungrateful son-in-law. Referring to her husband and to her sister's husband, she claimed, "All son-in-laws are bastards." According to her, her parents had paid for Roberto's and her own migration travel costs, and had shared their home when Roberto and Francisca first arrived. "Do you believe it?" she exclaimed in disgust. "He made them leave our place when they didn't have [money] to pay the rent."

The husbands in these families, compared with those in families that migrated in stages, played relatively minor roles in settlement. They did not command either substantial financial or social resources, and this fueled resentment toward their in-laws. Even though the men commanded less family authority and public status than they did prior to migration, they did not share in domestic chores. Based on what I observed in these six families, it was the wives, and to a lesser extent the daughters, who took responsibility for cooking, cleaning, and looking after the children. Although I saw the men care for and play with their children, I never saw any of them work in the kitchen, vacuum, sweep, scrub, launder, bathe the children, or otherwise be involved in "women's work." These women, most of whom were employed, sometimes expressed mild, simmering resentment at these inequities, but these reactions occurred infrequently and did not directly challenge household arrangements.

Of these six families, I came to know the Cerritos family best, as I visited them about once a week from February 1987 until May 1988. Jovita and Nacho Cerritos both worked graveyard shift in a bakery, and they had six children between the ages of three and fourteen. When I asked Jovita to describe her daily schedule, she described a routine I had witnessed on many occasions:

> Well, you know we go to work at 2:30 [in the morning], and we get home just before noon. I make lunch for Nacho and then he goes to his [auto-body shop] class. I rest a little, but soon the older children come home from school, and I make dinner for them. Then I clean up, sweep, maybe wash some clothes. Nacho comes home and I prepare his meal. Then it's time to bathe the children and lay them down to sleep. If Nacho and I sleep as much as four hours in one night, that's a lot and we feel we're really rested, but often it's only two and a half or three and a half hours. We're always tired. Sometimes after days of not sleeping enough, you get this numbing sensation on the forehead. And after not sleeping enough for several days, its hard to fall asleep.

In spite of the significant amount of housework which her twelve-year-old daughter performed, Jovita had no free time to herself. On weekends, when she didn't work, she often stayed up until one or two in the morning sewing dresses for herself and her daughters in order to save money by not purchasing store-bought clothes. In the afternoons, Nacho attended various vocational classes designed to prepare him for jobs as an auto-body painter and airport janitor, and in the evenings, he took English lessons. When he was home, he was exhausted, and he usually napped on the couch, or played with the children while he fiddled with the VCR. Jovita went about her routine cheerfully, but when her fatigue was exacerbated by the children's antics she would bitingly recite clichés such as "The man can arrive home and lay down, but not the woman" and "If the mother doesn't do it, who is going to do it?"

Despite the traditional division of labor, when these families were faced with major decisions—such as whom to seek for legal help, whether or not to move to another town, or the decision to lend money or make a major purchase—spouses seemed to exert equal authority. This did not, however, go uncontested. Intense processes of negotiations, sometimes erupting into fights, characterized these decision-making processes.

When the Cerritos family applied for legalization through the amnesty program, they discovered they had an eligibility problem, so they faced the difficult and risky decision of whether or not to stay with the agency with which they had begun the long and tedious application procedure. After weeks of discussion, Nacho and Jovita together decided to switch to a private attorney, who charged a considerably higher fee but also promised a greater likelihood of success. When their adolescent son was accused of looking at pornographic videotapes at a neighbor's house, Jovita took an assertive stand in first defending her son before the accuser, who came to the front door, while Nacho stood in the background. Later both parents together confronted their son and implemented punishment. Similarly, when Nacho signed up for his various vocational classes, and when he purchased an expensive automobile spray-paint machine, he did so after consulting with Jovita. Early on in their resettlement, Jovita said, she had taken the initiative and made the decision to find an apartment where the family could live alone, and her assertiveness continued:

> We were on Third Street. But I didn't like it there. [*Why?*] Because I wanted for us to live alone. . . . By then I wanted for us to live alone, just us. And we looked around at apartments, but they wouldn't accept children, or they said there were too many of us. And we couldn't find anything anywhere. Some *compadres* told us they saw a "for rent" sign on Woodrow. . . . I went to look and my *compadre* parked the car. The manager said that the size of our family wasn't a problem and he told us the rent was five hundred dollars. But they

also wanted the last month's rent and a hundred-dollar deposit. That's a lot of money. "Tell him to set it aside so Nacho can come see it," my *compadre* said. But I feared that they'd rent it to others, so I had to decide for myself there. I gave a deposit to the manager. I told him it's rented. And we came back, and he [Nacho] filled out the application.

Although their discussions were more conflictual than harmonious, Ausencio and María Mendoza also collaborated on major decisions which affected their family. They were even more inclusive, consulting their two eldest children, Tito, aged fourteen, and Rosalia, sixteen, for example, about putting a down payment on a home in another part of California. As María commented, "We have to see the children's point of view too."

Ausencio Mendoza claimed that his wife neglected the children and the family, that she was always "going to the street" with her community, church, and school involvements. Although she nostalgically recalled her life as an involved mother of young children in Mexico, María Mendoza, who had also worked in the family business in Mexico, claimed that an independent source of employment in the U.S. had given her new options that she would not trade:

> I don't know why, but all of the mothers there [in Mexico] do not work, they have more time to dedicate to their children. And everything is less expensive there. There is more time to get to know your children. Or perhaps it is because there are fewer jobs for women. Perhaps the women there are not well trained or oriented towards employment. Because I know now that in the present, if I were to go back there, if I could, I would work. I would work, because like any other, I've opened my eyes. Back there, they say no. You marry, and no, you must stay home. Here, it's different. You marry, and you continue working. Back in Mexico, it's very different. There is very much machismo in those men. There, the man says you cannot work because "you should not be employed. I am here to take care of you." So back there, its only what the men earn. But what the husband earns is not always sufficient to support a family.

María's income and employment as a paid domestic worker in the U.S. had given her more leverage with Ausencio, and in spite of Ausencio's insistence that she dedicate herself more as a homemaker and mother, she conducted her numerous public activities, often attending church and community meetings in the evening. Women like María Mendoza discovered that their own independent sources of income provided them with a modicum of authority in family affairs, and with a greater degree of independent spatial mobility. Even though—or perhaps because—their earnings were generally directed toward family expenses, women realized advantages. They compared this favorably with their options in Mexico. As Jovita Cerritos maintained, "Women's work is not valued in Mexico. . . . I had heard that here one can work, and this is the truth."

As María Mendoza noted, in the U.S., few Mexican immigrant men could afford to tell their wives, "I am here to take care of you." Trinidad Ochoa and Josefa Ramírez were the only two women in this subsample whose husbands prohibited them from working in the U.S. Felipe forbade Trinidad to work because of jealousy:

> I worked, and she dedicated herself to the home, as she does today. I've always been a jealous man. I didn't want her to work because I feared someone would steal her away from me. I would go to work and I would imagine that she was going to dances with her friends, and I would imagine all sorts of things. . . . I wanted to have a child with her so that way, no one would take her from me, so that she would stay home.

His jealousy became more pronounced when Trini's half brother urged her to work as a bar waitress at night. One might imagine that Trini would resent Felipe's restrictions, but Trini had worked hard all her life; after her first husband in Mexico left her, she had supported their sons, so she did not experience Felipe's commands as restrictive constraints on her own behavior. In fact, she welcomed the privilege of not having to work. Similarly, Josefa Ramírez stated that staying home was an appealing alternative given the limited job options: "I wasn't in a hurry to go to work in the [flower] nurseries in the winter, or to go clean other people's messes." Like many working-class women who face few opportunities for finding satisfaction and meaning in their jobs, Trinidad and Josefa found staying home with their young children to be a gratifying experience, a privilege made possible by their husbands' breadwinner capabilities.

Recall that these families, who migrated as a unit, were characterized by collaborative spousal decision making even before migration. This trend, however, became even more pronounced after migration, as women gained access both to financial resources in the form of wages, and to social resources, which were generally made available through their family of origin. These resources counterbalanced their husbands' power. This move toward greater egalitarianism in decision making and women's increased spatial mobility, however, was moderated by the continuation of a traditional division of labor in the household.

SETTLEMENT EXPERIENCES OF
SINGLE WOMEN AND MEN

Eight women and five men in my sample had migrated while they were single. With the exception of Milagros Aguilar, a widow who was then sixty-one years old, most of them were young at the time of migration—in their teens, twenties, and thirties. All of them migrated in the late 1970s and early 1980s. When I met them, four of the five men, and six of the eight women, either had married or were living with a common-law spouse.

SINGLE WOMEN

Women who migrated unaccompanied by either spouse or parents encountered a restricted range of jobs and residential situations. Five of the eight women's first jobs entailed "live-in" residential arrangements with their employers. Milagros Aguilar, María Alicia Navarro, Mariana Viñas-Valenzuela, and Margarita Cervantes all initially worked as live-in domestics, and María del Carmen Ochoa worked as a restaurant cook and lived with the employer's family.

Historically, live-in employment has been a common form of incorporation into a new urban society for single women migrants. Since the live-in employee does not spend earnings on rent, transportation, food, and utilities, she may initially view all of her earnings as savings, as Mariana Viñas-Valenzuela did: "I thought it would suit me and my needs. I didn't have to spend money on food or on rent. Everything I earned was for me, not for my bills." Margarita Cervantes echoed this with sentiments of gratitude:

> They gave me everything—food, a bed, and a roof over my head. . . . I didn't have to buy much [for my daily needs]. It immediately seemed very good to me, and as the family were Latinos, that is, of Mexican parents, and they spoke Spanish, it seemed magnificent to me.

These women initially rationalized the low pay because it freed them of living expenses, but the work was very poorly remunerated. Both Francisca Melchor, who first migrated while she was separated from her husband, and Margarita Cervantes had worked as live-in domestics for Latino families in the Oakview area in 1975. In exchange for a daily schedule that spanned at least from dawn until the evening, Francisca earned twenty-five dollars a week, and Margarita forty. Calculated on the basis of a five-day-a-week, twelve-hour workday schedule, their approximate hourly wages were, respectively, forty-two and sixty-seven cents. Their experiences were not uncommon; a survey conducted among return migrant women in Mexico in 1978 and 1979 revealed that 97 percent of women who had worked as domestics reported earning less than ten dollars a day (Kossoudji and Ranney, 1984:1,124–25).

In live-in arrangements there is no well-defined list of job tasks or workday schedule; thus, as Glenn has noted, there is "no clear line between work and non-work time" (1986:141). A live-in domestic's job does not necessarily begin with breakfast preparation and end with washing dinner dishes: she may be awakened in the middle of the night to clean a dog's vomit, or called to serve a meal at irregular hours or to provide baby-sitting for her employer's relatives. While a live-in domestic worker receives concrete, tangible room and board "privileges" and cash payment, there is an effective "hidden exchange" whereby the employee puts forth an ill-defined workday. This obscures the missing wages.

One of the defining features of domestic work is the highly personalistic relationship established between employer and employee, and this is generally intensified in live-in employment (Rollins, 1985; Glenn, 1986). Because they live with their employers, live-in domestics are deprived of a life of normal social interactions with friends and kin. Employers may assume a benevolent, protective, maternalistic stance toward their employees, posturing as a surrogate family in order to sustain the live-in domestic worker's loyalty and dependence. For single women alone in a new urban environment, "the myth of being 'like a daughter'" to their employers may be seductive (Young, 1987).

Some of these women nostalgically recalled this illusion of familial belonging. María Mendoza, who came from a poor rural family and later married into a middle-class family in Mexico where she herself was an employer of a domestic servant, had first migrated to California when she was single, and worked as a live-in:

> I really wanted to stay in the U.S. back then, because the lady I worked for told me to stay, she said she would fix my [immigration] papers. . . . She really loved me a lot because she told me she was going to Washington, that I was going with her, that she had to arrange for my papers first. . . . Today there are few people like that woman, because in reality, now the *Americanas* keep the Latinas around only for their own convenience; back then it was different. Back then, there were sincere people and that woman treated me like a sister instead of like a servant. Look, I had my nap, I had my lunch, and I had my outings with her—of course I went as the baby-sitter. But really, we would go shopping, we would go to restaurants. We were like sisters.

While María insisted that "back then" employers were kinder, she was in fact comparing a much more intensely personalized live-in arrangement with her current paid domestic employment, where she worked for several different employers. For María Mendoza, having been "like sisters" was also intertwined with the possibility that through dependence on her employer, she would obtain legal permanent residency. One of the most exploitative features that Latina and Caribbean undocumented immigrant women experience in live-in jobs is the promise of employer sponsorship in order to obtain legal status (Colen, 1987).

For newly arrived single immigrant women without kin or family in the U.S., live-in jobs held the promise of protection, security, and emotional support. Milagros Aguilar's first job was as a live-in maid/baby-sitter for a Latina woman, a single-mother professional. She stayed in that job for five years, cleaning house, cooking, and raising an infant until he was old enough to enter kindergarten. Milagros related that her employer provided the consideration and compassion that she had not received from her own family:

> I liked my new life here. She [her employer] paid me well. But more than that, she gave me compassion, understanding—and my children, they've practically forgotten about me! [*She starts crying.*]

Not all of these women characterized their Latino employers as benevolent. Even in situations where employer and employee were kin, live-in domestic workers remained in a disadvantaged position. Margarita Cervantes believed that when her aunt and uncle had employed her sister as a live-in, they intentionally prevented her sister from establishing employment or social relations elsewhere because they benefited from her services, and Margarita alleged that these confining arrangements were common:

> She was here as a baby-sitter with my aunt, caring for her children. But once she was here, my aunt imprisoned her. That is, she had her here exclusively for her. When there were advertisements on the radio that someone was looking for a baby-sitter or someone to clean house, or whatever, my aunt would say, "No, no, you are here caring for my children." And clearly, she was paying her what she [her aunt] wanted. This also happens in many families. Relatives, just because they help you to cross, because they make themselves responsible for us in some form, they also take advantage of us, they abuse us and they also don't allow us to search for work elsewhere. They don't let us buy a car, they don't let us separate from them because we are helping them as a baby-sitter, or as the person who cleans the house and cooks. So the baby-sitter is also cleaning and preparing the food, and the

señora that is out working, the aunt or the relative, she works and she comes home and the meal is already made. So why is she going to help her look for a job elsewhere? That would not suit her, and so she doesn't even take her out socially anyplace. She also doesn't allow her to go out with friends because the friends will say, "Are you still there [working] with so-and-so? Why don't you leave? Perhaps they will pay you more elsewhere." This also did not suit my aunt, and she had my sister there almost like a prisoner in her house.

These women chose live-in work because it lessened the risks they would be exposed to as women and as undocumented immigrants. Compounding the dangers faced by an "illegal" presence in the country, a young, unmarried woman unaccompanied by family or kin is easy prey for those who might take advantage of her sexuality. Not only men but women as well could take advantage of the migrants' circumstances, as Mariana Viñas-Valenzuela discovered during her first months in the U.S., when an older, more experienced immigrant woman suggested prostitution to her:

> Then that same woman, the one who brought me to that job, she wanted to use me to make business. [*What kind of business?*] Well, sell me, or I don't know what she wanted. Because she saw that I was alone, that I didn't have family here, well, she didn't know if I had family here or not, since I was renting in a house. So she would say to me, "Woman, fix up your appearance, put on some makeup, find a man, and everything will change. Fix your teeth"—my teeth were different then, one was missing and they were a little crooked. I saw that this woman was sly, so I didn't pay any attention to her. Others would say to me, "Don't be stupid, Mariana, make a deal with that woman." . . . And then she wanted me to come live in her place, but I never wanted to do that because she and her plans scared me.

Certainly not all women avoid prostitution, but given the stigma attached to this work, none of the women in the study said they had worked as prostitutes. When seventeen-year-old Anabel Castrillo arrived in Oakview in 1981, her first job was as a bar waitress, a job which she clearly still felt shameful about revealing to me. In fact, I only learned of this previous occupation after a Department of Motor Vehicles bureaucrat aggressively questioned her in my presence. One day some of her husband's kin, while maliciously joking about AIDS, suggested to me that Anabel had in fact worked as a prostitute.

Live-in work deprived women of normal social relations, but the flip side is that it effectively removed them from other potentially exploitative arrangements, such as prostitution. For newly arrived single immigrant women, live-in jobs offered the best option out of a limited number of alternatives. As Margarita Cervantes said, "When one comes without the support and protection of family, there is no other remedy [but to take a live-in job]." Yet exactly what kind of protection does live-in work offer?

These women's stories indicate that abuse and deception, at least as much as "protection," characterized their live-in jobs. With the exception of Milagros Aguilar and María Mendoza, the women held bitter memories of their live-in jobs. María del Carmen Ochoa lived at the home of her restaurant employers for three years, but early on, relations with them soured and her living conditions quickly deteriorated:

> They treated me very badly. At the beginning, they were all right. They even let me sleep in their daughter's bed. But then the daughters [aged seventeen and eighteen] complained, and I would hear them. Once I heard them, I preferred to sleep on the floor, and that's what they wanted.

Initially she also did household chores for the family, but when the disputes with the employers' daughters began, she stopped doing domestic chores and they moved her into their backyard, into what María del Carmen described as a dwelling more appropriate for an animal than a person:

> It was like a room for a dog. My bed and my suitcase and a chair is all that fit in that room. . . . After, I started fixing it up outside. I arranged, cleaned, threw out things. Later, when my friends would visit, they were shocked at what I called my "residence." I lived there for three years. They [her employer's family] would lock the door to the bathroom. . . . In winter, I sometimes felt as though my body would remain stiff forever [due to the cold]. There were nights when I couldn't sleep all night long. I'd pass my hand over my head and there would be ice.

When she recalled how these primitive living conditions had caused her to catch pneumonia, she cried. On another occasion, flipping through her photo album, she showed me pictures of what she had variously described as her "residence" and as a "room for a dog." The rudimentary structure consisted of a laminated tin roof, boards for walls, and a "ceiling" which was not even high enough to allow María del Carmen, who was approximately four-foot-ten, to stand up while she dressed. Like other immigrant women, she tolerated these conditions in hopes of achieving her goal: "I said to myself, 'Well, if I leave, I won't be able to save,' and that is what I wanted to do, to buy a house back there [in Mexico]."

While the other women did not reside in such extreme substandard shelters, the live-in job, by its very nature, imposed other problems.

Because these women lived with their employers, they enjoyed limited contact with kin and friends. Even the words they use to describe live-in employment highlight the seclusion and social isolation of the job: "*vivir encerrada*," "*puerta cerrada*," and "*adentro*" literally translate as "to live locked in," "closed door," and "inside." Some live-in domestic workers had Saturdays and Sundays off, while others were allowed only one day off during the week. On their days off, if they had kin nearby, the women generally went to stay with an aunt and uncle or a cousin. One woman, Milagros Aguilar, who felt abandoned by her kin in the U.S. and Mexico, took on another live-in job caring for an elderly couple during the weekends.

The enforced isolation during the workweek made the early period of resettlement especially difficult. Mariana Viñas-Valenzuela worked as a live-in maid for a Mexican family, and on the weekends, she stayed with her female cousin in Oakland. For Mariana, a short weekend spent with kin and friends barely compensated for a week spent in solitude and servitude:

> Once I was here, life became impossible. Here I was alone, closed up in the house, whereas in Mexico I was able to walk around in the open air, with my family. It was all so different. I came that [drought] year when there was no water, in 1977. Oh, lord, I'd think about how back home I could swim in the river. Sometimes I cried.

Margarita Cervantes's first job in Oakview was as a live-in for a Chicano family during the week, and on weekends she stayed with her three siblings and worked a second job as a motel maid. She recalled that on weekend evenings she and her sister busied themselves with various chores, so even during off hours, there was no time for social life:

> That was an era when we did everything hurriedly. We didn't have a social life, no, there was no time. There was nothing more than work and to the house, to clean the house, buy the food, and all those things one does. And also we didn't have a car, and there one wastes a lot of time . . . going to buy the groceries with those carts, taking the carts to do the laundry. . . . We didn't have time to talk with anyone, because we were really working too much, my sister and I worked too much, and we didn't start going to the dances until much later. Oh, my brothers, as I say, they did spend time in the street looking for diversions among other men.

María del Carmen Ochoa did not have kin, friends, or acquaintances nearby. On her weekly day off from the restaurant, she spent the day alone and had to go out and purchase her meals: "I didn't have friends.

I was always in the restaurant, with them [her employers], and at the house. I didn't have transportation then. . . . It was a long time before I got to know the streets."

The isolation and solitude intensified the effect of employers' harassment and intimidation of undocumented immigrant live-in employees. Several of the women reported that their employers had threatened them with calling the Immigration and Naturalization Service. María del Carmen Ochoa's employers even warned her not to sing in the shower, lest her voice attract INS suspicion, and Mariana Viñas-Valenzuela's employer told her that she was lucky to have a job at all given her unauthorized legal status. Employers attempted to reinforce loyalty by reminding the women that their inferior legal status allowed them few options.

Although none of these five women had employers who withheld their entire pay, many of the women experienced some type of deception from their employers. María Alicia Navarro earned ninety dollars a week when she arrived in 1984 to work as a live-in domestic in California's affluent Marin County. She had accepted the job on the condition that the employer would help her find part-time domestic work on the side, but these jobs, and the income she might have earned at them, were never forthcoming as promised. María del Carmen Ochoa, the woman who was recruited to work as a cook in an Oakview Mexican restaurant, earned the most: one hundred twenty dollars a week plus room and board. Still, the pay and the living conditions were below what she had been led to expect:

> Don't think that once I was here they paid me what they said they would. They were over one month late in paying me at all. Then they said they'd pay me one hundred twenty dollars a week, but I told them they had promised me one hundred sixty. They argued that since I didn't know how to do everything the old cook did, that's why they paid me only one hundred twenty. . . . They never raised my pay. I never earned more until the new owners took over three years later.

At the restaurant she worked six days a week, eight to ten hours daily.

Live-in domestic work has been viewed as an occupational bridge leading to upward social mobility or, alternately, as a dead-end occupational ghetto for rural-urban migrant women. In the U.S., the extent of mobility offered by domestic work has varied by race and ethnicity, with European immigrant women generally leaving the occupation after marriage, and women of color remaining in domestic work for a lifetime (Glenn, 1986; Romero, 1987). As has been the case for Chicanas, live-in work for these Mexican immigrant women was generally a stepping-stone to domestic day work, a process which Romero refers to as the "modernization" of domestic work (1988). The many drawbacks to live-in work—the ill-defined and expanded work schedule, the isolation and solitude, the highly personalistic employer-employee relationship, and deception over pay arrangements—made live-in work arrangements tolerable for only a limited time, generally the initial period of resettlement. Transitioning into day work allowed these women to participate in normal social relations with family and friends.

UNMARRIED WOMEN AND THEIR KIN SUPPORT

The three single women who did not take live-in jobs encountered a different kind of vulnerability. Although they had kin nearby, their kin were not especially helpful or supportive. Anabel Castrillo's aunt robbed her, Rosario Quiñones's sister-in-law asked her to leave the house, and Marisela Ramírez de Hernández's relatives returned to Mexico within months after they had arrived in Oakview. Anabel Castrillo's first residence in the U.S. was with her aunt and a single mother of three children, and although she avoided the worst aspects of live-in arrangements, she was equally oppressed by her aunt:

> I lived with my aunt for a while, but then we didn't get along, as she is one of these people that sells drugs and all of that. I lived with a woman who was renting the house, Roselia, and my aunt, and the woman [Roselia] had three children. But we had a fight because what I worked for, what I earned, she [her aunt] would grab it. My aunt would snatch it and when I went to look for it, I didn't know what was happening with the money, it was no longer there. She liked stealing other people's money. She also stole pots and pans and money from Roselia, and then she would always accuse me. . . . I lived with her for about six months, and then Reynaldo and I met. We got together and I don't know what happened to her, because they got her and sent her back to Mexico because of the drugs which she sold. Since then I don't know anything about her.

Left on their own relatively soon after their arrival, these three women moved in with male partners. For young women without the support of kin, attachment to a man offered one means of survival. The initial period of resettlement while her cousin/best friend and her aunt were still here was not altogether unpleasant for fifteen-year-old Marisela Ramírez de Hernández, as she enjoyed the companionship of her cousin on the job and in leisure activities:

It took me about fifteen days to find work. The woman [where I lived] knew people, and she recommended us, but cleaning work is all we got. The two of us [she and her cousin/best friend] would always go together to clean. We would walk to the houses, or sometimes they [their employers] would pick us up. . . . Sometimes we would clean two houses in one day, on other days, not even one. On those days, we would go do our laundry, maybe go to the park, walk around the city. We had no transportation and we didn't know the bus routes, but we still went out.

After six months had passed, Marisela's cousin and aunt returned to Mexico, and her cousin's brother-in-law, who had also accompanied them, moved to another part of California in search of work. By then Marisela had already met Carlos, so when the others departed, she moved in with him:

There were too many of us there, and then we each went our own ways, and I met Carlos, and when they went, I stayed with Carlos at his place. I went to live with him in a camper behind his uncle's house. I liked it better there. When I went to live with Carlos, I no longer worked because he didn't want that.

Anabel Castrillo, anxious to leave both her thieving aunt and her job as a bar waitress, also moved in with a man less than a year after her arrival:

[I worked at the bar] seven months. Seven, and as Reynaldo went there quite often, I got to know him and I told him I didn't want to work there anymore, that I was going to leave, because I didn't like that job; and he said okay, if you don't want to work there, and so I left and then he found me houses [to clean] as he worked as a gardener, and he would transport me to the different jobs. Then in 1984 when I was pregnant with the girl, I left those jobs.

When her sister-in-law asked her to leave the house, Rosario Quiñones and her two boys moved in with Armando, whom she had met at a dance. They moved into Armando's small trailer home, located on a ranch where he cleaned horse stables. She helped him sweep around the stables, but mostly she looked after the trailer and the boys.

These three women all withdrew from the labor force after they got together with their partners. Rosario did so immediately "because there were no jobs out there in the country," Marisela quit working "because he [Carlos] didn't want that," and Anabel worked for three years until she was pregnant. These women's vulnerability and lack of kin and friends in the area translated into greater dependence on their husbands. They became dependent not only on their husbands' income, but also on their husbands' kin to provide emergency financial assistance, information, and advice. Most of their social life centered around the men's kin as well.

These three couples were still living together when I met them, and all of them had children together. Anabel and Marisela were not employed but looked after their young children, and Rosario had begun cleaning houses in 1983, when her husband was incarcerated and she had to support the family. These women remained largely dependent on their spouses for income and social contacts. Household arrangements reflected a traditional division of labor. For women like Marisela, this was a welcome respite from a restricted labor market; she said that when she went to live with Carlos:

> I no longer worked because he did not like that. He likes me to do the things in the house. Some of the men have that idea, and he is one of them that likes his woman in the house and coming home to find me there. That's what they are accustomed to. . . . It seemed fine to me. I didn't have a job that I liked very much. It wasn't as though I had an important job, then perhaps I would have preferred to stay [employed]. Sometimes I would go with an old woman and I would help her, I washed her clothes, her things, but I never prepared meals. Because I didn't know how to do that. Later when I had children, I think that's why Fernando was always sick, because I didn't know how to cook. . . . It wasn't until one, no two years ago that Carlos's aunt arrived and she taught me to cook and to do other things that I didn't know. Because as I'd always been on the job and in the street, I never learned to do the things of the house. . . . He doesn't help me with any of the housework. He does nothing. Well, on Saturdays and Sundays he does help me because he entertains the children while I clean, cook, sweep, or change the sheets, or clean the stove. He doesn't help, though. If he feels like it, he sometimes bathes the boys.

As we saw earlier, women sometimes welcomed the privileges of domesticity and access to the support of a male breadwinner. In Mexico, Marisela's father had never provided any reliable economic support to her mother or to her and her siblings, so she was happy to care for her three young sons while her husband, Carlos, earned the family income.

This does not signify Marisela's complete subordination to her husband or to others in official positions of authority. One morning while I was interviewing her at a park, a schoolteacher reprimanded her chubby three-year-old for throwing sand in other children's faces. Marisela immediately rose to embrace the whimpering child and to directly confront the teacher. Moments later she said:

> I've always known how to defend myself. That person who mistreated the boy just now, sometimes they've treated me that way, but I don't allow for it. For example, if we go to an office and a secretary is badly assisting me, I just

ask if she wants to help me or not. There's no reason they should yell at the people. I think sometimes I defend myself better than Carlos.

Anabel Castrillo had made a similar transition to becoming a home-maker, but she expressed dissatisfaction with the performance of her husband, Reynaldo, as a breadwinner. On one evening when we visited kin, we enjoyed coffee and cake while discussing the impending birth of a friend's new baby and the responsibilities of fatherhood. Reynaldo's uncle had remarked that "most men would prefer a son. You think about all of the things you will give them that you didn't have as a child, you think about his first animal, his first horse, and the joy that will bring him. And later, you will leave him a little ranch." While the men nodded in agreement, Anabel snickered and, commenting as much about her own father as her husband, she added, "And in the end, they don't give their children anything." Although young women such as Marisela and Anabel struck fairly traditional patriarchal bargains with their husbands, they remained outspoken and assertive in both family and community affairs.

The women who had initially located live-in jobs later moved into live-out employment, a feat they accomplished through the help of other women. Even though many of these women did not have supportive kin in the U.S., they gradually established multiple social ties. After María del Carmen Ochoa left her restaurant job due to a job injury, she obtained, with the help of women friends, jobs as a domestic worker and then a job in an electronic assembly plant. Along the way she also established a relationship with a man she met in the restaurant; their sexual relationship was short-lived, but they remained friends and when she required surgery, he helped to cover the costs. María Alicia Navarro found emotional support with her male companion, and although they lived together, they were not committed to a long-term partnership and they kept strictly separate finances.

Unmarried women formed chains of support among themselves for help in finding new jobs and homes and in orienting themselves to the new society. These social ties played an important role in resettlement, yet the social transactions among these women had both negative and positive dimensions. The resettlement trajectory of María Alicia Navarro exemplifies the ambivalent nature of these women's networks. Although María Alicia had received various types of migration and resettlement help from other women, she insisted that "it's better to be alone. That is, I prefer not to get too close to friends. . . . [They] took advantage of me."

María Alicia secured her initial live-in job in affluent Marin County with the help of her brother's ex–mother-in-law, Carmen Maldonado. When the job did not yield the leads for domestic day work as expected, Carmen took María Alicia to meet another Mexican immigrant woman in Oakview, Demetria. Demetria promised to help María Alicia find her own *casas* [houses], but in the meantime, she said, María Alicia could share her home and accompany her on her own domestic work jobs.

María Alicia jumped at this chance, but her situation did not readily improve. Demetria took her on as as her domestic work helper, but she paid no wages to María Alicia, arguing that María Alicia did not pay rent. María Alicia recalled these days as being "full of exhaustion, anxiety, and nerves" as the job leads which she had expected from Demetria were not forthcoming.

> I helped her to work a lot, and she did not pay me. Nothing, nothing. I would help her do three or four houses a day. No, no, no, no, they were giving me nothing. It would have been better had I never accepted. Then she started taking me to work with her daughter, so I said, "Well, here I am going to charge." All I asked of her [Demetria] is that she understand that I am desperate, I need work. I was so desperate that finally I said to Amador [her boyfriend from Mexico] that I need to get out of here. I told him, "If you want, we can look for a room, something, and if you have money with which to pay the rent now, let's go, without saying anything to Demetria." So we went and looked for a garage [to rent].

After several months, María Alicia located a steady housecleaning job from another immigrant woman, Herlinda, but she was ambivalent about this favor:

> I am grateful [to her], but she also wanted to get out of that job and she charged me. When I arrived in Oakview, Demetria and Herlinda took advantage of me and my situation. . . . She [Herlinda] borrowed money from me, and she still owes me. She tricked me.

When María Alicia secured this twenty-five-hour-a-week job at an hourly rate of five dollars, she brought her three children from Mexico, as she feared her teenage daughter, who was unhappy living with her grandmother, might otherwise run away. She accomplished this by borrowing money from Carmen Maldonado, her brother's ex–mother-in-law. Her niece and her niece's infant accompanied the children on the journey, and they joined María Alicia and Amador in the rented garage, which was attached to the home of another immigrant family. Amador paid the initial rent, but he did not help to support them, and the couple kept their finances separate. When Carmen Maldonado returned to Mexico, she asked María Alicia to pay her back the money she had lent for the children's passage. María Alicia borrowed money from another woman, Amalia, in order to do this.

In all of these accomplishments, María Alicia Navarro relied on the help of immigrant women, and on Amador in obtaining this first rental. Yet in spite of the job contacts and leads, the information, shared residence, and money lent, María Alicia felt as much resentment as gratitude toward the various women who had helped her. While she acknowledged their help, she also believed they had taken advantage of her. She suspected that these women's own self-interest had deterred her own achievements.

Chain links of migration among women continue, and they are often extended before settlement is consolidated. While still in an extremely tenuous financial position, María Alicia Navarro helped her adult niece and later her older sister, Eulodia, to migrate illegally. Eulodia, the mother of four young-adult and adolescent children, was separated from her husband, yet when they were living in Mexico City he continued to pursue her from the taxi he operated, maintaining a daily, spylike surveillance of her as she left her home and traveled between her two jobs. Eulodia was not interested in spousal reconciliation, and with Mexico's deepening economic crisis, her standard of living was impossible to maintain despite her two jobs. Coaxed by her sister, María Alicia, who also funded her migration costs, Eulodia decided to escape both financial and spousal urgencies. She literally did escape, too, with the collaboration of her teenage children, who hid her in the trunk of their automobile so that their father would not see she was departing for the airport.

Women-to-women network ties are not characterized by absolute altruism or harmony of interests. For example, María Alicia helped her sister Eulodia to migrate, and they worked together doing housecleaning, but it would be months before Eulodia received remuneration. María Alicia felt conflicted about this, but she had undergone very similar work arrangements when she first arrived, and she justified it by citing the debts incurred in supporting her children in the U.S. and her sick mother in Mexico and in funding her sister's migration. María Alicia had also urged her adult niece to come north, but the two women held very different perceptions of life in the U.S., and the niece stayed only a short while:

> I had told her that here life was different, I said that here there are many opportunities [*facilidades*] if one has work and everything, because that is how I had seen it, that there were in fact many possibilities. . . . My niece

began working [cleaning] in a house where they paid her five dollars an hour, but she was very ill adjusted and so she said she was returning. It's not easy here. As my niece said to me, "No, I don't have the same spirit of a martyr as you. Having a steady job back in Mexico, I can't make such a great effort here." My point of view is, Yes, we had jobs in Mexico, but jobs worth nothing, and here by contrast, there is at least the possibility that one will advance, come out ahead.

Although I never met the niece who had returned to Mexico, I wondered if she suspected that María Alicia had urged her to come north out of self-interest, since it was the niece who accompanied the children on their journey north.

Women do help each other through the trials of resettlement, sometimes in unexpected ways. These include expressions of approval from nonmigrant women back home. Late one Saturday evening, after a long and relaxed meal, María Alicia played for me a tape-recorded, collective "letter" from her extended kin. I was deeply moved by the depth of admiration, affection, and respect expressed by her sisters, nieces, and sisters-in-law. They praised her courage, hard work, initiative, and efforts to provide a better life for her children, and they cautioned her not to overexert herself in her job cleaning several houses daily. One of the nieces, in between sniffles, stated how much she missed María Alicia and looked up to her. The comfort this provided for her—unmistakably visible in her facial expressions, although she had listened to the tape many times—illustrates how the extension of emotional support from women kin "back home" can mitigate the hardships both of being a single mother, and of working without legal authorization to support a family.

How did gender relations and roles change for these women? The women had managed to maintain fairly independent and autonomous lives in the U.S., even after they married. When I met them, some were single, while others were married or living in stable unions with men. Most of them had not assumed traditional subservient roles in their marriages. As Margarita Cervantes emphasized, she had craved and established autonomy, not separation from family relations:

The independence I was looking for was not just independence. I did not want to totally separate [from my family]. The independence I wanted was simply to feel useful and to know how to do things for myself.

This sense of independence accentuated their commitment to permanent settlement in the U.S. While they sometimes expressed nostalgia and longing for people and events "back home," they had no intention of returning to live in Mexico. Although Mariana Viñas-Valenzuela expressed ambivalence about the women's domestic world she had left behind in Mexico, she maintained that her earning power and independence in the U.S. outweighed this loss:

> Since I've been here, I've returned to Mexico only once, when my mother died in 1983. Yes, I miss it and I like life there. I like all of the domestic things which one [i.e., a woman] does in Mexico, knitting and everything. Here, one cannot do them. One comes home from work and one comes home tired. In Mexico I really liked to knit, embroider, and sew, I really liked washing by hand and taking care of my clothes. Here there are machines. . . . But I like it here more too because here one works, but one earns money. And I've never liked to ask anyone for money, not even my father.

SINGLE MEN

The literature on settlement, like that on migration, takes as its point of focus the experiences of single male migrants. Recall that in Piore's (1979) seminal framework, migrants are described as purely economic beings, working long hours to save and send money home, avoiding community or leisure activities. Once these migrants establish families in the new society, they begin to think and act differently. They work shorter hours, spend more on consumption, and they are less likely to return to their home country.

For the men in this study who had migrated while still single, getting married and having U.S.-born children increased the likelihood of settlement and redirected their income and future plans. Family formation or reunification, and the birth of children in the U.S., are important steps in the settlement process (Chavez, 1985, 1988; Massey et al., 1987), in part because the acquisition of family ties serves as a "resource drain" that prolongs U.S. stays (Villar, 1990). These analyses assume, but do not explicitly examine, single migrant men as men; most immigration research has considered men to be genderless beings. Here I discuss the initial settlement experiences of single men, and then go on to explore the character of gender relations in their newly formed families. Two factors distinguish single migrant men's experiences from those of their female peers: access to supportive, well-developed kin networks in the United States, and the postponement of return migration in order to sustain a particular image.

Upon arriving in the United States, four of the five single men in this study initially lived with kin. Male kin and friends were instrumental in these men's migration. When they arrived in California, most of these men stayed with their uncles' or friends' families, and the men came to depend on them for various job opportunities. Unlike the single unmarried women, these men were embedded in well-established, tightly knit kin networks that facilitated their incorporation into the new society.

Gerónimo López's initial settlement experiences were typical. He moved in with the family of his father's brother, initially worked in a car wash with his uncle, and then after several weeks, his male cousins helped him find a job in a Mexican chain restaurant. Gerónimo worked there for two years, first as a janitor and then as a dishwasher; later, with the help of a friend, he obtained a much better paying job, one with benefits, at a university cafeteria.

Men in Gerónimo's circumstances worked in a variety of jobs—in factories, in gardening, and in other services. Without exception they located these jobs with the help of male kin and friends. Their jobs afforded more opportunities for social interactions with other immigrants, and this facilitated their integration into community life. The men did not find themselves isolated from kin and community as did their female peers who worked as live-in domestic workers.

Like the women, these men came north with the intent of working a short time—perhaps six to eighteen months—before returning to Mexico with their pocketed earnings. Like all of the people in this study, they did not do so, but part of the reason they did not is that they dreaded what others in Mexico would think of them. Their accomplishment of masculinity and maturity hinged on living up to the image of a successful migrant. Settlement was prolonged as these men tried to earn and save money so that upon return they would be favorably viewed by peers and family in Mexico. If a man were to return home penniless he would risk being seen as a failure or a fool, as Reynaldo Castrillo affirmed:

> One cannot go back without anything, because then people will talk. They'll say, "Oh, look at this guy, he sacrificed and suffered to go north and he has nothing to show for it." Well, on the other hand, there are others who will talk too if one returns with fine clothes, a car, they'll say you are stuck-up, that you think you are better than them. Either way, people talk, but I think it's better when one returns with something to show for the effort he put forth.

Women did not report this sort of motive for prolonging their stays. Unlike men, the women did not have to live up to high expectations as successful labor migrants. In fact, by becoming autonomous immigrants, the women were in many ways breaking stereotypical female roles; failing to save enough money to return to Mexico "in style" would not threaten their personification of femininity. And even when the women did accumulate enough savings to achieve some target goal in Mexico, they rarely carried through with it, as they grew increasingly committed to staying in the U.S.

Most of these men initially sent money home to their families of origin in Mexico, but they usually stopped this practice when they started their own families in the U.S. Gradually, their obligations shifted from natal to conjugal family. And as they married and had children, they became increasingly anchored to living in the U.S.

Although the men expressed personal preferences for living in Mexico, they realized that the better options for their families in the United States hinged on employment opportunities for themselves and for their wives. Even men whose wives were unemployed or irregularly employed as occasional baby-sitters or domestic workers, such as Reynaldo Castrillo and Carlos Hernández, wanted their wives to learn English and obtain vocational training. Reynaldo hoped to achieve enough financial stability "to send her [Anabel] to school, so she can learn more," and Carlos expressed identical aspirations for both his wife and his children:

> I would like for her to study, to learn skills for a better job, to learn English. She could take English classes here in the high school, and then go elsewhere to learn something else, maybe computers. She could get a good job in an office working with computers. I want her to learn and to excel. She could earn more than those [women] who clean houses. When the children are older, perhaps we can make a down payment on a house of our own. Sure, I'd like to return to Mexico, as the rhythm of life is calmer there. But the boys are U.S. citizens. We want them to learn the language here, to study for careers. There are more opportunities for them to progress here. So for that reason, we will probably stay here.

This doesn't mean that return migration ceased to enter their minds. They thought about it, and talked about it, but the discussions generally remained at the level of fantasy. Reynaldo Castrillo, the man who lived with his family in the garage of an expensive home, frequently voiced an interest in returning to Mexico. One sunny afternoon when Anabel and I had driven to one of the luxurious country estates where Reynaldo was working as a gardener, he told me that it would only be a few years before he would buy a similar house in Mexico, where I would be invited to spend vacations horseback riding in open fields surrounded by panoramic views. I responded by saying, in effect, that it would be a "dream vacation." Then he quietly acknowledged, "And I am the one who dreams without being able to sleep."

For this group of immigrants, being in the United States coincided with gaining families of their own, as they had been single in Mexico. The men who started families in the U.S. sometimes blamed the accumulation of family ties for the impoverished conditions in which they lived. They sometimes romanticized bachelorhood, and implied that it had enabled them to live not only a free life, but one where they had enjoyed more disposable income. Fidencio Flores recalled that while single, he would be

> going out with the guys, going strong until the morning. If I had the desire to buy a round of drinks for my buddies and my *compadres,* I just did it. Now, it's different. With a woman and with children, one must think of their needs. Yeah, those days are gone.

Living in the United States and acquiring a family had constrained the men's spatial mobility and redirected their meager financial resources, and this created tension in the family.

This tension was again exhibited one summer evening when I accompanied Reynaldo and Anabel Castrillo on a series of visits to deliver home-grown vegetables to three different households of kin. At each stop Reynaldo told his kin of a new job and residential opportunity—a rent-free house available in exchange for cleaning horse stables and fixing fences. He weighed out loud the advantages and disadvantages, but since there was no guarantee of permanence, he reasoned, it would be too risky with a wife and child. The new situation might be temporary, and if so, he and his family would lose access to the rent-free garage. Together with his brother-in-law, Mateo, he reminisced and romanticized about the bachelor days that the two of them had spent together in Los Angeles in the early 1970s. At Mateo's house, a young man slept in the next room, and, nodding his head toward this presumably unattached young man, Reynaldo wistfully remarked, "Look at him, he has only his own self to worry about, to dress, to feed. He can sleep and do as he pleases, whenever he pleases. You and me, we've already limited ourselves." In front of his more comfortably situated cousins, Reynaldo felt ashamed of the substandard living conditions he provided for his family, and in an attempt to save public face, he blamed his wife and child for these conditions. Paradoxically, family responsibility required achieving financial security, yet the burden of supporting family members worked against this. Men like Reynaldo rationalized their precarious financial position in the U.S. by blaming their families.

In this context, men engaged in rhetoric designed to demonstrate their lack of commitment to remaining in the U.S. When they stated their preference for returning to Mexico for self-employment, or when they faulted their families for their financial position, they seemed to imply that they could easily reestablish their independence.

DIVERGENT GAINS AND PREFERENCES

Changing gender relations in the family help to explain women's and men's divergent preferences toward settlement. In terms of spatial mobility, household divisions of labor, and the balance of family power and authority as indicated by decision-making processes, women gain in the process of settlement while men lose. Women gain greater personal autonomy and independence, becoming more self-reliant as they participate in pubic life and gain access to both social and economic resources previously beyond their reach. Many women begin to partake in family decision making in areas where they previously had no say. In some families, women no longer perform 100 percent of the housework. In contrast, the men lose the monopoly they once enjoyed over family resources, and they exercise less authority over family members than they had in Mexico. The men enjoy less personal autonomy than before, and some participate in daily household chores.

These transformations highlight the ongoing relationship between the public and private realms. Women simultaneously expand their spatial mobility in the public sphere and exercise greater status in the family, especially in the making of decisions and the division of household labor. Compared with women, men still have more status and they are more mobile, but men have new constraints placed on their spatial mobility, and they lose power and status in the public sphere, especially as it is expressed at the workplace. As men lose their monopoly of control over resources, they lose some of their power and status within the family.

Patriarchy is renegotiated through migration and resettlement in a variety of ways, and family power relations take many new forms. While it would be premature to hail the end of patriarchy in these families, it is significant that there is a general trend toward more egalitarian relations. This is not a unilinear trend without contradictions; these transformations occur heterogeneously and appear in contradictory patterns.

Patriarchy, however, even when not contested or challenged in an organized fashion, remains susceptible to modifications exerted through the social processes of migration and resettlement.

In this chapter I have described people's initial resettlement experiences in order to show the effect of these experiences on gender relations in families. Through the process of settlement, relatively speaking, women gain and men lose in family politics. In the next chapter, relying more on the ethnographic data than the interview material, I show how women's position in their families is further consolidated on an ongoing, daily basis through their activities outside the household. These activities simultaneously strengthen women's position in their families and advance, indeed construct and define, settlement.

CHAPTER SIX

Women Consolidating Settlement

As traditional family patriarchy weakens, immigrant women assume more active public and social roles, and these activities ultimately advance their families' integration in the United States. In this chapter I examine three dimensions of women's activities outside the family, and I argue that in the aggregate, these activities anchor family settlement. Women advance settlement for their families, and in the process, they consolidate their own newfound status in the family.

First, settlement involves working at relatively stable, nonseasonal jobs. As others have noted, the presence of immigrant women allows immigrant men to work at permanent, stable jobs without interruptions caused by visits to see their families in Mexico. The vast majority of undocumented immigrant women also work at nonseasonal jobs.[1] Second, due to immigrants' low wages and because the family no longer resides in Mexico, settlement often entails use of public and private financial support. These families use private forms of assistance, including loans and credit, to purchase medical services and consumer goods. Women are central in seeking and mediating both private and public institutional assistance. Finally, long-term residence in the U.S. entails the creation of, and reliance on, culturally distinct immigrant communities, and women, through their informal and organizational activities, play a vital role in the development of these communities.[2]

Men and children also, of course, advance undocumented immigrant settlement, but in this chapter I primarily focus on women because their activities are crucial to establishing full family units and thereby fostering settlement. Moreover, newly reconstructed gender relations in the family provide women with incentives to organize and advocate for long-term settlement.

PERMANENT, NONSEASONAL WORK

Metropolitan and urban areas are conducive to settlement because they offer a diverse array of job opportunities, especially for immigrant women (Massey et al., 1987; Browning and Rodríguez, 1985). I now turn to the types of jobs Mexican undocumented immigrant women do in Oakview, as well as the strategies women use to stabilize their employment, and ultimately achieve long-term residence in the U.S. The ethnographic detail highlights how immigrant women informally collectivize and share information about paid domestic work, which is the most typical occupation for Mexican immigrant women in Oakview. Paid domestic work has historically played an important role in both "processing" migrant women into urban society (McBride, 1976; Jelin, 1977) and building settlement communities (Glenn, 1986). Before exploring these dynamics in contemporary Mexican immigrant settlement, I examine the area's changing structure of jobs for immigrant women.

IMMIGRANTS AND SERVICE-SECTOR JOBS IN OAKVIEW

Nearly all of the immigrant women and men I met in Oakview, including those not formally included in my sample, worked in low-end service-sector jobs, not in assembly or light manufacturing.[3] Characterized by relatively low wages, few advancement possibilities, and manual labor, these jobs required few English-speaking skills and no extensive interaction with English-speaking clients, customers, or bosses. Such work included jobs in small competitive businesses (restaurants, hospitals, laundries, car washes) and in private households, and self-employment—usually, providing goods and services to other immigrants. For immigrant women in Oakview, the likelihood of falling into a particular job category has changed over time, and is affected by both the growth of the immigrant community and the shifting job structure in the area.

When Mexican immigrant men first began settling in this area during the late 1950s and early 1960s, commercial and residential areas were expanding, fueled by postwar economic growth and westward migration. Mexican men who had worked as "illegal braceros" in the Salinas Valley and in northern-California fruit orchards found work in Oakview restaurants as busboys and dishwashers, and soon male friends and relatives from their *municipio* (town and surrounding rural county area) also began to seek restaurant work.

Restaurant businesses depended on these workers, so many undocumented men were able to become legal permanent residents by acquiring employers' letters of labor certification.[4] Restaurant employers needed employees who would work year-round, uninterrupted by biannual or unpredictably timed departures for family visits to Mexico, so they sometimes went out of their way to keep trusted and trained employees.[5] When Manuel Galván was deported in 1955, after working five years as a dishwasher in a local restaurant, his employer wrote to him in Mexico and offered to help him legalize his status if he returned to the U.S. Although the employer did not actively recruit Manuel Galván's wife, she insisted in migrating as well, and ultimately Manuel realized that if she did, he could sustain uninterrupted periods of employment. Manuel's wife, Sidra, migrated north in 1958, and Manuel then continued working at the same restaurant until his retirement in 1981.

When the wives of this first cohort of formerly undocumented men arrived during the late 1950s and early 1960s, they found work in flower nurseries and laundries, as did Sidra Galván. Although men worked in nurseries as well, these jobs increasingly came to be defined as "women's work." Only a minority of these women did paid domestic work.

This cohort of women entered the labor market with the benefit of legal status, which helped them find jobs.[6] Like their husbands, who worked in restaurants, these women stayed at the same jobs and place of work for many years. The sociability and friendships established at work overlapped into private and community life. They developed a workplace culture much like the ones described by Zavella (1985) among Chicana cannery workers in the Santa Clara Valley, and this contributed to their job tenure.

Beginning in the 1970s, as real-estate prices skyrocketed, the Japanese-American nursery owners sold their properties to developers building new suburban tract homes, and the nursery owners moved their operations to less expensive, rural land. This closed off a traditional source of employment for Mexican immigrants in Oakview. Hospitals and laundries, as well as nursing homes and motels, continued to provide job opportunities for immigrant women, but by the late 1960s, greater numbers of Mexican immigrant women were arriving in this area, and a significant proportion of them lacked legal status. Most of the undocumented immigrant women sought employment as paid domestic workers in private households. Mexican undocumented immigrant women now typically work as domestic workers in Oakview, a trend with several sources.

THE GROWING DEMAND FOR DOMESTIC WORKERS

During the 1970s and especially in the 1980s, particular areas of the United States, such as California, and cities such as New York and other urban centers with concentrated immigrant populations, witnessed a dramatic growth in the demand for paid domestic work. Census and Department of Labor data underestimate the expansion of the domestic occupation because they do not accurately capture situations where under-the-table pay arrangements and undocumented immigrants may prevail, but other evidence suggests that in recent years, the amount of paid domestic employment has increased (Rollins, 1985; Sassen-Koob, 1984; Wrigley, 1991).[7]

The demand for domestic work is closely connected to the mass entrance of women into formal sectors of the labor force. While proportionately few women earn salaries that one commonly associates with the ability to afford domestic workers, the demand for housecleaning services stems from the forty-hour-a-week absences of many of these working women from their homes, which occurs largely without major rearrangements by their male partners, government, and private employers.[8] The demand also stems from the greater purchasing power of dual-income families. In 1987, for example, families with employed wives had a median income of $40,422, a figure that is 50 percent higher than the median $26,652 for families where wives were not in the paid labor force (Rix, 1990:334).

Employers of domestic workers are a diverse group. They include middle-class and upper-income, dual-career families of the sort described by Hertz (1986), as well as dual-earner working parents and single mothers who constitute part of the bottom of a "two-tiered" domestic-service market (Salzinger, 1991:15). A large number of high-income families—the first group—live in the areas surrounding Oakview. Economic restructuring in the 1970s and 1980s expanded the number of high-income, professional service and managerial jobs, especially in the urban centers of global corporate management, of which San Francisco is a minor but nevertheless significant example, and this growth promoted demand for personal cleaning services (Sassen-Koob, 1984). For those at the high end of the income and occupational hierarchy in the San Francisco Bay area, the area surrounding Oakview is a desirable locale with highly rated public schools, a number of elite private day schools, and expensive boutiques, department stores, and gourmet shops. Proximity to corporate offices in San Francisco and the Silicon Valley, and the possibility of maintaining semirural estates with swimming pools and horse stables, also enhance the attractiveness of this elite residential area. Consequently, gardening and domestic work provide an important source of employment for Mexican immigrants in Oakview.

My inquiry focuses on how paid domestic work fosters permanent settlement for Mexican immigrant women and their families. The following section explores this question by examining how undocumented immigrant women obtain these jobs, the requirements of the work, and negotiations with employers over pay and control over the work. This discussion is based on participant observation in a range of public and private locales—at picnics, parties, and informal gatherings in people's homes—supplemented by interviews with seventeen of the undocumented women with recent experience as non-live-in domestic workers.

OCCUPATIONAL CHARACTERISTICS
AND INFORMAL WORK CULTURE

Most of the undocumented immigrant women in Oakview performed paid domestic work on a non-live-in basis, in arrangements that Romero (1987, 1988a) has termed "job work." In "job work," domestic workers maintain several employers and clean different houses on a weekly or biweekly basis, generally in exchange for a flat rate of pay. These arrangements allow for independence and mitigate deeply personalistic employer-employee relations—one of the potentially most abusive aspects of this type of labor. Job-work arrangements, however, introduce the extra burden of locating multiple jobs and juggling schedules (Romero, 1988a; Salzinger, 1991). Another problem is that the work itself occurs in isolation, and terms and conditions are generally negotiated between two lone individuals—the domestic worker and her employer. As Judith Rollins summarizes:

> The mistress-servant relationship is one of the more private labor arrangements existing: it takes place within private households between fairly isolated individuals. As multi-servant households become more and more rare,

the typical domestic works alone; as the nuclear neo-local family pattern becomes more prevalent, the employer administers the daily chores of her house alone. A sense of isolation surrounds the job and the relationship: there are no co-workers or co-managers on the spot to support, reinforce, compete with, or guide behavior. Consultations with others in similar positions must take place haphazardly during off hours; the job situation is typically one of a single employer dealing with a single employee. (1985:91)

The job does indeed occur in an isolated and privatized environment, and some women leave the work for this reason.[9] Moreover, a labor agreement established between two lone individuals who are operating without standard guidelines heightens the asymmetry of the employer-employee relationship. But the social interactions I observed among immigrant women domestic workers provide a sharp contrast to the solitary quality of the domestic worker's job negotiation. In various social settings—at picnics and baby showers, in people's homes, and at the parish legalization clinic—I observed immigrant women engaged in vigorous conversation about paid domestic work. Women traded cleaning tips, tactics about how best to negotiate pay, how to geographically arrange jobs so as to minimize daily travel, how to interact (or, more often, avoid interaction) with their bosses, how to leave undesirable jobs, remedies for physical ailments caused by the work, and cleaning strategies to lessen these ailments. The women were quick to voice disapproval of another's strategy and to eagerly recommend alternatives. These interactions were not embedded in formally organized cooperatives, as they are for a select group of Latina immigrant women domestic workers in the San Francisco Bay area (Salzinger, 1991), but neither were the consultations with one another as haphazard as those that have been described among African American women (Rollins, 1985; Kaplan, 1987).

Strong informational ties among these women mitigate the isolation and privatization of paid domestic work, and their interactions lessen the insecurity of piecing together myriad jobs. These employee networks also serve as informal training and advocacy centers for domestic workers. Well-organized albeit informal communication transforms the job situation from one of a single employee dealing with a single employer to one where a socially well-connected employee is informed by the collective experience of others. These exchanges constitute a largely sex-segregated work culture. To a lesser extent—because I had less access—I observed similar interactions among Mexican immigrant men who work as private gardeners and horse-stable cleaners.

THE JOB SEARCH

The women I interviewed most often located jobs not through agencies or classified ads, but through informal networks of employers. Employers, all of whom were women, recommended a particular domestic worker to friends, neighbors, relatives, and coworkers. Teresa Ibarra, for example, found her first domestic job at a county medical clinic, with a nurse. This employer passed along referrals to her coworkers, so that Teresa later worked for a number of public-health nurses who shared the same office but lived in different neighborhoods. Similarly, Rosario Quiñones found her first domestic job with the secretary at her son's school, and she later worked for two teachers employed at the same school.

Tapping employer networks was the primary technique for finding jobs, but obtaining the first domestic job was often difficult. Family, friends, and kin of the women seeking employment helped them over this initial hump. Immigrant men were more likely to pass along domestic-job referrals than were immigrant women because of competition among women for a limited number of jobs. Some women occasionally found work through other women, but unless a domestic worker had a surplus of desirable jobs—an unlikely occurrence—or was returning to her country of origin, she was unlikely to pass along a choice job. Many of the immigrant men in this community worked as gardeners, and a few in horse stables, and this provided them contact with prospective employers of domestic labor. In this regard, immigrant women do appear to benefit from the male-network ties of their husbands (Kossoudji and Ranney, 1984), and from cross-gender network links.

Women with ties to well-connected, established kin networks found initial employers without much difficulty, but immigrant women lacking these ties either were unable to break into domestic work, or languished on the margins of the occupation. As a single teen in the United States without close family ties, Anabel Castrillo's first U.S. job was as a bar waitress in a cantina, serving primarily Latino immigrant men; she managed to break into domestic work, which she viewed as preferable employment, with the help of Reynaldo, a man she met at the bar and later married.

The first difficult task in paid domestic work is breaking into the employer network and securing employers who exclusively contract with one person for services. Once a woman obtains a steady employer, there is the possibility—but no guarantee—that the job will snowball into more referrals and more jobs. Most women wish to maximize their earnings by securing as many jobs as possible. Due partially to the unpredictable turnover of employers, few women reached the point of saturation, of having the maximum number of jobs they could handle.

María Alicia Navarro, a single mother of three children, had a difficult time establishing steady and sufficient domestic employment. She initially came to the United States alone, leaving her children behind in Mexico under the care of her mother, so that she might assume a live-in domestic position with an employer who promised to help her find additional domestic job work as well. When the extra jobs were not forthcoming, she quit her live-in domestic position in order to work alongside another domestic worker who paid her little but promised in return to find María Alicia her own jobs. This domestic worker, a more established Mexican immigrant woman, exploited María Alicia's labor, and never did pass along any clients. Ultimately, María Alicia paid a fee to another domestic worker in order to obtain her first steady employer.

Many undocumented immigrant women were constantly on the lookout for more domestic jobs. Indeed, part of the occupation seems to be the search for more jobs and for jobs with better working conditions and pay. Although some undocumented immigrant women tried placing ads in newspapers and on community bulletin boards to secure domestic work, employer networks were the primary means of securing multiple employers.

SUBCONTRACTING ARRANGEMENTS

While employment with one party can multiply into several jobs, securing that first job is difficult. For this reason, many new immigrant women first find themselves subcontracting their services to other, more experienced and well-established immigrant women who have steady customers for domestic work. This provides an important apprenticeship and a potential springboard to independent contracting. Romero (1987) discusses the important training and recruitment functions of these apprenticeships among Chicana domestics, but she looks only at the advantageous features of the relationship. While subcontracting arrangements can be beneficial to both parties, the relationship is not characterized by altruism or harmony of interests. I found that immigrant women domestic workers who took on a helper did so in order to lighten their own work load, and sometimes to accommodate newly arrived kin, factors that often led to conflicting interests.

For the new apprentice, the arrangement minimizes the difficulty of finding employment and securing transportation, and it facilitates learning expected tasks. The "how-to's," such as how to use a variety of vacuum cleaners, knowing the names of various cleansers and polishers, and cleaning techniques, are sometimes learned in this context. These types of interactions are vividly portrayed in the movie *El Norte,* where the newly arrived Guatemalan undocumented woman works alongside the more established Latina woman.

Domestic workers must learn the ropes for negotiating their employment terms. Unlike office, retail, or factory settings, the work site lacks standard guidelines and coworkers, so the women learned employee strategies in informal settings and in the subcontracting relationship. When María Alicia Navarro's sister, Eulodia, arrived in the U.S. "without papers," María Alicia invited Eulodia to accompany her on domestic jobs and began teaching her the rigors and strategies used in paid domestic work. While I visited at their apartment one evening María Alicia related to Eulodia that the houses are typically disgustingly filthy when one is first hired—usually no one has cleaned them since the last domestic worker left. She warned her sister of the risks involved in taking on a new house under job-work terms: "You have to watch out with them [employers] because once their houses are nice and clean, then they say they no longer need your services."

María Alicia offered her sister protective advice, such as not to work too fast or be overly concerned with cleaning all crevices and hidden corners. She advised her sister to occasionally clean thoroughly and, on alternating visits to the same work site, to do maintenance routines so that she might minimize the strain of the work. To avoid losing time by talking with chatty employers, María Alicia advised Eulodia to simply smile, citing the language barrier as an effective deterrent to the sort of sociability about which the African American house cleaners in Rollins's (1985) book complain. The women did not want to engage in long conversations with their employers; they wanted to expeditiously do the work and then move on. María Alicia told Eulodia that when she wishes to leave a particular job because the pay is too low, or because the employer makes too many unrealistic demands, she simply tells the employer she is returning to Mexico.

A subcontracted arrangement is informative and convenient, especially for an immigrant woman who lacks her own transportation or has minimal English-language skills. The pay, however, is much lower than what a woman might earn on her own. For example, although Eulodia began working alongside María Alicia in her domestic work route, it would be months before Eulodia received remuneration. María Alicia felt conflicted about this, but she herself had experienced very similar arrangements when she first arrived. She rationalized not paying her sister by citing her various debts, her economic dependents, and her contributions to funding her sister's migration costs.

Subexploitation of other, more disadvantaged immigrant women is one way that more established immigrant women can improve their own earnings and working conditions. When Teresa Ibarra first began paid domestic work, it was as a helper to a Filipina woman who provided the transportation and the employers. Teresa later sought and established her own schedule of employers, and years later, after she began driving a car, she lessened the burden of domestic work by employing a newly arrived Mexican immigrant woman, who lived in her garage, to assist with the jobs.

In an apprentice/subcontracting arrangement the pay can be so low that it renders the experience exploitative and demeaning. María Gándara, a thirty-eight-year-old mother of three, told me that when she was working as a domestic helper to an acquaintance and had worked seven hours on one of the hottest days of the year, she received only twenty-five dollars, an amount reflecting less than four dollars an hour in pay. Contrasting this situation with her previous middle-class status, she concluded, "I never would have thought to clean houses in Mexico." Although subcontracting arrangements ameliorate isolation and help domestics secure employment with multiple employers, the relationship established between the experienced, senior domestic worker and the newcomer apprentice is often very exploitative for the apprentice. The apprentices, however, still acquired training and important information in this context. Sometimes the how-to's that women traded were as simple as relating a method of dusting with a damp rag, but a more serious and recurrent theme in these discussions centered on earnings.

NEGOTIATION OF PAY

The pay for domestic work varies widely across different regions in the country and even within a given area. For example, in El Paso, Texas, characterized by both a high rate of unemployment and the lowest per capita income level of any city with over one hundred thousand inhabitants in the nation, domestic workers averaged fifteen dollars for a day's work in the 1980s (Ruiz, 1987:63).[10] Undocumented immigrant women in my study averaged thirty-five to fifty dollars for a full day of domestic work, although some earned less and others twice that amount. This wide disparity reflects the dynamic economy in metropolitan California as well as the absence of a regulated system of payment.

What determines the pay scale for domestic work? There are no unions, government regulations, corporate guidelines, or management policy to set wages. Instead, the pay for domestic work is generally informally negotiated between two women, the domestic worker and the employer. The pay scale that domestic workers attempt to negotiate is influenced by the information that they share with one another, and by their ability to sustain a sufficient number or jobs, which is in turn also shaped by their English-language skills, legal status, and access to private transportation. Although the pay scale remains unregulated by state mechanisms, social interactions among the domestic workers themselves serve to informally regulate pay standards.

Unlike employees in middle-class professions, most of the domestic workers talked quite openly with one another about their level of pay. At informal gatherings such as a child's birthday party or at a community event, the women revealed what they earned with particular employers, and how they had achieved or been stuck with that particular level of pay. Working for low-level pay was typically met with murmurs of disapproval or pity, but no stronger sanctions were applied. Conversely, those women who earned at the high end were admired. At one baby shower, a woman who had recently moved from this community to the Silicon Valley and purchased a home with her husband told us that by working steadily on a job-work basis, she averaged fifteen dollars an hour. The women responded with awe and approval, but some of them grew discouraged when they learned that this visitor had obtained legal status and a car, factors that gave her distinct advantages in the domestic job market.

The exchange of information about domestic workers' earnings sometimes starts in the premigration phase, in Mexico. María Alicia Navarro, whose two office jobs had provided a middle-class status in Mexico until the inflationary crisis of the early 1980s, claimed that rumors of the high earnings in domestic work prompted her to migrate to California: "I had heard that here a woman could earn good money, that here a woman could earn fifty dollars by cleaning one house. I figured that if I could clean two houses, I could earn one hundred dollars with only one day's work. I had to see if it was true." This upper continuum of wages attracted women to domestic work, and such information flowed through transnational networks prior to migration.

Of course not all immigrant women can earn one hundred dollars a day in domestic work, and fewer still can sustain such relatively high earnings over time. Since most women obtain jobs through employer referrals, in their new job they generally ask for at least the same wage rate they are presently earning elsewhere or they ask for a slightly higher rate. The highest rates earned by women in my sample were fifty dollars for cleaning a three-bedroom, two-and-a-half-bath house, and thirty-five to forty dollars for cleaning a two-bedroom house. Some women were able to clean more than one house a day.

As live-out, day workers, these immigrant women were paid either on an hourly or on a "job work" basis, and most women preferred the latter. Although being paid on an hourly basis allows one to work at a slower pace, lessening the chance of accidents and injuries, most women tried to maximize their earnings by working intensively on a job basis. Physical pain and injuries were exacerbated by the intensified, rapid pace of work, a direct outcome and another drawback of the "job work" system of pay. Domestic work is indeed, as Rollins (1985) puts it, "hard on the body."

The pay earned each week is highly variable, and the weekly job schedule is constantly in flux. The job is typically performed for the same employer on a weekly or biweekly schedule, so domestic workers must patch together many different jobs in order to maintain a certain income level. Adding to the variability, domestic workers typically earn a different level of pay with different employers. A domestic worker may earn a set fee for cleaning some houses, and an hourly wage for cleaning others.

Sometimes the employer sets the price, but when the domestic worker has enough jobs, and if she is a fast worker, she is able to be more selective and assertive in setting the pay. One afternoon at María Mendoza's home, as she was preparing for an interview with a potential employer, who had been referred from another employer, I naively asked, "What kinds of questions do they ask you in the interviews?" She quickly retorted: "They don't ask me anything, it's me who interviews them! I decide how much needs to be done, and I set the conditions: no washing laundry and ironing, and I tell them I charge fifty dollars for four hours a week." María Mendoza was confident in asking for a certain wage level because she already had six steady employers, and in addition she worked in a produce-vending business operated by her family.

Access to private transportation also affects wage rates. Women who do not drive are simply unable to hold as many jobs, since they spend many hours walking, waiting for and riding buses, or waiting for family members to transport them to semirural and suburban residential areas where no public transportation is available. When I first met Teresa Ibarra in February 1987 she calculated that she spent as much time walking, riding the bus, or waiting for a ride as she did "on the job." She prompted many family fights when she tried to obtain early-morning rides from her son, who worked late nights in a restaurant and needed to sleep in the morning. Once while we watched television ads for weight-loss programs she quipped, "I've got a solution for people who want to lose weight: just give me your car!" By the spring of 1989 she had learned to drive. This allowed her to take on more jobs, which in turn gave her the leverage she needed to demand raises or leave the lowest-paid jobs. Eventually, she took on a "helper."

A survey conducted in Los Angeles indicates that undocumented immigrant women earn less in domestic work than do women with legal status (Simon and De Ley, 1984). In Oakview, I found that earnings were also mediated by an employee's ability to communicate at some rudimentary level with her employers, her ability to efficiently arrive at numerous work sites without wasting time on excessively long bus rides and walks, and, importantly, by her ability to utilize information available through social networks. The woman in my study who consistently earned the highest income from domestic work, María Alicia Navarro, constantly drew on the domestics' networks for cleaning tips and advice. Her favorite topic of conversation was domestic work, and with friends, family, and acquaintances she discussed how to approach an employer for a raise and how to deal with problematic employers; she also drew on the employers' networks for new job referrals. In spite of her undocumented status, her resourcefulness paid off. At any given time, she could unfold a large calendar page stored in her purse, where she recorded whose house she cleaned on which day of the month; with the exception of Sundays, each calendar date block bore two or three penciled-in names. María Alicia cleaned approximately fifteen houses a week, and on a good week she earned approximately five hundred dollars.

Since the number of jobs and hours worked per week fluctuates, earnings do not always yield anticipated amounts necessary to cover bills. This is a serious problem for women who are not well connected in the domestics' networks, and for those women who are primarily or centrally responsible for meeting household expenses. Teresa Ibarra best illustrates this precarious dilemma. When I first met her, she was desperate to find new employers, and when she learned that I was a student at a local university, she asked if I knew of students who wanted to hire domestic help. At that time she had only three jobs lined up for the week. Gradually, she found new domestic work jobs, but they were sporadic, and organized on a biweekly or monthly basis. On one occasion when I asked Teresa about her weekly earnings, she could not specify, but she was certain that it always remained below $200. Later, when I interviewed her during an exceptionally good work period, we tallied up the projected hours and earnings for the following five-day work week and came up with a total of $170. She figured that on alternating weeks she would earn only $115 with three days of work. Two weeks later, she lost her best-paying job, lowering her "good week" earnings to $124. Her low-week earnings thereafter sank to $73. Doing in-home child care for a neighbor's children, taking in boarders, and pooling income with her children enabled her to pay the bills during that period. When I visited Teresa two years later, she had promoted herself into the forefront of domestic work; her earnings had increased and she now employed a young "helper." I believe that she advanced within the occupation because she learned to drive and because of her greater exposure and her use of network resources, a process facilitated by her attendance at evening English classes.

Undocumented status and lack of English facility sometimes cause women to lose jobs. In the spring of 1988, after the employer sanctions provisions of the Immigration Reform and Control Act (IRCA) went into effect, Tola Bonilla started a new job cleaning an enormous, filthy house. The employer implied this would be a steady job, but when she asked if Tola was a citizen or legal resident, Tola told the truth and the following week was told she was no longer needed.[11] Later, Tola's friends chastised her for not having lied about her legal status. Rosario Quiñones lost a housecleaning job because she mistakenly heard the employer ask her to clean the "lobby," and although she searched the house for the lobby, the employer had in fact said "oven"; another woman lost a steady, three-times-a-week housecleaning job because she was unable to verbally defend herself in English against an employer's unfair accusation.

Domestic work is inherently volatile. Women who are not well connected to networks of employers who provide referrals, and to other domestics who offer strategic advice, run the risk of severe underemployment. To minimize this, some women combine paid domestic work with other jobs, such as in-home day care for other immigrant women's children, vending, or other wage employment. Similarly, several women supplemented their primary income, which they earned working forty hours a week at jobs in restaurants, laundries, or motels, by cleaning one or two houses for pay on their days off. María Carmen Ochoa had maintained this type of arrangement for nearly fifteen years. Josefa Ramírez, who worked the graveyard shift (2 A.M. to 11 A.M.) in a bakery, was carefully taking on one or two domestic jobs in order to see if she could muster enough employers so that she might eventually leave the bakery job.

DOMESTIC WORK AS PERMANENT EMPLOYMENT

While the immigrant women in this study work relatively permanent, year-round jobs, domestic work offers little job security. With the institutionalization of multiple employers and the decline of personalistic employer-employee relations, employers are less obligated to loyally retain the same employee for many years. Job stability remains vulnerable to employers' whims and personal lives; for example, an employer's prolonged vacation, illness, house remodeling, or fickleness can abruptly terminate a substantial portion of expected earnings. The informal work culture among immigrant women minimizes this insecurity, which gives these ties significance in the process of settlement; informal social ties sustain and enhance women's employment as domestic workers. In nearly all of these undocumented immigrant families, without the women's earnings, settlement in Oakview would not be possible. The domestic workers' networks stabilize employment for immigrant women, and in turn this constitutes part of the social web that fosters settlement.

UTILIZATION OF PUBLIC AND PRIVATE ASSISTANCE

Among the settled, undocumented immigrant population, women and children have the greatest need for institutional resources. Mexican immigrant families with young children face particularly high living costs (Browning and Rodríguez, 1985), and the initial stages of settlement require substantial investment as well (Chavez, 1990; Villar, 1990). Housing, and a minimal amount of furniture, clothing, and utensils, are expensive acquisitions. Additionally, unemployment arising from disability, illness, or lay-off may complicate a household's ability to meet monthly expenses. The burden of supporting non-income-earning dependents, especially children, and unexpected breaks in steady employment can quickly lead to urgent financial situations.

To cope with these circumstances, undocumented immigrant families combine various strategies. They try to cover expenses by employing as many wage earners in the family as possible, or they cut living costs by sharing residences with other families, or by taking in boarders who sleep in living rooms and garages. Individuals and families share and borrow resources among kin and *comadres* and *compadres* (godparents) in their social network; and for child-care solutions, sometimes older women kin from Mexico come to look after the young children of working parents.

But immigrants live in a market economy. The vital necessities for immigrant families—such as housing, clothing, medical attention, household utensils, and other goods—are available only on a cash basis. Reciprocity among immigrant kin and friends may stretch scarce resources, but sharing and borrowing does not produce needed resources. These must be purchased in a capitalist economy.

Due to undocumented immigrant workers' low wages, the high cost of living in metropolitan areas like Oakview, and the burden of supporting non-income-earning dependent children, family settlement sometimes requires use of institutional forms of public and private resources. These resources can be grouped into three categories: credit and installment purchases, assistance from private charities, and public assistance. Looking at these activities goes beyond the exploration of immigrant "nonmarket" reciprocity and bartering exchanges in order to examine how formal U.S.-based institutions enable undocumented immigrants to get by in the U.S. I found, as have other researchers (Chavira, 1988; O'Conner, 1990), that it is primarily women who become adept at utilizing and seeking out these resources in the new society.[12] By doing so, they advance settlement.

CREDIT AND INSTALLMENT PURCHASES

Not all undocumented immigrants are easily persuaded to purchase goods and service with credit. Many undocumented immigrants retain an ideological preference for cash purchases, which are often a source of pride (Villar, 1990). As Roberto Melchor said, " I never take out loans! If I need something, then I save my money, cent by cent, dollar by dollar. If I don't have enough money, well, then I just don't buy it." Regardless of ideological preferences, I found that many undocumented immigrants in Oakview had purchased or were making purchases on credit. The most common items purchased on credit were medical services and consumer goods.

Medical Services   Although maternal and child health services are the most important health-care needs of the settled immigrant population, Mexican undocumented immigrant families underutilize health services, especially preventative health care, in the U.S. (Cornelius et al., 1982; Chavez et al., 1986; Rumbaut et al., 1988).[13] Undocumented immigrants do not qualify for Medi-Cal coverage, except for emergency and pregnancy services, and most of them do not have medical insurance, so they generally pay for their medical services.[14] Nearly all of the women in this study who had obtained obstetrical care in the United States had paid for the treatment received, or were in the long-term process of paying such bills, and families with small children incurred sizable debts for the treatment of routine ear infections and immunizations.

The Mendoza family, with six children, told me that they owed over twenty thousand dollars to the county hospital (they owed thirteen thousand dollars alone for their son's arm operation). The Macías family was paying similarly large debts to a well-known research hospital where their son had undergone several eye operations. While some relatives and acquaintances advised these families to simply default on their payments by returning to Mexico, the families remained determined to stay in the United States and honor their debts.

The high cost of obstetrical care placed a double burden on those young families where mothers of infant and toddler-aged children were not employed. With only one income earner (the father/husband), these families encountered difficulties in making medical payments. When I met them, Trini Ochoa and Felipe Palacios, parents of two U.S.-born boys aged three and six, were still paying a bill of $450 for the birth of their first son, and a $2,900 bill for the birth of their second child, who had required special postnatal care. Each month they paid $30 toward these combined debts. They also had a running tab of $1,460 at the local community medical clinic, which had accumulated as the boys required attention for immunizations, ear infections, and childhood diseases. When the couple received a notice to appear in court over this bill, I accompanied them to court, to the medical clinic's accounting office, and finally to the county collections agency. The bureaucrats at that agency ultimately decided that Trini and Felipe must make a minimum $20 monthly payment. According to this agreement, in each payment, half of the sum would go toward interest only. When I protested to the collections-agency official that Felipe Palacios earned $5 an hour as a dishwasher and that Trini had not yet obtained the temporary legalization card necessary to secure employment, and that out of approximate monthly earnings of $800, they paid $575 for rent and that they were already paying $50 monthly toward their medical debts, he replied: "They aren't the only ones in this situation."

Marisela and Carlos Hernández faced similar debts incurred over child delivery. For the birth of their eldest child, Marisela had returned to Mexico to deliver among her family of origin and the neighborhood *partera* (midwife); her other two sons were born in a U.S. hospital in 1984 and 1986. Due to complicated deliveries, the bills had totaled thousands of dollars, but they were whittling this down with periodic but substantial payments. Marisela looked after the three pre-school-aged children and did not work outside of the home. Although Carlos earned relatively high wages, as much as one hundred dollars a day, in his job digging foundation trenches, his earnings varied from week to week.

One day, while spending several hours in the hospital billing agency with Marisela, I caught a glimpse of the labyrinth of bureaucracy in which her family was enmeshed. As we tried to iron out a billing discrepancy of nearly a thousand dollars, I saw Marisela produce a meticulously organized stack of canceled checks showing that they had already paid thousands of dollars toward their medical bills. Marisela argued that Medi-Cal had covered her baby's costs (not her own), because Carlos was underemployed when the baby was born, and the baby had been sickly and required special neonatal care. The billing discrepancy was not resolved that day, and the imposing bureaucracy—including two collections agencies in separate cities, a not very helpful hospital clerk who spoke only English, and the hospital's computer billing system that concealed more than it revealed—allowed for little optimism.

Many undocumented immigrant women in Oakview had returned to Mexico to give birth, as Marisela chose to do with her firstborn. Some women reported that they did so because they wished to be with their mothers during childbirth, and because they feared U.S. medical practices, or being discovered as "undocumented" persons, but others said they did so in order to avoid enormous medical costs.[15] This common practice of returning to Mexico for childbirth was often financially motivated.[16]

Jovita Cerritos had successfully avoided exorbitant medical costs by returning to Mexico for the birth of two children, and by having a home birth in the U.S. Still, as the mother of six children aged three to fourteen, Jovita Cerritos was continuously investigating the possibilities of obtaining medical insurance. She and her husband worked at a bakery restaurant that offered medical benefits only to Anglo, citizen workers, and she was anxious to receive her legalization card and legitimate Social Security number so that she might seek a new job that offered medical insurance. When I visited their house they frequently asked me to read and translate junk mail that advertised life insurance or special "emergency accident insurance" for injuries involving automobile accidents. None of these promotional insurance plans covered what the Cerritos family needed most—routine medical care.

Many of these women were clearly unhappy about the quality of medical care that they had received in the U.S., and the seemingly surreptitious way they became indebted. More than a few of them denounced the culture of U.S. medical services, medicine, and, of course, the exorbitant cost of medical attention. Trini Ochoa claimed that U.S. doctors "don't know anything," and María Mendoza complained that "here in this country, if you or your family get sick and must enter the hospital, they charge you for everything, even the Kleenex. And the worst part is that they don't cure you." In contrast to these positions, Rosario Quiñones had no complaints about the obstetrical care and bills incurred over the 1978 birth of her youngest daughter, as she stated: "I had good care with lots of doctors and nurses, so what if it cost a lot of money? My husband would have just drank it anyway."

The purchase of basic medical attention on credit graphically illustrates a key difference between sojourners and settlers. In sojourner migration, women and children either remain in Mexico or return there when the harvest season ends, thus avoiding the high medical and reproductive costs in the U.S. By contrast, young settler families require medical care, which is so exorbitantly priced that purchase is possible only through credit or installment purchases. These undocumented immigrant families enter a Sisyphean cycle of seeking medical attention, amassing debts, and then wage-earning in order to pay for past costs of subsistence and reproduction.

Undocumented immigrant women in Oakview played an important role in this process, primarily because medical care was required for their children's as well as for their own personal needs, and also because women took a more active role than their husbands in record keeping, tracking medical bills, and negotiating payments. Marisela Hernández explained: "I've always taken care of the papers because I talk more than Carlos does. He says I can talk better than he does, since he was raised on a rancho and is timid." These continual efforts to pay off medical debts further strengthen institutional ties to the United States.

Installment Purchases   Consumer activities are an important part of settlement, and many undocumented families purchase consumer goods through installment payments or credit.[17] These goods include merchandise that is vital to earning a livelihood in the United States, such as special work-related tools and automobiles for transportation to jobs, as well as consumer durables, some of dubious value. Many undocumented immigrants pay exorbitant prices for merchandise sold by door-to-door salespersons. In Oakview, cosmetics, jewelry, and housewares, including a line of sensationalized pots and pans called Cenaware (a pseudonym), were sold in this manner. Nearly everyone in my study could cite a neighbor, friend, or relative who had purchased Cenaware.

During the eighteen-month period of my fieldwork, the Cenaware salespersons were young Salvadorean women and men who were shuttled in vans from San Francisco to various suburban Latino neighborhoods to sell the pots and pans on a door-to-door basis. The typical cost of a package consisting of seven to eight pieces of pots, pans, and lids was five hundred to eight hundred dollars. The vendors, who worked on commissions, carried small cases equipped with sample wares and magazine folios. They promised that cooking in these pots improved food's taste and nutrition, and that due to the special "silicon gel" built into the pots, the food cooked in half the normal time, promising savings in utility bills.

Many people purchased overpriced goods on installment payment plans hoping that this would lead to credit for automobiles, plastic cards, and perhaps, ultimately, a house (one undocumented family in my sample had secured a mortgaged house). Latino-owned and -operated neighborhood jewelry stores and furniture stores commonly sold merchandise in this manner, as did Spanish-speaking door-to-door vendors of expensive vacuum cleaners, encyclopedias, and English learning sets. The Cerritos family purchased their Cenaware set because they thought that by doing so they would receive a credit card. They did, but it was only good toward the purchase of more Cenaware products; they had erroneously believed it would be honored at major department and discount stores. Hoping to establish more credit, Jovita purchased a $500 watch at a local jewelry store for Ignacio's birthday. Patricio and Blanca Macías paid $395 for an English-language series that included three instructional audiotapes, two very thin English books, and a "free" complementary dictionary. The series offered the option to purchase additional tapes at $80 each.

Sometimes children and teens pressured their parents to provide up-to-date clothes and other consumer items, and this was at times possible only through reliance on credit or installment purchases. María Alicia Navarro's teenage daughter insisted that she needed a presentable environment to entertain prospective boyfriends, and eventually María Alicia bought a complete living-room set of furniture through an installment payment plan. Little boys as young as age five refused to wear out-of-fashion bell-bottom pants purchased at secondhand stores, and insisted instead on the more up-to-date ankle-tight jeans they saw on their peers. Children wanted popcorn poppers, VCRs, and color televisions. Although parents did not indulge all of their children's consumer preferences, children did make consumer demands that often could be met only through credit or installment purchase.

Loans for work-related apparatuses were not uncommon, especially for men. Women in this study did not distinguish themselves in this area, as the main type of employment for the women, domestic work, required no significant investment in tools. After Luis Bonilla's gardening tools were stolen from his home, he applied for a six-hundred-dollar loan to replace his stolen leaf blower and power mower. The Mendoza family made monthly payments of eight hundred dollars toward the purchase of their produce-vending truck. In December 1989, they finished making payments on the truck which, with interest, totaled fifty thousand dollars. Patricio Macías purchased a vacuum cleaner costing eleven hundred dollars at 12 percent interest from a door-to-door vendor because he needed it for his job as a janitor. Several families had taken out larger loans for the purchase of automobiles and pickup trucks.

During the period of my field research (November 1986 to May 1988), the most typical form of installment payment was for the purchase of amnesty-legalization services, an employment prerequisite in the post-IRCA employer-sanctions era.[18] Many undocumented immigrants in this study, as well as those I assisted at the legalization clinic, paid for these legal services on an installment basis.[19]

The purchase of automobiles, clothing, and education on credit is so common in the U.S. that it hardly seems extraordinary that undocumented immigrants make use of this option. Yet the purchase of goods and services through loan arrangements with U.S. firms and agencies signals an important mode of societal and economic integration. On the one hand, it signifies acceptance of American consumerist standards and aspirations. These are not absent in Mexico, but they are most fully realized in the United States. Credit also marks one's financial establishment in the U.S. The purchase of services and consumer goods on credit is an important achievement, one that reflects the accumulation of employment stability, references, and experience with institutions in the United States. As Ignacio Cerritos described it, "When we first arrived, we had nothing. We didn't have all of the necessary contacts and papers [to obtain credit] that we do now."

Personal accumulation of goods and debt in the U.S. suggests that an individual or family has decided to remain in the country, at least for the immediate future. It also signifies a rejection of sojourner labor migration, where immigrants attempt to save money in anticipation of financial needs in their country of origin. Seen from the creditor's perspective, extending credit for consumer purchase is viable only if profitable, and this rests on the expectation that the debtors will continue to pay off their debts.

Assistance from Private Charities   The majority of Mexican undocumented immigrants buy all of their food and consumer goods, and so stimulate consumer demand and contribute to tax revenues.[20] Most undocumented immigrants in my study had purchased cars, furniture, and electrical appliances. A minority of them, however, had not purchased big-ticket items and had received donations of food, used clothing, toys, and household items from private nonprofit charitable organizations. Although reliance on donations from private agencies occurs only during periods of financial urgency and is much less widespread than are purchases bought on installment, this pattern represents an important transfer of necessary resources. The private organizations that provided donations to people in this study either were operated by locally based Catholic priests and nuns, or were religious-affiliated, such as Good Samaritan House.

Families with several children and only one income earner were most likely to use these resources. In most cases, these were families where young mothers did not work outside of the home—due to child-care responsibilities or lack of jobs and/or lack of legal work authorization. One exception was the Valenzuela family, where Héctor Valenzuela was unemployed, disabled from a work accident, and his wife, Mariana, supported the family, including six of the ten children from his previous marriage.

Typical food and clothing donations were modest, generally a box of food containing staples—rice, beans, flour, oil, and canned goods—or used clothing or, at Christmastime, toys for children. Gaining access to these goods was not always easy, and sometimes required a reference from a social worker or community worker. Young mothers passed along information about where and when to obtain goods. For some families, the small donations provided emergency aid and stretched scarce resources.

One evening, as we watched the California state lottery winners announced on television, I discussed with the Quiñones family what each of us would do as a winner of the California lottery. Herman Quiñones said that if he won the lottery, he'd return to Mexico. His wife, Rosario, did not hesitate to differ: "Not me! Leave me half of your winnings, and I'll stay here." When I asked why she expressed this preference, she explained that even poverty in the United States would be preferable to wealth in Mexico because of the charity and social-welfare assistance available in the U.S.:

> I like the stores and the help available here. I would prefer to be poor in the United States than rich in Mexico, because here if you are poor, you can still get bread at the community center, food and clothing at the church; there is help. In Mexico, it's different.

I would be remiss if I did not discuss the undocumented immigrants who, through their volunteer work with church-based or neighborhood organizations, spend many hours collecting and donating food, clothing, and money to help others less fortunate than themselves. Undocumented immigrants in Oakview organized a number of benefit dances and benefit food sales on behalf of others in need—for people who could not raise the money to submit their amnesty-legalization application, for Salvadorean refugees, and for Nicaraguan earthquake victims. This community participation fostered social integration, but here I emphasize that the private transfer of resources proceeded in more than one direction.

PUBLIC ASSISTANCE

Immigrants are considerably less likely than the native born to receive public assistance (Blau, 1984; Tienda and Jensen, 1985; Jensen, 1988). As a group, Mexican immigrants underutilize public services; this is especially true of undocumented immigrants, who fear apprehension and deportation. Moreover, eligibility requirements exclude undocumented immigrants from AFDC (Aid to Families with Dependent Children), SSI (Supplemental Security Income), unemployment insurance, food stamps—and from Medi-Cal, except for emergency and pregnancy services.[21] Yet many immigrant families consist of undocumented immigrant parents with U.S.-born, U.S.-citizen children. It is families with infants and small children that are most likely to be in need of assistance, and families with U.S.-citizen children are eligible for some public programs. A minority (six) of the families headed by undocumented immigrants in my study had received some form of public, government assistance. These undocumented immigrants sought public assistance only in extremely urgent situations and for periods lasting a short time. Still, this is more than the survey literature would lead one to believe.

A significant body of survey research conducted during the 1980s concluded that public-resource utilization by Mexican undocumented immigrants is negligible, that only 2 to 6 percent have ever received any type of AFDC, Social Security payments, or food stamps (Cornelius, 1981; Massey et al., 1987; CASAS, 1989.)[22] These conclusions were all based on self-reported answers, a method that is not necessarily conducive to gathering sensitive data. Studies employing participant observation or community workers suggest higher rates of public-assistance utilization.[23]

Although I did not systematically collect information on the use of public assistance among all of the undocumented immigrants in my study because of the sensitive nature of this information, I did witness or learn of several instances of the utilization of public resources among families headed by undocumented immigrant parents.[24] The following section discusses two broadly defined types of government assistance.

Tax-supported Programs   Programs supported by tax revenues, which are paid into by immigrants as well as citizens, include AFDC, WIC (Women, Infants, and Children—a nutritional program), food stamps, Medi-Cal, and Supplemental Security Income/State Supplemental Payments.[25] Six undocumented immigrant women in my study either were presently receiving assistance from one of these programs, or told me that they had done so in the past. In all instances they sought assistance for U.S.-born infant children. During pregnancy, the mothers of these children had been advised by public-health nurses, friends, or informal *servidoras* (community workers) to seek assistance that would enhance infant well-being. In these cases, WIC, food stamps, Medi-Cal, and AFDC were used for a relatively short period of time—a maximum of six months. Typically this was during a period of underemployment or unemployment, when young mothers were unable to work, and/or when they were receiving little support from their husbands.

Paid-into Funds   Assistance from "paid-into" programs consists of cash supplements from programs funded by paycheck deductions, such as Social Security, pension programs, unemployment compensation, and disability. Although undocumented immigrants routinely pay into such funds, they rarely receive the benefits to which they are entitled. For example, in one survey, only 20 percent of Mexican undocumented immigrants reported ever having received unemployment compensation (Massey et al., 1987:262). Undocumented immigrants underutilize the funds that their direct payments support because they fear that their undocumented status will be detected if they apply for benefits.

In spite of these constraints, two legal immigrant men, two undocumented women, and one undocumented immigrant man in my study were presently receiving Social Security, disability, or unemployment-insurance compensation. Three had worked in restaurants, one in a flower nursery, and the other as a motel maid. They received anywhere from $250 to $500 a month. Payments helped to sustain these women and men until they could work again or find other solutions, and this further integrated them into U.S. society.

WOMEN'S ROLES IN SECURING INSTITUTIONAL ASSISTANCE

As families accumulated time and experience in the U.S., they became better acquainted with U.S. institutions. They learned to maneuver within these interactions both through direct contact with various institutions and through advice from kin, friends, and neighbors. In both areas, women played vital roles.

Women were much more likely than men to come into direct contact with private charities, with social workers and informal *servidoras*, and with medical clinics. The men in my sample were by no means negligent toward their families' well-being, but when a family sought assistance, the most typical family division of labor assigned to the women the task of accompanying the sick to the doctor's office, negotiating with collections agencies, acting as the recipient of nutritional advice for the children, or securing toys or secondhand clothing from charitable organizations.

Women were also central to this mode of integration because they passed information along to one another. Women, as friends, neighbors, sisters, and kin, told one another where emergency medical care might be obtained, where and when to go for prenatal clinics, and how to obtain legal services, food, and clothing. Undocumented immigrant women established relations with other women that facilitated this informational process.

In Oakview, four women—"informal" social workers, or *servidoras*—played an important role in directing undocumented immigrants to various resources. Two of these women were Chicanas, one of whom worked in a formal capacity as a community social worker, and the other as a public-health nurse, but their assistance to undocumented women clients extended far beyond the range of their official duties. Two others, a Guatemalan woman and a Mexican woman, were naturalized U.S. citizens. Although one worked as a paid domestic worker and the other in a hospital cafeteria, they had worked in community-service jobs in the past, and informally, as individuals and through their work in neighborhood organizations, they continued to provide undocumented immigrants with valuable information about institutional services.

The initial settlement period is a difficult and expensive time of transition. In subsequent years, the difficulties of getting by are complicated by the arrival of more children, inflation (especially in the price of rental housing and food), illness, and temporary periods of unemployment and underemployment. Briody (1987:40) has suggested that the receiving of public assistance might be a factor in lowered rates of return migration. If we take into account a much wider array of institutional forms of assistance—such as credit, installment purchase plans, and assistance from private charities—we see that together these further advance settlement by integrating undocumented immigrants into U.S. social and economic institutions.

COMMUNITY

Popular images portray undocumented immigrants living "underground," with undocumented immigrant women in particular cowering in fear behind locked doors and closed curtains as they attempt to minimize interaction with the dominant society. Undocumented immigrants do try to avoid detection and apprehension, and many immigrant women do indeed work behind closed doors in sweatshops or in private homes, whether these be their own or their employers'. Yet the cocoon image is misleading because it suggests that undocumented immigrants, especially women, live in suspended isolation, in a domestic capsule void of community.

I began my fieldwork with some of these preconceptions, but they were quickly dispelled. Instead of socially inactive lives, I witnessed a good amount of informal sociability, participation in formal groups and organizations, and contact with various institutions and agencies. Instead of anonymity, I observed and experienced an environment where the intensive scrutiny of personal life from kin, friends, and acquaintances at times reached stifling levels.

Undocumented immigrants arrived in Oakview primarily in search of work and wages. Yet in the process of pursing these goals, women and men created informal webs of friendship and kinship, and some of them joined voluntary organizations. A distinct immigrant community, one permeated by ties of kinship and friendships, and characterized by shared ethnicity as well as ties to more formal organizations, emerged over time.

WOMEN AND COMMUNITY

Women have played a central role in the development of immigrant communities. During the bracero era (1942–64), many areas in California were initially settled by a "pioneer" cohort of Mexican immigrant men, and their interactions developed the groundwork for many immigrant communities (Mines, 1981). In this study, I suggest that if men are the community pioneers, it is women who are the community builders. In Oakview, dense community ties emerged only with the migration of entire families. Women constituted community directly through their interactions with one another, and they did so indirectly as well through the multiplicity of ties to other families, friends, and institutions. In Oakview, women were socially active in the private sphere of family and home, as well as in the public sphere, in various church groups, in parents' school groups, and with coworkers.

Observers have suggested that Mexican immigrant men's soccer clubs are the most important mechanism of community integration in the U.S. (Massey et al., 1987). But soccer clubs, like pool halls or bars, are often limited by an exclusively male participation (Rouse, 1990).[26] My portrait of the Oakview immigrant community focuses on the women. Women do not constitute community on their own, independent of men. They do so in consortium with men and children; in fact, often it is because of their family members that they are drawn into various organizations and social interactions. Strong community ties both emerge from and foster family settlement.

PARTICIPATION IN CIVIC AND
EDUCATIONAL ASSOCIATIONS

Many undocumented immigrant women and men in Oakview participate in voluntary, formal associations.[27] Among my respondents, Luis
Bonilla and María Mendoza, two middle-aged siblings, were the most
active participants. I first met Luis Bonilla during an evening meeting at
the local community center when he presented the history of the Migrant
Education Program, a nationwide program devoted to serving the educational needs of Mexican migrant workers' children. As he summarized
the history of parental involvement in the supporting organizations, I
assumed that Luis Bonilla was a naturalized U.S. citizen, perhaps even a
U.S.-born Chicano who spoke impeccable Spanish. He was a skillful
public speaker, and he blithely referred to his participation in statewide
conferences held in Sacramento, San Diego, and Anaheim.

Later, as I participated with Luis Bonilla in other community and
church groups, I learned that he personally knew all three of the local
elementary school principals, the various parish priests, and the director
of the community center. Still later, at a meeting of Latino parents and
high school administrators and resource teachers, I noticed that he was
on a first-name basis with the superintendent of schools. As the father of
seven children, he was deeply committed to improving the quality of
local education. He moved easily in public circles, his baseball cap proclaimed "100% Chicano," and he maintained a wide extension of social
ties with both the immigrant community and various administrators.
Given his visibility and membership in various organizations, I was very
surprised when I learned Luis Bonilla and his family were undocumented
and would be applying for amnesty legalization.

Such patterns of civic and community participation are certainly not
exclusive to men, although in Oakview, as in other Latino communities,
men more often served in positions of high public visibility and leadership (Hardy-Fanta, 1993; Pardo, 1990). María Mendoza, Luis Bonilla's
sister and the mother of six children ranging from twin five-year-old boys
to a seventeen-year-old daughter, was equally involved with various
church, school, and community groups. Like her brother, she attended
meetings nearly every evening, and on the weekends, she and her husband volunteered to teach prebaptismal classes to groups of thirty or
forty adults. During the days, she worked as a paid domestic worker,
tended to the needs of her home and children, and in the afternoon she
frequently worked with her husband in their produce-vending business.

It was on the weekends and during the evenings that she immersed herself in formal community activities.

While few of the respondents in my study were as intensely involved with community organizations, more than half of the forty-four respondents were either currently attending meetings of a local self-help group, attending instructional classes, or participating in a civic organization, or they had done so in the past. Many of them worked with some community group, volunteer organization, or self-help group. These were groups that held meetings for instrumental purposes. They included an Alanon co-dependency group organized exclusively for Latina women, Alcoholics Anonymous, various parents' school and educational support groups, neighborhood organizations, and several groups which emerged in response to IRCA and amnesty legislation.

I attended meetings of all of the above groups (except AA), but during my field research, I was most involved with a small grass-roots immigrant-rights group, and with the parish-sponsored immigration legalization clinic. The number of active participants in both of these groups dwindled over time, reflecting the period of crescendoed uncertainty and urgency experienced by undocumented immigrants immediately after passage of IRCA. But throughout the duration, women constituted the majority of volunteers in both groups.

The legalization clinic was established to facilitate the processing of applications at a reasonable fee, and it was staffed by approximately ten to twenty-five community volunteers and one paid paralegal, a middle-aged Salvadorean man. The volunteers were primarily undocumented immigrants who were also applying for legalization. As time passed, the legalization clinic became an important place for informal socializing. The social environment became a magnet for the volunteers on weekday evenings and Saturday afternoons. This was especially true for many women. Friendships among volunteers formed, and they arranged to meet their neighbors and acquaintances at agreed-upon hours in order to assist them. A good deal of time was spent chatting—talking about topics such as paid domestic work, children's schoolteachers, or disciplinary problems with children and adolescents. Among volunteers and clients, a shared social position as applicants for *la amnistía* (amnesty legalization) who faced similar problems in obtaining legal status turned into a lively source of conversation and social identity.

On several occasions I attended the evening meetings of the Migrant Education Program, affiliated with the local high school and elementary schools, as well as meetings of another Latino group of concerned parents of high school students. These were attended by anywhere from twenty to sixty adults, generally accompanied by their children, and more mothers than fathers attended. Most of the parents were immigrants, and "illegal" status did not seem to deter attendance.

During my field research, I worked most intensively with a group called El Comité (the Committee). This grass-roots group formed as a direct response to the Immigration Reform and Control Act in November 1986, and it became a combination mutual-aid-like society and advocacy group for recent immigrants. Its diverse membership included legal immigrants, naturalized U.S. citizens (from Mexico and Guatemala), one U.S.-born Chicana, and a couple of academics (Latinos and Anglos) like myself, but the majority of members were undocumented Mexican immigrants.

The Comité's biweekly Friday-night meetings, held in an elementary school classroom, were attended by women, men, and children, but a core of married women regularly attended without their husbands, while only one man, in the absence of his wife, maintained a regular profile at these meetings. Leadership was assumed by men, who were more at ease in public speaking, but women were by far better represented in any project participation, and sponsored events.

The Comité's success in organizing public informational forums (two of which drew over four hundred people), drawing new people to meetings and social events, and organizing benefit dances and tamale sales was due to members' reliance on primary group affiliations and their relations with friends, neighbors, acquaintances, and co-workers. Women were particularly resourceful in these activities. The women used ties to their children's schools, to their neighbors, and to kin in order to attract other people to these events. Whenever benefit events featuring food were organized, women played a central role in planning, calculating expenses, shopping, and cooking and serving the food.

English classes were another gathering point for many undocumented immigrants. English classes served as popular meeting places for same-sex friends, and for some, a place to begin a prospective romance. I first began visiting English classes as a representative of the Comité, in order to give "know your rights" oral presentations for those people who would remain ineligible for the amnesty-legalization program. Later, during the spring in 1988, this was part of my job as the coordinator of an information and outreach program for the San Francisco–based Coalition for Immigrant and Refugee Rights and Services.

Each time I visited the English classes, I saw a good deal of hallway and classroom sociability. Women and men seemed about equally represented in the English classes that I visited. Three married women in my study, mothers of young children, were not employed, and they attended local daytime English classes, where child care was available. For these women, school attendance was a way to improve one's language skills, and it offered a place to interact and to make friends with others. Marisela Hernández explained, "I like going to the English classes, since I don't know that many people here," and Anabel Castrillo said, "I was never able to study in Mexico for lack of resources, but here I am learning a lot, to read and to write, and how to make conversation with other people."

Research conducted by O'Conner (1990:82) among Mexican immigrants in another California community documents "an increase in involvement by women in Latino community activism," and Hardy-Fanta found that in Latino neighborhoods in Boston, Latina immigrant women were "the majority of the participants and activists at political events" (1993:2). As I conducted this study in Oakview, women were also intensifying their participation in many community organizations. Undocumented Mexican immigrants who participated in self-help groups, special classes, and civic and educational organizations gained two things. They consciously worked toward improving both the quality of their own lives, and those of their families' members. Some groups were organized as self-help groups, such as the women's Alanon group, while parents' groups aimed at improving the quality of their children's public-school education, and the immigrant-rights groups targeted problems more broadly shared by the local undocumented immigrant population. In all of these endeavors, members gained a sense of satisfaction at bettering the quality of life for themselves, their children and families, and others in the neighborhood. This active emphasis on self-improvement lessened the sense of feeling powerless or helpless, and increased the sense of having something at stake—an emotional and social investment in Oakview.

From their participation in various self-help, civic, and educational organizations, members also gained a sense of group belonging and shared identity. Friendships formed internally in various groups, and these sometimes developed into or solidified smaller primary groups and friendships.

SOCIAL VISITING PATTERNS

Women routinely organized social gatherings for kin and friends, and they undertook many activities that tied together different households, which di Leonardo (1987) refers to as "kin work."[28] Women planned and prepared food for Sunday outings in the park, organized parties with games for the baby showers, and similarly organized baptismal and first-communion celebrations. Women, however, did not monopolize this kin work. In several families men seemed more active in kin work, especially when this fit the family stage pattern of migration, and the men's family of origin lived nearby. Yet insofar as we consider the role of women and the community of undocumented immigrants, it is the presence of women and entire families which makes it possible for men to participate in kin work.

Community is not a social phenomenon relegated to public spaces. Community interaction occurred in the domestic realm as well. Friends and neighbors visited frequently, and, together with temporary boarders and houseguests, they contributed to an extremely social environment in many undocumented families' residences. Even the door-to-door salespeople might remain for as long as two hours.

Compared with the more privatized style of middle-class life, where visiting generally occurs only with prior notice, a great deal of informal sociality occurred in the domestic sphere of Mexican undocumented immigrant families. Not all of the families in my study lived in such socially busy residences. Some of the families' households were quieter and less active than others. Yet during my field research, there was not one household where I never encountered visiting kin, neighbors, friends, vendors, coworkers, and boarders or houseguests.

As the weather warmed during the spring and summer months, many families left their front doors wide open in order to capture the late afternoon and evening breezes. This was common for families with small children who lived in relatively small (six to twelve unit) apartment buildings. Children played together outside and entered each others' family residences, and often when it was time for them to return, their parents—usually mothers—came to fetch them. Neighbors and kin might also stop by to arrange for someone to look after their children, or simply to chat.

More formal visiting and gathering occurred on Sundays, which was, for most people, the only day off from work. Typical Sundays for church-attending families began with preparation for attendance at one of the Spanish-language Masses. Mass was often preceded and always followed by informal socializing outside church doors. After the Spanish-language Masses on Sunday mornings, hundreds of people congregated in small groups on the Santo Domingo Church patio to greet kin and friends, and to exchange personal news and gossip. Afterward, some families shopped for groceries or perhaps made a more elaborate shopping trip to the flea market before returning home for the main meal of the day. The afternoons were spent either at home—usually watching Spanish-language videos on television, visiting relatives, or receiving kin—or at the park with the children. More elaborate socializing occurred at the park.

SUNDAYS AT THE PARK

On Sunday afternoons the park served as the most popular public gathering place, rivaling the traditional plaza in many towns and villages in Mexico. During the warm months, festivities celebrating baptisms or first communions, or children's birthday parties, complete with piñatas and balloons, were commonly held in park settings, which provided an alternative location to cramped apartments and small houses. These informal social events were largely organized by immigrant women.

For those families embedded within a local-based kin network, regular visits to the park offered a place to socialize around shared food and drink, in a setting where children could run and play among open fields and swing sets. These networks were not limited to kin, as I learned one day when I was gently chastised by Reynaldo and Anabel Castrillo because I had not automatically assumed that we would meet at the park on Sunday (my middle-class expectations had led me to expect prior verbal notice). For those families not intimately connected to a tight network of kin, Sunday visits to the park were an accessible and affordable means of family entertainment, and the park was a safe and convenient place to take the children.

THE CATHOLIC CHURCH

Mexican undocumented immigrants, like previous generations of legal immigrants from Europe, looked to the church to express their faith and seek others with whom to share these practices. Of the forty-four adults in this study, all but two men, and one couple with two young children, attended Mass at one of the two Catholic churches. Most attended Mass regularly, and more women than men participated in the church-affiliated groups.[29]

Families with young children became directly involved with the local parish. Catholic children receive a series of sacraments, beginning with baptism and then first communion, and this required the participation of both parents and children. For baptism, the parents and prospective godparents attended instructional seminars that explained and emphasized the religious obligations and symbolic meaning of baptism. To receive first communion, children were required to participate in a two-year program of instructional preparation. Parents, especially mothers, became involved here also, most minimally by attending orientation meetings and taking the children to and from the classes, but some deepened their participation by serving as instructors or classroom assistants. In those families where boys served as altar boys, or adolescents participated in youth groups, family ties to the church and its priests became more personalized. Priests visited the homes of some of these families at Christmastime and other religious holidays.

On the one hand, the church served to advance community integration and Mexican immigrant settlement. In this respect it coalesced family members, and further integrated them into the parish community. Yet at the same time, many conflicts and divisions developed among segmented groups within the same parish.

I witnessed these divisions most graphically during the parish fall festival, a weekend family-oriented event held outdoors on the parish grounds. Parish members, mostly women accompanied by several men, sold food and beverages, and organized games and rides for children. The volunteers were divided into eight separate booths, and these represented separate church organizations: the Legion of María, which dedicated itself to visiting the sick; charismatic prayer groups, which met on Friday evenings to collectively pray and "talk in tongues" as they received the word of God; Christian base communities, where members met to "read the Bible, reflect, and act," according to the canons of liberation theology; and so on.[30]

At this particular festival, these groups were all working toward the same purpose—to raise money for the parish— yet they acted as competing entities. Subtle undercurrents of disapproval ran throughout the groups. "*Los carismáticos*" in the prayer groups looked down on those in the base communities for being too involved in what they perceived as communist-influenced, secular projects, while those in the Christian base communities criticized "*los carismáticos*" as ignorant and foolish to believe in a hierarchical concept of God. While these church organizations and their diverse approaches to Catholicism served to further integrate members into the larger church community, the separate groups reflected the segmentation of identity in the immigrant community, even within the same church.

This segmentation was also reflected by the particular Mass and church which one chose to attend. Two churches, organized under the same parish, served the Latino immigrant community in Oakview. Both Santo Domingo, the main church and parish, and San Jose del Obrero (St. Joseph of the Worker), commonly referred to as the *capilla chica* (the little chapel), held Masses serving the local Spanish-speaking population. Many of the people in my study preferred San Jose. They claimed there were less social pressures placed on appearances there, and they felt comfortable worshiping in the more intimate, simple surroundings. San Jose was small, freshly painted, and outfitted with simple metal folding chairs that seat about 125 people. The selection of what church to attend reflected subtle hierarchies expressed among Mexican immigrants of the same faith and parish.

CLASS DIVISIONS

Internal community stratification occurred not only between legal immigrants and undocumented immigrants, but also among undocumented immigrants. In Oakview, those undocumented immigrants who were literate often looked down on those who were illiterate or semiliterate. More than once, some of the more schooled people in my study called my attention to the poor slang or grammar used by another person. Similarly, those who had migrated from urban centers in Mexico sometimes ridiculed the dress, mannerisms, or speech of immigrants from rural areas. Undocumented immigrants who had worked in Mexico as civil employees or entrepreneurs were anxious to highlight their class and occupational backgrounds. These internal cleavages are virtually identical to what Villar (1990) found in a Mexican undocumented immigrant community in Chicago.

All Mexican immigrants experienced racial discrimination in their daily interactions in the dominant Anglo society—with employers, children's schoolteachers, public bureaucrats, and police and other authorities. Their responses to this discrimination, however, were not uniform, but were mediated by class background. Undocumented immigrants from middle-class, urban backgrounds developed a keen critique of the injustices which Mexican immigrants experience in the U.S. In community and church groups or at social events, people like the Mendozas and María Alicia Navarro denounced racism and discrimination. Ausencio Mendoza complained:

> The Anglo doesn't like the Mexican, especially the illegal ones. They pay us less than the *Americanos* because they know we can't protest [*reclamar*]. This is a form of discrimination. They say this country is a democracy, but no, this is racism.

In contrast, Mexican undocumented immigrants from poor, rural, peasant backgrounds expressed less critical views. Their previous social status in Mexico did not afford them a better comparison to life in the U.S. In fact, some of the immigrants from poor backgrounds perceived that blanket discrimination served as the great equalizer for all Mexicans in the U.S. Margarita Cervantes best expressed this view:

> Here, we [Mexicans] are all equal. You know, there are millionaires who come here, rich people who don't have the necessity of migrating but come here to check it out, and here they are treated just like everyone else. They are the same as the poor Mexicans. Here we are all equal.

In the same conversation, Margarita Cervantes had recalled that in Mexico people in her village had discriminated against her because of her indigenous features, because she had been poor, and because she wore long, ugly skirts and her hair in braids. In the U.S., she took satisfaction in realizing that those same people were treated just as negatively by the dominant Anglo society. Still, class stratification continued to reproduce itself in unanticipated venues within the community, even when undocumented immigrants were structurally situated in similar occupational positions.

MEXICAN IMMIGRANT AND CHICANO SYMBIOSIS

In the Oakview community, undocumented immigrants did not socially interact much with Chicanos or Mexican Americans. Second-, third-, and fourth-generation Mexican Americans and Chicanos, as well as immigrants from South and Central America, owned and operated the commercial infrastructure of local stores, barber shops, bars, bakeries, and markets in the community that were patronized by Mexican immigrants, but beyond commercial transactions, or meeting with teachers or nurses, there was not much social interaction between Mexican undocumented immigrants and U.S. citizens of Mexican descent. In fact, there was thinly veiled hostility expressed by some of the undocumented immigrants toward the Latino merchants. Some of the merchants organized a neighborhood association called Hispanos Unidos (United Hispanics) for the promotion of commerce, college scholarships, and local politicians. Their meetings were open to the public, and I attended two of them, as did a few of the people in my study. One undocumented immigrant man, disgusted with what he perceived to be self-serving business interests in this group, suggested that a more appropriate name for the group would be Hispanos Jodidos, which translates to "Fucked-up Hispanics."

Is there an immigrant community among the undocumented? My observations and experiences suggest that, rather than an immigrant community, there are many immigrant communities within the Oakview barrio. Many pockets of diversity coexist, some intersecting and overlapping, some in conflict. Community ties characterized by both tension and collaboration connect these pockets within the barrio.

Women were critical to developing and maintaining these community ties. Women—through the informal work culture of paid domestic workers, as mothers of school-aged children, as neighbors, as active parish members, and as participants in and members of self-help groups and civic, religious, and school organizations—were active community builders. Men participated in these social and community activities as well, but women were central to establishing and sustaining these connections.

What is the significance of these community ties for undocumented Mexican immigrants? These social and community ties deter return migration. As women, men, and children establish face-to-face relationships and friendships with neighbors and coworkers, as they join church, civic, and educational groups, they become socially integrated into U.S. society, and less inclined to return to Mexico. The web of social relationships and organizational ties in which undocumented immigrant women participate intensifies social integration, and ultimately this serves to consolidate settlement.

This chapter began by noting that due to the weakening of patriarchy, which occurs as a result of migration and resettlement, women are generally more in favor of prolonging long-term settlement in the U.S. than are men. Reconstructed gender relations provide women with incentives for staying in the U.S., but incentives alone do not accomplish settlement. Concrete actions and practices lead to settlement.

Settlement is actively constructed and consolidated on a daily basis. Working at stable jobs, utilizing public and private institutional forms of support, and building social and community ties in the U.S. are three features which distinguish undocumented immigrant settlement from sojourner migration. Women play key roles in these activities.

All of these activities and practices deter return migration and enhance women's status in the family. Through these activities, women provide more resources for their families. They mobilize these resources both directly, through employment and by tapping public and private institutional assistance, and indirectly, by participation in social and informational networks. Undocumented immigrant women construct settlement on a daily basis, and in the process, they solidify their own position within their families.

CHAPTER SEVEN

Gendered Immigration

Every day throughout California and other states, Mexican undocumented immigrant families struggle to balance work, family, and community activities. As they work long hours at their jobs, attend church and school, and relax in the park on Sundays, these women, men, and children are building strong ties to their new communities in the United States. This study set out to explain these developments, and in this chapter I return to the initial queries about migration, gender, and settlement. This chapter also summarizes the study's findings and addresses some of the broader implications that the study of Mexican immigrants in the Oakview barrio holds for other recently settled immigrants.

GENDER ORGANIZES MIGRATION

Macrostructural rearrangements go a long way toward explaining the increasing numbers of Mexican women and entire families who migrate and settle in the United States without legal authorization. Since the late 1960s, the United States has generated many low-wage jobs centered in urban areas, constituting a feature of the global economic restructuring process that Sassen-Koob (1982) calls "peripheralization at the core." Small competitive firms in services and manufacturing, as well upper-income professionals and managers, increasingly rely on the labor provided by Mexican immigrants. Although many commentators have recognized these developments, they have not always observed that a significant number of the U.S. informal-sector occupations that grew during the 1970s and 1980s—paid domestic work, child care, garment and electronic assembly—recruited primarily female immigrant workers. An objective labor demand for immigrant women, one that is solicitous of workers with particular configurations of class, gender, ethnicity, and legal status, partially explains the increased participation of Mexican women in undocumented immigration and settlement. In Mexico, the ongoing economic crisis intensified and encouraged northbound migration from sectors of Mexican society previously not drawn to the U.S. These same economic pressures also propelled more women into a Mexican labor market that could not produce a sufficient number of jobs. As economic problems deepened, permanent immigration emerged as an increasingly viable response for Mexican women as well as men.

But macrostructural factors alone do not explain how people respond to these new opportunities and pressures. Theories based on structural transformations cannot explain who migrates, when migration occurs, or how people organize migration. And while structural explanations can help account for the changing sex composition of the immigrant population, they cannot account for the distinctively gendered way that immigration and settlement occur. As I stated at the outset, political and economic transformations may set the stage for migration, but they do not write the script.

Taking the household as a unit of analysis offers a more grounded approach for developing an explanation of the recent changes in Mexican immigration, as this approach recognizes that social actors live in particular social contexts, not in a vacuum outlined only by huge structures. Yet, immigration is not the outcome of households strategizing or adapting to macrostructural economic pressures, but of the exercise of multiple interests and hierarchies of power that come to life within households.[1] Migration is not calculated at the household level in terms of costs and benefits that will accrue to household members. People make migration decisions in a context of uncertainty and imperfect knowledge about economic opportunities—even if they have a specific job waiting for them up north—and similarly, they can only speculate about the subsequent behavior of those who are assisting them. Resources are not always equally shared and automatically pooled within the household or family unit, and this is especially true of that crucial resource for immigration: social networks.

This study suggests that a more fruitful approach requires looking inside the household and inside the social networks to see how gender relations shape migration experiences. Although people live in house-

holds, the cultural meanings, ideologies, emotions, and beliefs they experience as most salient are embedded in family relations. Gender relations in families and social networks determine how the opportunities
and constraints imposed by macrostructural factors translate into different migration patterns. Although patriarchal systems and ideals influence the migration process, patriarchal gender relations are fluid and
exerted heterogeneously in different contexts.

Strictly defined patriarchal relations of family authority and male-
dominated networks promote family stage migration. The implicit rules
of patriarchal family authority constrain women's actions, but enable
married men to act independently and relatively promptly when they are
invited to accompany a friend or relative on the journey north. Yet it
would be erroneous to see patriarchal privilege as necessarily strength-
ening class privilege under capitalism. For Mexican undocumented immigrant men, the contrary occurs. Patriarchy allows men to depart, but
it also mandates that men serve as good financial providers for their
families, which they attempt to do by migrating and assuming jobs that
are typically low-paying, physically arduous, and without opportunities
for upward mobility. Thus, male migrant labor is produced by patriarchy
for the benefit of U.S. capital.

Exclusively male networks favor the migration of men. But in the
process of migration, patriarchy in the family sphere is realigned, as the
women, out of necessity, act autonomously and assertively in managing
household affairs. This new sense of social power—and later, for another
cohort of migrant wives, additional access to women's networks—enable
the wives to go north. Until the late 1960s, the married women I interviewed struggled to convince their husbands to help them migrate, although a minority of women were (and still are) coerced into migration
by their husbands. By the 1970s and 1980s a substantial number of
immigrant women had established themselves in the Oakview barrio.
New immigrant women circumvented reliance on male-dominated networks by appealing to the assistance of immigrant women already established in the United States. And as more women migrated and settled in
the U.S., women's social-network ties emerged and widened.

Women and men involved in family stage migration do not enter the
process equally. Yet given the diverse historical and social contexts in
which migration occurs, women in the same culture and in similar circumstances encounter different types of patriarchal obstacles and hence
improvise different responses to migration. The women's contrasting
migration trajectories are related to the establishment of a permanent

immigrant settlement community, an accomplishment that reflects political and economic transformations. The legacy of the bracero program, passage of the 1965 amendments to the Immigration and Nationality Act, economic restructuring in Mexico, and the diversification of labor demand for Mexican immigrants in the U.S. encouraged the development of settlements such as the Oakview barrio. As more women and entire families settled in these urban communities, they helped to facilitate the migration of their friends and families. The women's variegated responses to family stage migration illustrate some of the ways in which gender interacts with macro-level political and economic transformations to produce particular immigration outcomes.

While others have noted that the range of immigrant social networks expands with the entry of each new migrant into the migration process, and that the networks subsequently embody more social capital (Massey et al., 1987; Mines, 1981), it is important to add that the networks themselves do not automatically become equally accessible to women and men. Immigrant social networks are highly contested social resources, and they are not always shared, even in the same family. Single women's networks are undeniably effective, but this study also reveals strong network ties developing among married women, a factor that cannot be underestimated in explaining the increase in the migration of both women and entire families.

The scenarios that emerged from this study also draw attention to several overlooked features of Mexican immigration. Contrary to what is posited by the household model, the men in this study often engaged in very little calculation about migrating. Many of them did not consult about their migration decisions with their spouses or families, nor did they invest considerable time in strategizing or planning their northward sojourn. Most of the men reported that they decided to migrate rather abruptly, when presented with an invitation or opportunity that had to be acted upon quickly. While they may have discussed and pondered this alternative earlier, they did not necessarily plan their move in advance. For many of these men, the social-network contact was all that was necessary to precipitate their departure. The wives of these men, precisely because they faced obstacles of patriarchal authority, reported investing time and energy in calculating and strategizing their immigration plans. Moreover, the women's motives for immigration arose over time. Interests are fluid, and decisions and actions are embedded in specific contexts. The unitary-household model cannot explain these changes because it does not recognize gender and generational power relations between women and men sharing the same household. Women praying for the Border Patrol to capture their husbands, and families in which spouses rely on different network resources and on separate income funds to cover their migration costs, call into question assumptions about unified household migration strategies.

Nuclear families who migrated together were characterized by a less rigid form of family patriarchy than were the families who migrated in stages. These families were characterized by shared decision making between spouses, and also by access to social networks composed of the wives' kin. Unlike the pattern of family stage migration, in these families the men did not enjoy uncontested, unilateral power, and the women participated in decision making about migration. These women were well positioned to act assertively in the migration process because of their income-earning work and their experience in sharing family authority.

Class affected this form of migration in two ways. First, the relatively more class-privileged backgrounds of some of these families appear to have allowed for more egalitarian practices of authority. This is because the families in this study who had achieved some semblance of a middle-class life-style in Mexico had done so only by relying on women's labor, often in a family business. This reliance legitimized the women's participation in decisions about migration. Negotiations about migration in these families were not necessarily harmonious, as they were characterized by some degree of bargaining, persuasion, and sometimes ultimatums, but they provide a sharp contrast to family stage migration, where unilateral decision making characterized the men's initial departure.

Another reason that women in these families played a primary role in migration decisions is that usually their kin provided the important social-network assistance for migration. In several cases, the women had accumulated direct migration experience when they were unmarried. Women's immigrant kin and, in a few instances, women's prior migration experience served as important social leverage for women, allowing for this pattern of family migration to emerge. These women avoided the "stay-at-home" scenario partially because they had access to decisive resources.

Class privileges also affected family unit migration in yet another way, as it afforded these families the financial ability to pick up and move the entire family at once. International migration is an expensive proposition, one that is generally not available to the poorest of the poor. Families that owned homes, small businesses, or apartment buildings were able to liquidate property, apply for loans based on their equity, or derive income from rent, and these financial resources funded migration costs for entire families.

Contrary to what much of the literature proposes, the immigrants in this case study who came to the United States while single were not "sent" or elected to migrate by their families or households. While many of these women and men did send money to their families in Mexico, at least during the initial part of their stays, their families' collective needs did not prompt their migration. In fact, patriarchal rules of authority often worked against the migration of sons and daughters, but this produced mixed results.

It is well known that throughout many areas of Mexico, young men are seeped in a culture of northbound migration. Sustained by vibrant transnational social networks and by the glories of return migrants, popular folklore defines a journey northward as a rite of passage. For many a young man, moreover, a journey northward signifies an important patriarchal rite of passage, as it reflects a young man's defiance of his father's authority and a step toward his own independence. These young men are departing not as family emissaries, but as independent seekers. Cohesive, patriarchally organized families may try to dissuade their sons from going north, but they are not always successful due to the strong social networks and the peer culture of migration that encourage this behavior, and due to patriarchal rules that see young men's autonomous actions as legitimate.

By contrast, the women in this study who migrated while single were either free of, or able to manipulate, familial patriarchal constraints. Most of these women came from relatively weakly bound families, characterized by lack of economic support and the absence of strong patriarchal rules of authority. When highly motivated women did encounter their fathers' resistance, they eventually negotiated their right to go north, suggesting the malleability of patriarchal power. For single women, the assistance of other women is often the key to migration. In the Oakview barrio, exclusively female social-network ties emerged in the 1970s and strengthened during the 1980s, a factor that cannot be discounted in explaining the increase in female migration to the community. This confirms survey materials collected in Mexico that suggest the formation of single women's immigrant networks in the 1970s. In the analysis developed in this book, I have tried to explicate both the context in which the networks arise and their dynamics.

This analysis of single and married women's networks underlines not only how the social capital embedded within social networks encourages migration by providing financial resources or job contacts, but more importantly, how these networks may allow women to circumvent or contest domestic patriarchal authority. This aspect of immigrant social networks, to the best of my knowledge, has not previously been acknowledged. The ramifications of this are significant for future increases in migration when we consider the broader realm of changing gender relations in Mexico and elsewhere.

Network ties dominated by men continue to operate and sometimes include the female kin of male participants, but new, women-centered networks have gained momentum. The ongoing economic crisis and contested gender hierarchies in Mexico, as well as occupational segregation by gender, have fed these new networks, giving further impetus to immigration of women and entire families.

While this study considers how generational dynamics operate within gender relations, a shortcoming of the study is that I did not examine children and adolescents as actors in the migration process. While a substantial body of literature examines immigrant children's educational needs and progress, no systematic research has examined how children actively influence their parents' decisions about migration, return migration, and settlement. Including children and adolescents in a research agenda may alter long-established beliefs about immigration.[2]

Labor migration is a process shaped in multiple ways by dynamic gender relations. One can, in short, conclude that migration is gendered. Women and men do not share the same experiences with migration, and their gender relations—patterns of separation, conflict, and cooperation—produce distinct migration patterns. Decision making about migration that occurs in families and the dynamics within the social networks are key in distinguishing migration routes and how immigrants are incorporated into the new society.

The onslaught of capitalism is often equated with the fortification of patriarchy. Yet in this study, both single and married Mexican women are contesting patriarchal dictates in the process of U.S.-bound migration, and men, as fathers, husbands, and brothers, are responding in various ways. Just as women often comply with their own subordination in patriarchal institutions, so conversely do men participate, albeit sometimes unwittingly, in the dismantling of patriarchy. Migration and settlement introduce new challenges and pressures for change in both women's and men's behavior.

IMMIGRATION RECONSTRUCTS
GENDER RELATIONS

What are the implications for gender relations among Mexican immigrants who settle in the United States? Patriarchal relations do not automatically disintegrate or break down once immigrants adapt to new ways of life in the United States, yet neither does patriarchy remain preserved intact. People construct their lives out of cultural resources within a social structural context, but through the process of migration and resettlement, cultural ideals and guidelines for appropriate behavior change.

Patriarchal gender relations undergo continual renegotiation as women and men rebuild their families in the United States. Gender is reconstructed in different ways, guided by the limits imposed by particular contexts and patterns of migration, but family and community relations exhibit a general shift in the direction of gender egalitarianism. This was indicated in the study by shifts in women's and men's spatial mobility, patterns of family authority, and, in some instances, by transformations in the gendered division of household labor. These changes do not occur in ways that conform to any formulaic linear stages. They happen unevenly, and often result in contradictory combinations of everyday practices.

While they have been amply studied, immigrant men have not been examined in the immigration literature as men—i.e., as gendered persons. An exception is the work of anthropologist Roger Rouse (1990), who argues that Mexican immigrant men, especially those who are undocumented, experience limited spatial mobility in their daily lives, which compromises some of their patriarchal privileges. The public spaces open to the men in the Oakview barrio were indeed limited to certain street corners, and a few neighborhood bars, pool halls, and doughnut shops. Although the men tried to create new spaces where they could recapture a public sense of self, the goal was not so readily achieved. As undocumented immigrants, these men remained apprehensive of harassment by the Immigration and Naturalization Service or the police, their jobs typically afforded little in the way of autonomy or mobility, and, as poor men who worked long hours at jobs as gardeners, dishwashers, or day laborers, they had very little discretionary income to afford leisure activities. While Mexican immigrant men may exhibit bravado and machismo, these behaviors are best understood as personally and collectively constructed performances of masculine gender display, and so should be distinguished from structurally constituted positions of power. Their displays are indicators of marginalized and subordinated masculinities (Hondagneu-Sotelo and Messner, 1994).

While cultural rules that segregate women in the domestic sphere are no longer as strictly enforced in rural and urban Mexico as they once were, a number of the women in this study had been, to some extent, secluded from public life in Mexico. After arrival in the U.S., some of these women stayed cloistered in their homes, usually due to fear of their new foreign surroundings and potential INS apprehension, but these practices changed quickly. In the U.S. nearly all of these immigrant women were employed. Many of the women in this study worked as paid domestic workers in private households, but job transportation typically required a combination of taking buses and walking substantial distances—practices that placed them outside of traditional normative expectations and squarely "in the street." The women also accompanied their children to school and medical visits, they shopped and visited friends, and they attended afternoon and evenings meetings for informal associations and organizations, often unaccompanied by men and unrestricted by rules relegating them to the home or market.

Transformations in patterns of family authority occurred following immigration. Some of the men had acted as the undisputed patriarchs in all family decision-making processes in Mexico, but in the United States, these processes became more egalitarian. This trend toward more egalitarian patterns of shared authority occurred because many Mexican immigrant women became more autonomous and assertive through their immigration and settlement experiences. Egalitarianism was also promoted by the relative increase in women's and the decrease in men's economic contributions to the family. As the balance of relative resources and contributions shifted, the women assumed more active roles in key decision-making processes. Where the family might live, how to budget finances, where to go for legal advice—these are all decisions in which the women commonly participated. Similar shifts occurred with the older children, who were now often reluctant to subordinate their earnings and their autonomy to a patriarchal family hierarchy.

The household division of labor is another arena that in some cases reflected Mexican immigrant men's diminished status. An orthodox household division of labor proved to be quite resilient, as most families continued to organize their daily household chores along fairly traditional, patriarchal norms. But in the families that had experienced family stage migration and where the men had lived for many years in "bachelor communities," the men took responsibility for some of the housework. These changes of course are modest if we judge them by feminist ideals of egalitarianism, but they are significant when compared with the patriarchal family organization that was normative before immigration. And they are a striking departure from stereotypical views of Mexican immigrant families.

Changes in Mexican immigrant families' gender relations do not result from any "modernizing" Anglo influence or acculturation process. Most Mexican immigrants live their lives in the United States encapsulated in relatively segregated jobs and well-defined immigrant communities. Yet limited contact with Anglo society doesn't mean that past practices and beliefs are sustained intact. Nor is the trend toward greater egalitarianism among Mexican immigrant families elicited by feminist ideology. The immigrant women in this case study were not immersed in any self-conscious feminist movement, but still they have achieved goals, however modest, consonant with feminism. Immigrants are not unique in this respect. Research by Rosanna Hertz (1986) on high-income, dual-career couples—people who lie at the opposite end of the occupational hierarchy—also testifies to the absence of feminist ideology in fomenting more egalitarian conjugal relations. Hertz found that high-income, professional couples generate new family forms in order to accommodate employer demands and realize individual desires for career success, and that in turn, these new spousal relations foster more egalitarian ideologies.

Key to the movement toward greater equality within immigrant families was the change in the women's and men's relative positions of power and status in the larger social structure of power. As we have seen, Mexican immigrant men's public status in the U.S. is very low, due to racism, insecure and low-paying jobs, and (often) illegal status. For those families that underwent long periods of spousal separation, the women often engaged in formal- or informal-sector paid labor for the first time, developed more economic skills and autonomy, and assumed control over conducting household affairs with other societal institutions. In the U.S., nearly all of the women sought employment, so women made significant economic contributions to the family. And in the instances of family stage migration, these transformations in gender relations began once the men departed but before the women left Mexico. All of these factors tend to erode men's patriarchal authority in the family and empower women either to directly challenge that authority, or at least to negotiate "patriarchal bargains" (Kandiyoti, 1988) that are more palatable to themselves and their children.

While it would be premature to proclaim the demise of patriarchy and the triumph of gender egalitarianism in Mexican immigrant families, there is a significant trend in that direction. Immigration and settlement processes temper the expression of family patriarchy, eliciting a general trend toward greater egalitarianism. Women still have less power than men do in families, but they generally enjoy more autonomy, resources, and leverage than they previously did in Mexico. Empirical study thus contradicts the stereotypical image of dominant macho males and submissive females in Mexican immigrant families. While patriarchal authority is not entirely undermined, immigration diminishes the legitimacy of men's unchallenged domination in families.

In spite of, or perhaps because of, these new gender arrangements in families, the issue of settlement remains highly politicized: men generally indicated a desire to return to Mexico, while women most often expressed intentions of staying in the United States. While these stated preferences bear little on what people actually do, these statements are significant in that they suggest the diminished power that patriarchy exerts in the United States. For many men, the dream of the ultimate return to Mexico seems to provide social and psychological relief from the indignity of restricted control in both public and private spheres. Through the process of migration and resettlement, men lose monopolistic control over family resources, decisions, and privileges, and women gain social power and newfound autonomy within families. The gendered orientations to settlement reflect these losses and gains, and they echo the findings of Sherri Grasmuck and Patricia R. Pessar (1991) in their study of Dominican immigrants, many of them from the middle class, in New York City.

In the case of Mexican immigrant families, it is not feminist ideology but structural rearrangements that promote social change in spousal relations. This observation may lead to strategic reconsiderations for the feminist movement in the United States. Most immigrant women in this study did not identify as feminists or with any feminist organization. For many of these women, forms of oppression which derive from their class, ethnic, and legal status were experienced as more decisive than gender oppression. Immigrant women in this study reported that being poor, "illegal," overworked, nervous about meeting bills, and unable to obtain satisfactory medical assistance for their children were far more trouble-

some than gender inequality. Their responses reflect the findings of a
needs-assessment survey conducted in San Francisco in 1990, where 345
Latina undocumented immigrant women identified housing assistance,
employment training, and medical care as their most pressing needs
(Hogeland and Rosen, 1990). While none of the immigrant women identified "gender subordination" as a primary problem, rearrangements
induced by migration do result in the diminution of familial patriarchy,
and these transformations may enable immigrant women to better confront problems derived from class, racial/ethnic, and legal-status subordination. Their endeavors may prompt more receptiveness to feminist
ideology and organizations in the future.

Latina immigrant women, however, are not silently waiting to be
organized; they are already organizing to address problems specific to
their class, gender, ethnic, and citizenship status. In the Oakview barrio,
undocumented women mobilized their kin, friends, and neighbors to
push for school reform for their children and to ensure that community
members received access to legal permanent-resident status available
through IRCA, and informally, they exchanged information that bet-
tered their occupational mobility as paid domestic workers. Larger institutional efforts are also under way.

In October 1991, the first national conference on immigrant and
refugee women drew more than three hundred women, most of them
Latina and Asian immigrants representing myriad organizations and
agencies.[3] For three days, women convened panels on issues as diverse as
domestic violence, alternative employment strategies, labor rights, lead-
ership-training models, and health care. Although these organizations
are not prevalent in every immigrant community, Latina immigrant
women do participate in a range of advocacy groups—in domestic workers' cooperatives, church groups, street vendors' associations, anti-
domestic-violence agencies, voter-registration drives, housing projects,
and child-care cooperatives. Latina immigrant women enroll in special
programs to develop self-esteem and learn political-leadership skills at
the Dolores Mission Women's Cooperative and Leadership Training Program in Los Angeles, and at Mujeres Unidas y Activas (United and Active
Women), a Latina immigrant and refugee women's organization in San
Francisco's Mission district. At the Mujeres Unidas en Acción (Women
United in Action) organization in Boston, Latina women learn English
and participate in community politics (Young and Padilla, 1990). In Los
Angeles, Latina immigrant women have mobilized on behalf of their
rights as street vendors (Sirola, 1992), have joined Mexican American

women to protest against the proposed placement of a state prison and a toxic-waste incinerator in a low-income residential neighborhood (Pardo, 1990), have joined together with men in union drives (Delgado, 1993), and have demanded that local businesses contribute to the fight against drugs and violent crime by providing jobs for gang youth (Amado, 1990). The diverse methods and organizing issues that Latina immigrant women have used reflect both the exclusion of immigrants, Latinas, and impoverished women from traditional avenues of political mobilization and electoral politics, and the vitality that comes from using interpersonal relationships. In fact, Hardy-Fanta (1993) argues that Latina women have been especially effective in political organizing precisely because of their strong interpersonal relationships and skills, which allow them to mobilize others, and thus serve as "connectors."

While these women's activism often derives from their traditional responsibilities for their children, families, and community, their activist practices—marching in the streets, raising their voices, and confronting authority—certainly break with tradition. Other Latinas and poor, working women are also challenging and expanding traditional forms of political expression. A range of unorthodox, creative political activities and motives have been documented among Mexican women in Guadalajara, Mexican American women in Los Angeles, and Puerto Rican women and other Latinas in the northeastern U.S. (Logan, 1984; Pardo, 1990; Naples, 1991; Hardy-Fanta, 1993). While women's motives for becoming political actors and neighborhood community activists may be rooted in their traditional identities as mothers, their actions provide a rich source of support for fundamental change in multiple arenas. And because of the range of embedded networks of kin and friends, Mexican immigrant women are well situated to become effective political actors.

HOW WOMEN CONSOLIDATE SETTLEMENT

Mexican undocumented immigrants must leap over a veritable obstacle course to establish themselves in the United States. Daily encounters with language difficulties, racism, poverty, vulnerability at the workplace and harassment in public areas due to the lack of legal status, the problems associated with missing loved ones "back home" and becoming accustomed to new social circles in a foreign environment—all of these factors may conspire to encourage sojourner, not settler, migration. Yet in spite of these challenges, millions of Mexican undocumented immigrants have incorporated themselves into U.S. society. In this study, I placed women at the forefront of analysis in order to understand this process.

My ethnographic materials suggest that immigrant women advance settlement along three structural dimensions that constitute and define it. These are the construction of community-wide social ties; employment in relatively stable, year-round jobs; and the utilization of private and public institutional forms of assistance, including credit.

Immigrant women need to earn income in order for their families to achieve permanent settlement in the U.S., and in Oakview most of the long-staying immigrant women work as paid domestic workers, an informal-sector occupation characterized by variable schedules and tenuous security. Their employment was generally arranged according to terms that sociologist Mary Romero (1988a) calls "job work," where a domestic worker maintains several employers and cleans a particular house on a weekly or biweekly basis in exchange for a flat rate of pay. While they are not as severely underpaid or as deeply enmeshed in paternalistic employer relations as are live-in domestic workers (a job more typical for newly arrived immigrant women), the job-work situation exacerbates the privatized nature of domestic work, and it also confronts domestic workers with having to secure multiple employers. The women in this study dealt with these challenges by sharing information through informal networks of support. Cross-gender links are also initially helpful in securing jobs. What appears to be an extreme atomization of the occupation is in fact mitigated by a work culture transmitted through many social interactions. In the process, the jobs in private households become a stable source of employment, which strengthens the conditions for permanent family settlement.

Historically, paid domestic work has been a key institution through which rural-urban migrant and international immigrant women become integrated into a new society. Since domestic work is generally viewed as a second-class job, studies have typically investigated the extent of upward mobility, both individual and intergenerational, out of domestic work, concluding that the work either constitutes an "occupational bridge" or serves as an "occupational ghetto" (Broom and Smith, 1963; Katzman, 1981; McBride, 1976; Glenn, 1986). The findings from this study suggest that there is mobility within the occupation itself, and that networks partially govern this mobility. A domestic worker's position within the occupation is not static but subject to change, and may improve as she gains experience, learns to utilize the informational resources embedded in social networks, and establishes a set number of

casas (houses) to clean. While the occupation remains largely unregulated by formal bureaucratic agencies, the domestic workers themselves
create an informal but intensive social system of regulation.

The domestic workers' networks, however, also have a downside, and
they are particularly constraining for newly arrived immigrant women
who are trying to break into domestic work. These women generally face
two alternatives: taking a live-in position, or working as a subcontracted
helper to another domestic worker, usually a well-established immigrant
woman. Both circumstances leave the women vulnerable to exceedingly
low pay and trapped in an exploitative relationship, yet subcontracting
can serve as a springboard to obtaining their own jobs. In this manner,
paid domestic work can be conceptualized as a career, with the networks
governing both entry into the occupation and internal occupational mobility. As one advances in the career, the network system becomes more
advantageous and settlement is fortified.

What implications does immigrant women's concentration in domestic work hold for other sectors of society? Research by Hertz (1986) and
by Hochschild (1989) indicates that the greater household equality enjoyed by class-privileged couples often relies on the exploitation of poor
minority women, many of whom are immigrant women. Women in
class-privileged couples purchase their way out of some aspects of gender
subordination, which allows them to pursue conjugal relations that are,
as the title of Hertz's book suggests, "more equal than others." The
number of Mexican undocumented immigrant women working as domestic cleaning women in the U.S. will, in all likelihood, increase in
coming years. As immigrant networks expand, bringing Mexican undocumented immigrant women to diverse points of destination in the
U.S., we may see a more widespread use of immigrant women as paid
domestic workers in diverse regions of the country, and we may see them
employed by families less class privileged than those that employ them
at the current time. Research conducted in San Francisco already indicates that seniors living on fixed incomes, dual-earner working parents,
and single mothers are no longer unusual employers of Latina immigrant
domestic workers (Salzinger, 1991).

In addition to employment, immigrant women stabilize settlement
by utilizing various institutional resources. The fact that some immigrants use public forms of support can be integrated into a conceptual
framework for understanding Mexican immigrant settlement, a topic
which is already controversial. This does not imply that all undocumented settled immigrants rely on public and private forms of assis-

tance. Rather, the conceptual scheme highlights the fact that in settlement, the resources for daily maintenance and survival originate only in the U.S. While sojourner migrants often rely on the family "back home" as a refuge and a source of financial support during hard times, settlers do not always have access to these ties. Long-staying immigrants cannot always rely on kin in Mexico, and, coupled with undocumented immigrants' vulnerable economic status and low earning power, this results in the need to seek supplemental sources of support which include credit, charity, and sometimes modest uses of public assistance, which is mostly available for U.S.-citizen children. This raises questions for further research regarding generational privileges and resources in immigrant families.

As undocumented immigrant families stay in the U.S. for prolonged periods of time, their livelihood may depend, in part, on their ability to seek institutional forms of assistance that stretch scarce resources. In turn, the availability of publicly funded social services, private forms of credit, and installment purchase plans may serve to anchor immigrants in the U.S. Through the utilization of public and private forms of assistance, including private credit, immigrants become further integrated into the U.S. economy and society. Immigrant women actively seek out these resources.

In the case of northwestern Europe, Freeman (1986) has argued that the availability of social services and support provided by both public and private agencies helps to transform temporary migrants into permanent-settler immigrants. According to Freeman, the shift from temporary solo sojourner migration to permanent settlement of immigrant families signals a transition from immigrants constituting a fiscal bonus to a net drain on state welfare programs. An exception, Freeman notes, is when there is a predominance of young adults in the immigrant population (1986). Research supports this conclusion in the case of Mexican immigration to the United States. Demographic projections rendered by Hayes-Bautista et al. (1988) indicate that young Mexican and other Latino immigrants, including their children, will constitute a substantial portion of the U.S. labor force in coming years, and it is these future workers who will shoulder the burden of Social Security payments for the aging baby-boomer population. In this scenario, Mexican immigrants are an overall bonus—indeed a key—to social welfare, in spite of their temporary needs. In the case of Mexican immigrants and their children, public investment now will have a tremendous positive impact in the next century. The Oakview study suggests that women are the key people to reach with respect to delivery of social services in the immigrant community.

Women play a vital role in the efforts to build community among Mexican undocumented immigrants. An appreciation of men as the community pioneers, as the first migrant sojourners and settlers, must be complemented by a recognition of women as community builders. Women create important linkages with bureaucratic institutions, such as schools, medical offices, and other public and private organizations, and they also weave webs of interpersonal social ties among themselves and their families. These social webs hold immigrant settlement in place.

Many observers have posited a strong symbiosis between Chicanos and Mexican immigrants, as various waves of Mexican immigration provide cultural replenishment for U.S.-born Mexican Americans or Chicanos, renewing language, and religious and culinary traditions. Certainly the settlement of Mexican immigrants fortifies Spanish-language media and prompts the opening of ethnic markets, yet during eighteen months of fieldwork in the Oakview barrio, I observed minimal interaction between Mexican undocumented immigrants and Chicanos. The interactions that I did witness generally consisted of immigrants' brief, bureaucratic or service transactions with Chicano clerks, shopkeepers, teachers, nurses, or social workers. Although the second-generation children of immigrants, who experienced childhood and adolescence in the U.S., sometimes came to identify with and gain acceptance in Chicano culture, this was not true of their parents and kin, who came to the U.S. after adolescence.[4] None of the study participants thought of themselves as Chicano, and they did not seem to be directly replenishing Chicano culture.

Research conducted in two Texas cities—Austin and San Antonio—by Rodríguez and Nuñez (1986) sheds light on this issue, as their comparative study of these cities suggests that the relative and absolute size of the undocumented immigrant concentration affects this relation. In instances of relatively small undocumented immigrant concentrations, there are few resources within the undocumented population, so undocumented immigrants are more likely to go outside their group for economic and social resources. This pattern was borne out in the Oakview community during the early stages of male settlement, when many of the undocumented immigrant men relied on assistance from Chicanos and Euro-Latins—the Spanish, Portuguese, and Italian shopkeepers.

When the immigrant community has grown and matured, newly arrived immigrants depend on established Mexican immigrant friends and family, not on Chicanos. Moreover, as Rodríguez and Nuñez point out, social, economic, and cultural differences also mitigate against the establishment of personal relationships between the two groups. In Texas, the proximity to Mexico helps undocumented immigrants maintain their cultural identity. In the Oakview barrio, the encapsulation of the undocumented immigrant community accomplishes this.

How does gender affect these processes? Using the woman-centered model of settlement that I have proposed highlights not only the role of women in ameliorating the hardships of settlement, but also the manner in which a demographically diverse immigrant community is better able to access and share diverse resources. As more women and families settle, the immigrant community becomes more self-reliant. This is largely due to women's abilities to mobilize various resources, and also to the cross-generational and neighborhood ties that emanate from varied family members.

A significant number of Mexican undocumented immigrants participate in civic groups or secondary associations, belying the notion, which is deeply rooted in sociology, of conflict between primary groups and secondary organizations among immigrants. I found not only organizational participation among immigrants—even those lacking legal status—but also a symbiotic relationship between primary groups and the more formalized political and community organizations. Ties among family and friends feed the vitality of formal associations and organizations. Importantly, women's social ties among kin and friends bind many of the secondary associations together.

Undocumented immigrant women's participation in self-help groups, instructional classes, parents' organizations, and in church and neighborhood groups solidifies settlement in two ways. First, these activities are aimed at improving the material conditions of life in the United States for both the participants and their families. As such, these activities represent an investment of time and effort toward the end of permanent settlement. Second, in the process of participation, immigrants widen their circles of *conocidos* (acquaintances), construct social solidarity, and gain a sense of belonging which furthers the project of social integration.

Women play a fundamental role in consolidating settlement. Through their efforts in establishing stable forms of employment for themselves, seeking institutional modes of support for themselves and their families, and creating community ties, women forge linkages between their families and institutions and people in the U.S. As such, immigrant women concretize long-term family settlement.

Through settlement, women improve their own position in their families. The income which they earn in their jobs, the public and private resources which they tap for family use, and the social and community ties which they build further strengthen women's position in families. Immigrant women solidify the likelihood of permanent family settlement as they enhance their own status in their families.

The case of Mexican immigrant settlement in the United States parallels the trajectory followed by Algerian, Italian, and Turkish immigrant workers in Western Europe. These migrations began with primarily male migrant workers, unaccompanied by women and families. Institutionalized state mechanisms—the bracero program in the U.S. and the "guest worker" programs in Western Europe—recruited male migrant workers, and thus fostered men's temporary migrant sojourns while explicitly discouraging immigrant family reunification and permanent immigrant settlement. These programs operated under the assumption that migrant workers would fill a seemingly temporary labor shortage, but as many commentators have noted, the programs responded to and eventually constituted structural features of U.S. and European labor markets.

One crucial factor distinguishing immigrant integration in Western Europe from that in the United States is the role played by the immigrants' home countries. Countries such as Italy, Turkey, and Yugoslavia sponsor immigrant organizations in Western Europe which address immigrants' legal, social, educational, and cultural needs.[5] Due to these efforts, Western European immigrant communities resemble immigrant exclaves more than enclaves, as the organizations strengthen immigrants' ties to social and political institutions in their home countries (Heisler, 1986). These institutional ties reinforce the ideology, indeed the plausibility, of return migration, leading to the indeterminacy of settlement.

The Mexican government has traditionally not sponsored such popular organizations for Mexican immigrants in the United States. Hometown organizations and soccer clubs, and more informal transnational social-network ties, certainly connect Mexican immigrants to Mexico, but these institutions do not appear to have the same impact as the more official organizations do in Western Europe. While in Europe a myriad of government programs and agencies fosters the indeterminacy of settlement, the Mexican government has not instituted similar organizations for Mexican immigrants in the United States. This may be changing as the electoral challenges faced by the PRI (Partido Revolucionario Institucionalizado), the ruling political party in Mexico, have prompted the Mexican government to take an active role in providing services to and defending the rights of Mexican citizens in the United States. Since 1988, the Mexican consuls have taken a more aggressive role, for example, in defending Mexican immigrants who are targets of violent hate crimes, in supporting regional and hometown clubs, and in promoting literacy programs and bilingual education for Mexican residents in the U.S. (Gutiérrez, 1993). These relatively modest efforts, however, still pale in comparison with the cumulative daily activities of immigrants that anchor settlement.

The permanent incorporation of new immigrants clearly signals the creation of new types of multiethnic and multiracial societies. Recognition that permanent immigrant settlement is well under way brings up both old and new questions regarding citizenship, nationhood, and membership, and an important area of future analysis lies in establishing how gender both conditions and intervenes in these processes.

The phenomenon of undocumented immigrants who are homeowners, taxpayers, school attendees, and small-business owners presents a challenge to the traditional dichotomous fashion in which we think about citizenship and "illegal aliens." The phrase "illegal alien" denotes not only unlawful, criminal activities but also marginal involvement in societal institutions. Long-term-staying, undocumented immigrants who are integrated into social and economic life in the U.S., who have developed strong, sometimes irreversible ties to their new home areas, cannot be equated with newcomer undocumented migrant workers, although both would technically fall into the same legal-status category. Given the current political and historical context, the critical category now is not citizenship, but membership. Questions of membership concern persons already well integrated into the economic, social, and cultural life in the territory, but excluded from the rights and obligations of citizenship and legal permanent-resident status. Like settlement, membership is not a neat category, but develops over time as immigrants establish ties while living and working in a particular country (Brubaker, 1989).

Long-staying undocumented immigrants are developing new social identities that are increasingly rooted in their migration and settlement experiences. As undocumented immigrant women and men mobilize to obtain fair labor conditions, to secure voting rights in school-board and other local elections, or to demand crime-free neighborhoods, their voices are not always well received. At times, the demands for enfranchisement and community empowerment have been met with blatant hostility.

The revival of xenophobia in Western Europe and the United States in the 1980s and the early 1990s targeted the unanticipated but seemingly permanent stay of undocumented immigrant workers and their families. Contemporary allegations that immigrants compete with citizens for jobs and depress wage levels, that immigrants are culturally unassimilable, and that immigrants threaten to become a permanent underclass, a drain on society's resources, are all directed at long-staying immigrants. Not incidentally, these allegations focus on the structural features of settlement, namely, nonseasonal employment, cohesive communities, and the use of institutional resources, both public and private. Contemporary nativists distort these features in their efforts to mobilize support against the permanent integration of Mexican immigrants.

Both the bracero program and Europe's "guest worker" programs provide stunning examples of immigration policy gone awry. Social policies designed to engineer particular outcomes often fail, pointing to the vitality of human agency and social dynamics—including gender relations—at the family and community levels. This serves as an important reminder to those who would dismiss as inconsequential for social outcomes or explanations the gendered activities in families and communities. Legislative measures may provide pressures and opportunities for migration and return migration, but the way people respond to these pressures is not so easily predicted.

Notes

INTRODUCTION

1. IRCA sought to reduce undocumented immigration through employer sanctions, an increased budget for apprehending undocumented migrants at the southern border, and by legalizing a large proportion of undocumented immigrants already well established in the U.S., and a proportion of undocumented migrants who had worked in U.S. agriculture. Because of its two legalization programs—the Special Agricultural Worker (SAW) plan and amnesty—IRCA became popularly known as the "amnesty law." The media went even further in advancing this representation, as many newspaper articles repeatedly and erroneously reported that the legalization program offered citizenship, when in fact it conferred legal permanent residency status, one constrained by special limitations. The general amnesty program required continuous "illegal" residence in the U.S. prior to January 1982 as the major eligibility criterion, and the SAW program required applicants to have worked a minimum of ninety days in U.S. agriculture between May 1985 and May 1986. The SAW program, with relatively easy eligibility criteria, attracted far more applicants (1.3 million) than the number (250,000 to 350,000) which policymakers had anticipated (Cornelius, 1989a:236; Martin and Taylor, 1988).

2. These figures are drawn from "Racial/Ethnic Make-up of Schools," a report sponsored and conducted by the Oakview (a pseudonym) School District.

3. The figures in the text refer to the two census tracts where the commercial core of the barrio is situated. Many Mexican immigrants and their families, however, live in adjacent areas of Oakview, and if the barrio is thus more broadly and inclusively defined, it includes an area of about three square miles with a total population of 31,586, approximately half of whom are of "Mexican-origin" (unpublished data from *1990 Census of Population and Housing* CPH-3 100 Percent Data Tables, Population and Housing Characteristics for Census

Tracts and Block Numbering Areas. San Francisco, CA: Primary Metropolitan Statistical Area, Table 1 and Table 8).

4. Many of them did become successful candidates in one of IRCA's legalization programs.

5. Conventional random-sampling techniques are not feasible when researching an undocumented immigrant population in the U.S. (Cornelius, 1982), and locating and gaining access to undocumented immigrant respondents is not always easy. I met some of the respondents through previous contacts established when I worked in the community from 1979 to 1982 at a nonprofit immigration legal-services agency and in a bilingual-education and literacy-skills program serving parents of Spanish-speaking children. Later in 1983, for my master's thesis research, I traveled to a village in Michoacán, Mexico, where many of the immigrants originate, and these contacts also widened my circle of acquaintances. But it was primarily through my participation in various community organizations during the field research and through personal reciprocity that I elicited and maintained continuity with respondents.

6. In an article entitled "Can There Be a Feminist Ethnography?" (*Women's Studies International Forum*, 11 [1988]: 21–27), Judith Stacey argues that researchers acting as friends or advocates leave subjects open to betrayal, exploitation, and abandonment. This is a complex issue, but I believe that reciprocity in field research can attenuate some of the more asymmetrical aspects of field research. The traditional appeal to nonexploitative research generally argues that the finished research project justifies the means, and the standard human-subjects protocol that I read to all respondents did in fact state that the research might ultimately inform policy and benefit undocumented immigrants. Yet I believe that people participated in the study less in expectation that by doing so they would contribute to new immigration policies than in the expectation that their research relationship with me could be a nonthreatening and perhaps even a personally beneficial one.

CHAPTER ONE: IMMIGRATION, GENDER, AND SETTLEMENT

1. The Immigration Reform and Control Act (IRCA) enacted in 1986 included major provisions in the areas of employment and legalization for undocumented immigrants in the U.S. The employer sanctions provisions require all employers to check the work authorization of all new persons hired, and the regulations impose fines and penalties for those employers who do not comply with the letter of the law. The legalization component of IRCA allowed undocumented persons to obtain legal resident status if they met a series of criteria. By May 1991, the INS had processed 1.7 million amnesty-legalization applications from people who had lived in the United States unlawfully since January 1, 1982, and nearly 1.3 million SAW (Special Agricultural Worker) applications from people who worked in agriculture for a minimum of ninety days prior to May 1986. Mexicans submitted 1.2 million applications for amnesty legalization, and over 1 million applications for the SAW program (U.S. Immigration and Naturalization Service, 1991:91).

2. For studies analyzing the establishment of Mexican settler immigration, see Browning and Rodríguez (1982, 1985), Chavez (1988), Cornelius (1992), Massey (1986) and Villar (1990). By the 1980s, demographers estimated that the Mexican undocumented settler population in the United States included approximately 2 to 3 million people (Passel, 1986; Passel and Woodrow, 1987). Demographic tabulations of the size of this group are based on data from the 1980 U.S. and Mexican censuses, and derive from extrapolations placing the settler and long-term sojourner population at about 2 million in 1980, and projections which estimate annual growth of one hundred thousand to three hundred thousand during the 1980s (Bean et al., 1983; Passel, 1986). See Bean et al. (1986), Heer (1990), and Heer and Passel (1987) for a discussion of the problematic methodological issues involved in estimating the size of the Mexican undocumented immigrant population.

3. In California, the "Hispanic origin" population increased 69.2 percent from 1980 to 1990, while total population growth amounted to 25.7 percent and the Anglo population grew 8 percent during the same period (U.S. Census, P.L. 94–171 File, March 1991). According to Cornelius (1992), Mexican immigrants continue to go to diverse places in the U.S., but California is an increasingly preferred destination for both undocumented and documented Mexican immigrants. Cornelius (ibid.) cites several investigations which corroborate this, and the following discussion summarizes these findings. Since the 1970s, about half of the total flow of legal immigrants from Mexico to the U.S., as indicated by visas, go to California. California, however, appears to be more attractive to Mexican undocumented immigrants, as approximately 67 percent of all undocumented Mexican immigrants censused nationwide in 1980 lived in California (Passel and Woodrow, 1984:651). In the CENIET (Centro Nacional de Información y Estadistica del Trabajo) household survey conducted in Mexico in 1978, California also emerged as the place of destination for nearly 50 percent of long-staying Mexican migrants in the U.S. IRCA's two amnesty-legalization programs, one based on length of continuous residence and the other on prior agricultural work, also drew the greatest number of Mexican applicants from California. California accounted for approximately 55 percent of Mexican applicants to both programs, leading to perhaps as many as 1.5 million newly legalized Mexican immigrants in California's labor force (CASAS, 1989:1).

4. A number of studies published in the 1980s noted the significant presence of women and entire families among long-term Mexican immigrant settlers (Baca and Bryan, 1981; Briody, 1987; Cárdenas and Flores, 1986; Cornelius et al., 1982; Flores, 1980; Guendelman and Pérez-Itriaga, 1987; Portes and Bach, 1985; Reichert and Massey, 1980). One study suggests that women may constitute a majority of the Mexican undocumented immigrants who settle in the United States (Woodrow and Passel, 1990).

5. When Cornelius (1978) catalogued the undocumented Mexican immigrant population into four categories, he found an equal ratio of women and men among long-term migrants, a dramatic contrast with the male-female ratio among chronic temporary migrants, where men composed 85 to 90 percent of that group. North and Houstoun (1976) also found that men predominated in circular migration from Mexico to the United States. More recently, IRCA legali-

zation applications may reflect these trends. Among the Mexican amnesty-legali-zation applicants who had resided continuously and unlawfully in the United States since January 1, 1982, women accounted for nearly half (517,388) of the 1.2 million applicants. In contrast, women represented less than 15 percent (160,780) of the 1.1 million Mexican applicants for the Special Agricultural Worker (SAW) legalization program, where applicants had to prove a temporary work period of ninety days (U.S. Immigration and Naturalization Service, 1992). I appreciate the help of Maria Blanco, attorney at Equal Rights Advocates in San Francisco, for sharing these INS data with me; any errors of calculation or analysis are my own. In this analysis I am using SAW applicants as a proxy for seasonal migrants. Women may in fact represent far fewer than 15 percent of valid SAW applicants, as most indicators suggest that fraudulent applications were widely submitted for this legalization program. Martin and Taylor (1988) assemble data that suggest that half or more of the six hundred thousand SAW applications submitted in California may have been fraudulent. During the field-work for this study, I met people who successfully applied for SAW status, some of whom had never worked in U.S. agriculture, or who had not done so during the critical period specified by IRCA regulations. Information about the price and sale of fraudulent documents circulated widely throughout the Oakview community, and women and men alike traded instructions on how to respond to questions which might be posed by legalization adjudicators (i.e., information on the harvest of particular fruits and vegetables). If indeed women and men participated about equally in the submission of fraudulent SAW applications, the sex balance of SAW applicants may be more skewed than the official figures indicate. For a divergent view, arguing that seasonal agricultural labor is more conducive to family migration than is urban employment and residence, see Durand and Massey (1992). Successful recipients of SAW legalization may in fact be solidifying ties to the United States and moving out of agriculture and into urban occupations and residences.

6. In the 1980s, a number of anthologies and special issues of journals were published on the topic of women and migration. See, for example, "As the World Turns: Migration, Work, and International Migration," special issue of *Women's Studies* (vol. 13, no. 3 [1987]), guest editors Karen Brodkin Sacks and Nancy Scheper-Hughes; "Women in Migration," special issue of *International Migration Review* (vol. 18, no. 4 [1984]), guest editor Mirjana Morakvasic; Rita James Simon and Caroline B. Brettel, editors, *International Migration: The Female Experience* (New Jersey: Rowman and Allanheld, 1986); A. Phizacklea, editor, *One Way Ticket: Migration and Female Labor* (London: Routledge and Kegan Paul, 1983). See also Donna Gabbacia, editor, *Seeking Common Ground: Multidisciplinary Studies of Immigrant Women in the United States* (Westport, Conn.: Greenwood Press, 1992).

7. Recent advances in theorizing intersections of race, class, and gender have furthered a more complex understanding of gender, but have been hampered by a prevailing biracial model. Baca Zinn (1992) suggests that research on Latina and Asian women may serve as an important step for moving beyond biracial thinking, and for developing a more qualified understanding of these intersecting inequalities. More attention to immigrant legal status may be one route toward

advancing these analyses. An insightful study of Mexican workers in California agriculture shows how legal status affects workplace labor processes and social inequality (Thomas, 1985). In another publication, I argue that legal status is also an important category that intersects with race, class, and gender to shape the livelihood of Latina immigrants who are employed in domestic work (Hondagneu-Sotelo, forthcoming).

8. For analyses that examine gender inequality in the context of global economic development, see Benería and Roldán (1987), Fernández-Kelly (1989), and the collection of papers edited by Ward (1990).

9. Rayna Rapp (1978) defined the "household" as an empirically measurable unit of analysis where production, reproduction, and consumption occur, and distinguished the "family" as a normative, ideological construct that recruits people into households and prescribes their behavior.

10. Reification of the male sojourner as the stereotypical Mexican immigrant arises from methodological strategies employed due to the problems in locating "illegal" or criminalized respondents. Studies of undocumented immigrants conducted in Mexico oversampled short-term sojourner male migrants, but often conclusions were generalized as universal to the larger undocumented population. Similarly, as Baca and Bryan (1981) suggest, research based on apprehended undocumented Mexican immigrants has tended to oversample the least experienced newcomers and sojourners, especially those captured in raids at workplaces where men predominate. One of the first studies to examine Mexican undocumented and unapprehended immigrants in the United States is the study conducted in Los Angeles by Van Arsdol et al. (1979).

11. Many sociologically informed critiques have faulted the "push-pull" approach for presenting an overly reductionist, static view of human behavior (Bach and Schraml, 1982; Dinerman, 1978; Portes and Bach, 1985; Wood, 1982.)

12. More eclectic than the competing framework, the macrostructural approach is represented in a variety of models that emphasize the political economy of immigration. Discussion has focused, for example, on how foreign investment in third-world countries disrupts established economic structures and generates emigration (Portes, 1978), on how capital mobility from core to periphery induces labor migration in the opposite direction (Sassen-Koob, 1978; Sassen, 1988), and on the significance of labor migration for capital accumulation in the societies of immigrant destination (Castells, 1975).

13. For example, Massey et al. (1987:141) state that "the most important kin relationships in migrant networks are those between fathers and sons, uncles and nephews, brothers and male cousins." Brettel and deBerjeois (1992) note that the concept of social networks is used in two ways in the immigration literature: with regard to chain migration, and with regard to the community-based support systems that emerge in the new society. While gender and women's presence are generally ignored in the study of transnational chain migration (e.g., Mines, 1981; Massey et al, 1987), there is a large literature in anthropology, history, and sociology documenting immigrant women's activities in work and community-based networks (Deutsch, 1987; Glenn, 1986; O'Conner, 1990; Yans-McLaughlin, 1977; Yanagisako, 1977; Zavella, 1987).

14. Perhaps the most succinct indictment of urban immigrant life is found in Robert Park's "Human Migration and the Marginal Man," first published in 1928. In this essay, Park portrays the immigrant in the city as a permanently pathological, unstable character, as a person plagued by "spiritual instability, intensified self-consciousness, restlessness and malaise" (Park, in Sennett, 1969:142). In this essay, Park went so far as to compare the social disruption caused by migration with the violence of full-blown revolution: "The first and most obvious difference between revolution and migration is that in migration the breakdown of the social order is initiated by the impact of an invading population, and completed by the contact and fusion of alien with native peoples." (Park, in Sennett, 1969:134–35). Park examined the "changed type of personality" created by migration and the breakdown process, and he concluded that the marginal man experiences a permanent state of crisis. Louis Wirth further developed this line of thinking in "Urbanism as a Way of Life" (1938), as he maintained that the city pulverizes traditional family values and patriarchal authority. Historian Oscar Handlin (1973) also concluded that European immigrants "lived in crisis because they were uprooted. In transplantation, while the old roots were sundered, before the new were established, the immigrants existed in an extreme situation . . . the effects of the shock persisted for many years." Similarly, W. I. Thomas and Florian Znaniecki argued in their multivolume *The Polish Peasant* (1927) that social disorganization occurs as the individual is released from kinship bonds, obligations, and duties, and as family norms and values weaken. For them, this outcome did not necessarily have a pejorative connotation, as they speculated that such conditions were as likely to lead to greater individual freedom and autonomy as they were to deviancy and destruction.

15. As Baca Zinn (1975) has pointed out, this revisionist argument prevailed not only within the confines of academia, but in politics as well, as some activists in the Chicano movement claimed that the tradition of "la familia" served as a basis of cultural resistance to discrimination and accommodation. These analyses cast traditional family and patriarchal gender relations as instruments of political resistance. For example, in "Machismo: Rucas, Chingasas y Chingaderas" (*De Colores*, 6 [1982]): 17–31), Alfredo Mirandé juxtaposes the pathological view of machismo "with a reassessment that casts machismo as a symbol of resistance of Chicanos to colonial control, both cultural and physical. . . . [Machismo] symbolizes most importantly, resistance to acculturation and assimilation to Anglo society" (p. 27). See also Peña (1991), who argues that Mexican undocumented immigrant men's displays of machismo reflect symbolic displacements of their class antagonisms.

16. A significant body of social-science research focuses on the character of patriarchal gender relations among Mexicans and Chicanos in the United States (Cromwell and Ruiz, 1979; Fernández-Kelly and Garcia, 1990; Guendelman and Pérez-Itriaga, 1987; Horowitz, 1983; Peña, 1991; Segura, 1988; Ybarra, 1982, 1988; Zavella, 1987; Zinn, 1980). See also the articles compiled in de la Torre and Pesquera (1993).

17. Machismo may also be characterized by extreme verbal and bodily aggression toward other men, frequent drunkenness, informal polygamy, and sexual aggression toward women (Paz, 1961; Peña, 1991).

18. It is instructive to consider the underpinnings of Mexican patriarchal ideologies, especially as they relate to Mexican women's subordination. According to Shirlene Soto (1986), three cultural prototypes, one positive and two negative, have played a historical role in controlling Mexican women's conduct. The Virgin of Guadalupe, the indigenous virgin that appeared in 1531 to a young Indian boy and for whom a major basilica is built, provides the exemplary maternal model, *la mujer abnegada* (the self-effacing woman), who sacrifices all for her children and religious faith. *La Malinche*, the Aztec woman that served Cortés as translator, diplomat, and mistress, and *La Llorona* (the weeping one), a legendary solitary, ghostlike figure reputed either to have been violently murdered by a jealous husband or to have herself murdered her children by drowning them, are the negative and despised models of femininity. *La Malinche* is blamed and stigmatized as a traitor and a whore who collaborated with the Spanish conquerors, and *La Llorona* is the archetype evil woman condemned to eternally suffer and weep for violating her role as mother and wife. Legends of these three female figures are passed from generation to generation in an attempt to socialize young Mexican and Chicana women by inculcating clear-cut images of good and evil femininity (Soto, 1986).

19. For specification and analysis of the dynamics in classic patriarchy in North Africa, the Muslim Middle East, and South and East Asia, see Kibria (1993), Kandiyoti (1988), and Wolf (1990).

20. As Adaljiza Sosa Riddell (1986) has noted, many observers who believe Mexico to be the most backward stalwart of patriarchal institutions were surprised when the Mexican government hosted the International Women's Year World Conference in 1975. In fact, Mexican women have a long history of pursuing political, economic, and social change on their own behalf, and the first wave of feminism in Mexico coincided with the first women's movement in the United States (Macías, 1982; Sosa Riddell, 1986; Soto, 1990).

21. The key to women's mobilization in the territorially or residentially based groups is their identity as mothers and their desire to improve material living conditions by demanding city services. Toward this end, they stage public demonstrations, organize delegations, and circulate petitions—actions that may be leading to what Kathleen Logan (1988) calls "an activist interpretation of motherhood." For analysis of similarly mobilized actions among Mexican peasant women, see Browner (1986) and Martin (1990).

22. A number of studies have examined Mexican women's participation in rural-urban migration, and in the construction of new urban settlements. See, for example, Arizpe (1978, 1979), Logan (1984), Lomnitz (1977), and Niembro Díaz (1988). For a more recent analysis that contrasts patterns of men's and women's rural-urban migration in Mexico, and its relation to U.S.-bound migration, see Patricia Arias, "El tiempo de las mujeres: El campo y la migración a EEUU," in *New Perspectives on Mexico-U.S. Migration*, proceedings of the conference organized by the Center for Latin American Studies and the Mexican Studies Program, University of Chicago, October 23–24, 1992.

23. For studies of Mexican women working in export agribusiness in Michoacán, see Arias and Mummert (1987), Arizpe and Aranda (1981), and

Mummert (1990); Zabin (1992) has studied Mixtec women's employment in Baja California agribusiness.

24. *Maquiladoras* are foreign-owned assembly plants located along Mexico's northern border. These labor-intensive, export-processing plants receive investment incentives from the Mexican government, and tariff duties on products exported to the U.S. apply only to the "value added" outside the U.S.

25. While Lourdes Benería (1992) concurs that the ongoing economic crisis of the 1980s sent more youth and women into the labor force, she suggests that mothers with husbands or male partners were the last to join the labor force, due to their male partners' income and opposition to female employment. Still, in Benería's (ibid.) study of lower- and middle-class households in Mexico City, fully 60 percent of mothers with male partners were involved in some type of income-earning activity.

26. The bracero program was a contract-labor program initially designed to meet wartime agricultural labor shortages in the Southwest.

27. A number of community studies conducted in Mexico indicate how men's migration to the U.S. has accelerated women's employment and income-earning activities in Mexico. See, for example, Ahern, Bryan, and Baca (1985), Alarcón (1988), Arias and Mummert (1987), Moreno (1986), Baca and Bryan (1985), Crummet (1987), González de la Rocha (1989), and Mummert (1988, 1990). See also a study based on interviews conducted in the U.S. by Curry-Rodríguez (1988).

28. For studies of women's occupational status in Mexico, see Escobar Latapí and González de la Rocha (1988), Salazar (1980), Elu de Leñero (1980), Fernández-Kelly (1983), and de Oliveira (1990).

29. These ideological beliefs are often internalized by both women and men. A study conducted in the 1960s indicated that married Mexican working women typically expressed guilt over employment, and 57 percent of women surveyed and 74 percent of men believed it was up to a woman's husband to decide whether a woman should work (Elu de Leñero, 1980:55).

30. Little is know about how migration affects sexual practices and sexual mores, and this is one of several topics meriting investigation. In Mexican and Chicano society, family honor has traditionally—although this is changing—hinged on unmarried women's virginity and on married women's fidelity (Horowitz, 1983; LeVine, 1993; Ruiz, 1992), but research has not systematically examined the relationship between these beliefs and practices and contemporary migration. Georgina Rosado's research suggests that in the context of men's migration northward, women's beliefs about traditional double standards of sexuality are weakening. One of the young, single working woman that Rosado interviewed in a rural, migratory village of Michoacán discussed the issue of spousal sexual infidelity with her friends and her mother, and then concluded, "I don't believe as my mother does that you must put up with your husband forever if he cheats on you and turns out bad" (Rosado, 1990:67, translated by Hondagneu-Sotelo).

31. As Vicki L. Ruiz (1992:151) eloquently states, "There is not a hermetic Mexican or Mexican-American culture, but rather *cultures* rooted in generation, gender, region, class and personal experience." Similarly, there is no monolithic

form of Mexican patriarchy, but a multiplicity of patriarchal legacies and manifestations.

32. A substantial literature on rural-urban migration in Latin America indicates the tenacity of family ties (Balán et al., 1973; Peattie, 1968; Lomnitz, 1977; Perlman, 1976).

33. Piore (1979) argued that in the initial stages, labor migrants are driven by purely utilitarian concerns, as their drive to rapidly earn and save income prompts them to work long hours at undesirable jobs, live frugally, and avoid leisure activities. But as time passes, and as they establish families and households in the new country, these same migrants work shorter hours, spend more and save less, and begin to congregate socially and enjoy leisure pursuits. No longer obsessed with returning to the home country as quickly as possible, the increasingly anchored immigrants are then concerned with job stability and social position in the new society. Patricia Pessar (1986) has noted that this is an essentially androcentric framework, as it does not distinguish between the gendered spheres in which men and women locate social identity. Pessar identifies these as community and household, respectively.

34. While formation of some type of extended family household is an important mechanism in the initial phase, the formation of nuclear family households signals an important achievement of settlement (Chavez, 1985, 1988).

35. The finding that children of Mexican immigrants often do not wish to return to Mexico was documented as early as the 1920s and 1930s by sociologist Emory S. Bogardus (1934) and anthropologist Manuel Gamio (1971b).

CHAPTER TWO: THE HISTORY OF MEXICAN UNDOCUMENTED SETTLEMENT IN THE UNITED STATES

1. The Mexican population living in the Southwest in 1848 numbered between eighty thousand and one hundred thousand people. While the Mexican citizens living in the newly conquered Anglo territories were formally granted civil, language, religious, and land rights under the Treaty of Guadalupe Hidalgo, these rights were rarely and selectively conferred (Acuña, 1981; Barrera, 1979; Weber, 1973).

2. For analyses of these cyclical migration patterns, see Bustamante (1975), Portes and Bach (1985), and Cockcroft (1986).

3. Chicano historians have chronicled a significant presence of Mexican women working in southern California and Texas during the late nineteenth century, but it is not clear how many of these women came from Mexico and how many were descendants of the original Mexican inhabitants, born in the conquered territories. See, for example, Griswold del Castillo (1984), Barrera (1979), Camarillo (1979), and Garcia (1981). On New Mexico and southern Colorado, see Deutsch (1987).

4. By 1910, communally owned properties were illegal and the majority of Mexico's rural population lived in debt peonage, working as sharecroppers; 97 percent of rural families were landless (Cardoso, 1980:7).

5. In response to pressure from southwestern agricultural growers, the secretary of labor exempted Mexicans from the head tax, and the literacy tax imposed

by the Immigration Act of 1917, and instituted special contract-labor provisions for Mexican workers (Kiser and Kiser, 1972:127–31). Labor shortages in agriculture occurred when more than 1 million U.S. citizens were conscripted into the military, drawing poor white and black workers from agriculture to urban jobs (Cardoso, 1980:45–48).

6. The Cristero Rebellion, a popular Christian backlash to the Mexican government's attempt to undermine the powerful hegemony of the Catholic church, consisted of a series of battles and random violence perpetrated in the western area of Mexico.

7. These new urban settlements also drew the attention of "Americanist" groups. Americanization projects targeted Mexican immigrant women with the intention of changing Mexican cultural values and practices (Sánchez, 1990).

8. The recruitment of Mexican family labor in Colorado sugar-beet fields began as early as 1908, and after 1910 the Great Western Sugar Company institutionalized a policy of recruiting only family labor. Many of these Mexican-origin families came from northern New Mexico villages (Deutsch, 1987:34).

9. The lyrics of a popular song from the 1920s, sung from the perspective of a returning migrant worker, suggest men's greater willingness, when accompanied by family, to comply with employer demands. The lyrics tell of a migrant worker who, upon returning to the U.S. with his wife, proclaims: "What do you say, my contractor? Didn't I tell you I'd be back? Send me wherever you will, because now I bring someone with me." (Gamio, 1971:90).

10. See Durand and Massey (1992) for a discussion of historical and contemporary debates over the number of persons migrating from Mexico to the U.S., and for debates over the numbers of Mexican immigrants remaining in the U.S.

11. Carreras (1974) reports that between 1931 and 1933, two-thirds of the deportees were women.

12. In Los Angeles, local welfare agencies aggressively promoted the repatriation of men, women, and children (Kiser and Kiser, 1979; Hoffman, 1976). Mexicans did not respond passively to these attacks. Mexican communities organized mutual-aid societies that provided assistance, and that protested the massive raids and the boycotts against hiring Mexicans. And Mexican government officials, under the leadership of President Lazaro Cardenas (1934–40), welcomed the *repatriados* (repatriates) by granting land and tools to help them reestablish themselves (Balderrama, 1982).

13. García y Griego reports that U.S. and Mexican government statistics show that more Mexican immigrants returned to Mexico than remained in the U.S. during the first three decades of the century, indicating "a strong component of seasonal labor migration" and "the relative impermanence of Mexican settlement in the United States," especially after the Great Depression (1983:50). As García y Griego (ibid.) and others have noted, however, accurate figures on the number of Mexican immigrants settling in the U.S. are difficult to ascertain because of lax practices in recording border crossings, poor census records, and the undercount of braceros and Mexican workers who migrated illegally.

14. The first bilateral agreement in 1942 allowed U.S. government representatives to recruit in Mexico and assign contract workers to selected employers. In initial negotiations, the Mexican government required that employers pay

the cost of the workers' round-trip transportation and subsistence en route, provide adequate housing in the labor camps, and provide minimum standards of wages, working conditions, medical care, and insurance against accidents (McWilliams, 1968). Some growers resented these government interventions, preferring instead a "laissez-faire" open border, and by 1947, employers were allowed to directly recruit workers, which they often did at the border. While provisions for workers' rights were included in the 1947 agreement, government regulation of employer practices decreased, wages declined, and employer abuses rose. During this period, Mexican undocumented immigrants apprehended by the INS were returned to Mexico and then immediately "recruited" under employer contract, a process then crudely known as "wringing out the wetbacks"— that is, authorizing the immigrants for work (Samora, 1971:47). When the Mexican government threatened to negate these accords because of widespread abuse and the absence of government supervision, the program was formally institutionalized by the U.S. Congress as Public Law 78 in 1951. During this last phase of the bracero program, 1951–65, fewer than 2 percent of commercial farmers received bracero workers (Hawley, 1966:157). See García y Griego (1983) and Samora (1971) for an assessment of the bracero program's operations and legacy.

15. Men accounted for 98 percent of former braceros surveyed in Michoacán and Jalisco by Massey and colleagues (Massey and Liang, 1989:207).

16. For analyses of these outcomes of the bracero program, see Corwin and Cardoso (1978), North and Houstoun (1976), Massey et al. (1987), Massey and Liang (1989), and Mines (1981).

17. From 1961 to 1970, 453,937 Mexicans legally immigrated, 887,635 entered as braceros, and 1,017,719 were apprehended by the INS. While the number of apprehended undocumented Mexican immigrants had decreased between 1957 and 1964 from thirty-eight thousand to twenty-three thousand, in 1966—two years after termination of the bracero program—the number jumped to seventy-one thousand and then steadily increased until 1977, when the INS apprehended over 1 million undocumented Mexican immigrants (Jenkins, 1977). From 1971 to 1980, 640,294 people legally immigrated from Mexico, but more than ten times that number of undocumented Mexicans (7,473,248) were apprehended. See U.S. Immigration and Naturalization Service (1983), and Pedraza-Bailey (1985:77, table 4).

18. Many of the Mexican undocumented immigrants in the U.S. did not qualify for either the legalization-amnesty program, which required proof of continuous illegal residence in the U.S. dating from prior to January 1982 as the major eligibility criterion, or the Special Agricultural Workers (SAW) program, that required proof of having worked a minimum of ninety days in U.S. agriculture from 1985 to 1986. Many other undocumented immigrants feared that the bureaucratic procedure would place them in jeopardy with the authorities, and did not file applications. Using data from the 1988 Current Population Survey, Woodrow and Passel (1990:55) indicate that approximately one-third of the Mexican undocumented immigrants living in the U.S. prior to January 1982 did not apply for amnesty legalization. Hence Durand and Massey (1992) suggest that the 2.3 million Mexican applicants confirms these estimates of the Mexican

undocumented immigrant population, accounting for approximately 75 percent of the 3.1 million.

19. See, for example, Cárdenas and Flores (1986), Curry-Rodríguez (1988), Fernández-Kelly and Garcia (1990), Solórzano-Torres (1987), Simon and de Ley (1984), and Villar (1990).

20. See Cornelius (1989b:31) for a list of sixty-six goods and services produced by 177 Mexican immigrant–dependent firms studied in metropolitan areas of California. The list includes fish, duck, and chicken processing; electrical machinery; plastic, vinyl, and textile products; and household appliances.

21. From 1921 to 1965 U.S. immigration law mandated the selection of legal immigrants on the basis of national-origin quotas. These racist quotas were designed to exclude Asians and other groups deemed undesirable. For example, the Emergency Quota Act of 1921 established a 3 percent limit on each nationality group already resident in the U.S. when the 1910 U.S. Census was taken, effectively privileging immigration from northwestern Europe. The 1952 McCarran-Walter Act justified quotas on the basis of assimilability. Quotas for the Western Hemisphere were established for the first time with the 1965 amendment, and national-origin quotas were phased out. (Keely and Elwel, 1983:181).

22. While from 1900 to 1965, 75 percent of all legal immigrants to the U.S. came from Europe (Massey, 1981:58), this changed radically after 1968, when the 1965 amendment went into effect. Asia, Latin America, and the Caribbean accounted for approximately 75 percent of all U.S. immigrants during the 1970s, and for 80 percent by the 1980s. (U.S. Immigration and Naturalization Service, 1989).

23. Mexico had previously accounted for approximately forty thousand legal immigrants annually, and with this figure halved in 1976, severe backlogs encouraged many would-be legal migrants with pending applications to come as undocumented immigrants. In 1977, 1978, and 1979, apprehensions of Mexican undocumented immigrants totaled more than 1 million each year (Portes and Bach, 1985:63).

24. IRCA also allowed for a 50 percent increase in budget allocations to the Border Patrol, and provisions to benefit U.S. agriculture, such as a temporary contract-labor program for sugarcane workers.

25. For an evaluation of IRCA, see Bean et al. (1989). One commentator noted that IRCA was a "product of the new restrictionist mentality, in terms of its origins and the symbolic message of control that it transmits to the American public, if not in terms of its actual impact" (Calavita, 1989:162). One can also surmise that even restrictionists recognized that a large proportion of undocumented immigrants were irreversibly established in the United States.

26. Although the acquisition of permanent legal residency facilitates integration into U.S. society, it does not necessarily mandate it. In fact, acquisition of legal status facilitates return trips to Mexico, as crossing the border becomes less problematic with legal papers. Also, many elderly Mexican immigrants retire to Mexico. I am grateful to Maria de Lourdes Villar for this observation.

27. In 1987, an increasing proportion of women were sighted at Zapata Canyon, a popular crossing point in Tijuana for Mexicans illegally migrating into the United States (Bustamante, 1990), and by 1988 and 1989, the propor-

tion of women and children apprehended by the Border Patrol in California had significantly increased (Bean et al., 1990). Other investigations of undocumented border crossers in Tijuana sponsored by El Colegio de la Frontera Norte also indicate a growing presence of women without prior immigration experience. Daily interviews conducted in Tijuana between September 1987 and July 1989 indicate that more than 80 percent of the women interviewed (N=718) were coming to the United States for the first time. Investigations simultaneously conducted in Ciudad Juárez reveal that the vast majority of Mexican women crossing the border illegally had previous experience in doing so. This is because the majority of the women crossing in Ciudad Juárez are border residents who routinely commute to work in Texas. These women typically do paid domestic work, and may cross the border on a weekly, biweekly, or even daily basis. In Tijuana, the majority of illegal border crossers stem from the interior of Mexico (Woo, 1993).

28. In this regard, Bean et al. (1990) suggest that the labor demand for domestic work and child care may coincide with the end of summer and the start of a new school year. They observe that the peak months of apprehensions for female Mexican undocumented immigrants are July and August, and note that "it would be an ironic twist if IRCA leads to decreased undocumented migration among males, but increased migration of undocumented females" (1990:149). Donato (forthcoming), on the basis of data gathered in ten Mexican communities and in the United States, suggests that during the 1980s Mexican women were more likely to participate in undocumented migration than legal migration, with one exception. The exception is 1988 and 1989, and this is explained by the temporary deterrent effect of IRCA during those years. Donato (ibid.) found that by 1989, Mexican women's likelihood of migrating north "without papers" on a first trip rose back to 1985 levels.

29. For analyses of labor-market impacts of immigrant workers, see Thomas R. Bailey, *Immigrant and Native Workers: Contrasts and Competition* (Boulder, Colo.: Westview, 1987); Thomas Muller and Thomas J. Espenshade, *The Fourth Wave: California's Newest Immigrants* (Washington, D.C.: Urban Institute Press, 1985); George J. Borjas, *Friends or Strangers: The Impact of Immigrants on the U.S. Economy* (New York: Basic Books, 1990); and Alejandro Portes and Robert L. Bach, *Latin Journey: Cuban and Mexican Immigrants in the United States* (Berkeley: University of California Press, 1985).

30. Cross and Sandos (1981:52) add that higher education and military conscription in the 1960s also removed many young men from the U.S. labor force. While domestic sources of cheap labor were withdrawing from the labor force, Sassen-Koob (1980) argues, the availability of immigrants spared employers from upgrading jobs in the secondary labor market necessary to attract citizens. Hence the dual labor-market structure was effectively reorganized with undocumented immigrants at the bottom.

31. For example, until the mid-1960s, U.S.-born workers filled lower-level service jobs in Los Angeles hotels, but by the 1980s, only "the least mobile native-born workers (older minority women and uneducated minority men)" remained in these positions, which are now filled largely by Mexican undocumented immigrants (Cornelius, 1989b:39). See also Rick A. Morales, "The Utili-

zation of Mexican Immigrants in the Restaurant Industry: The Case of San Diego County," and Gary R. Lemons, "Hiring and Employment of Undocumented Workers in the Roofing Industry of Albuquerque, New Mexico," in Wayne A. Cornelius, *The Changing Role of Mexican Labor in the U.S. Economy: Sectoral Perspectives* (La Jolla, Calif.: Center for U.S.-Mexican Studies, University of California at San Diego, forthcoming.)

32. Cornelius's study (1989b) of 177 immigrant-dominated firms in California indicates that foreign competition has also been key to the "Mexicanization" of the work force in rubber and furniture manufacturing and in food processing.

33. For analyses of how rapid-paced development in Mexico has contributed to U.S.-bound migration, see Alba (1978) and Arizpe (1981). See also Portes (1978).

34. Between 1940 and 1965, the agricultural sector in Mexico boasted an annual growth rate of 5.7 percent (Arizpe, 1981b:629). Agricultural outputs increased over 100 percent between 1940 and 1960, and industrial outputs, stimulated by advertisements promoting "modern" standards of consumption, increased by 120 percent during the same period (Cockcroft, 1983:150).

35. The government invested heavily in a series of *grandes obras de irrigación*—enormous irrigation projects—located primarily in northwestern Mexico, where export crops were cultivated on a large scale (Schumacher, 1981). Investment in irrigation and green-revolution technology supported growth in modernizing commercial agriculture, and this provided the dynamic behind Mexico's postwar growth (Hewitt de Alcántara, 1976).

36. Arizpe (1981b:629) cites Banco Nacional de Comercio Exterior data indicating that the proportion of federal investment in irrigated, large-scale agriculture was twice that directed at small-scale, rain-fed agriculture in 1960, but that by 1966 it was seven times greater. For studies on the modernization of commercial agriculture in Mexico, see Hewitt de Alcántara (1976), Esteva (1980), and Grindle (1986).

37. By 1970, the distribution of cultivated land was so highly skewed that 3 percent of all agricultural units accounted for 54 percent of total agricultural production. At the bottom of the hierarchy, one-half of all agricultural units controlled only one-eighth of the land and produced approximately 4 percent of the total value of agricultural production (Esteva, 1980:38–39).

38. From 1970 to 1980, the economically active population in Mexico increased by 62 percent, constituting an "overall absolute surplus of labor" and severely exacerbating unemployment by the early 1980s (Alejo, 1983:87).

39. Many commentators agree that Mexico's economic problems in the 1970s and 1980s grew directly out of the development model pursued in the 1940s and 1950s (Cockcroft, 1983; Hamilton and Harding, 1986). Capital flight, overextension of credit, and wage suppression were familiar problems, yet it was the incremental, quantitative growth and continuity of these trends that resulted in a crisis of qualitatively different proportions. Chant (1991:183) reports that consumer prices in Mexico rose 981 percent between the second half of 1982 and 1986, while the daily minimum wage rose only 573 percent.

40. The changing class composition is explained by the effects of the economic crisis on different sectors. Employees in the formal sector of the economy

may have suffered these blows more intensely than workers in the unregulated informal sector (Escobar Latapí and González de la Rocha, 1988:554). As far as geographical diversification goes, Cornelius indicates that as late as 1973, 48 percent of undocumented Mexicans apprehended near the Tijuana crossing originated in the traditional immigrant-sending states of Jalisco and Guerrero (Dagodag, 1975), but in a survey conducted in 1987–88 in southern California with 200 recently arrived undocumented immigrants, the Federal District ranked as the top sending area, followed by Puebla (Cornelius, 1988). Research based on interviews conducted in Laredo, Texas, with 656 apprehended undocumented immigrants in 1986 found the Federal District to be the third most important state of origin (Fatemi, 1987).

41. Although public-sector spending has been curtailed, the Mexican government's lobbying expenditure for NAFTA constituted one of the most expensive foreign lobbying campaigns waged in the U.S. From 1989 to 1993, the Mexican government spent at least $25 million on NAFTA-related activities. For a report on these lobbying activities, see Charles Lewis and Margaret Ebraham, "Can Mexico and Big Business USA Buy NAFTA?" *The Nation*, June 14, 1993, 826–39.

42. By 1987, the minimum urban wage diminished to 58 percent of what it had been in 1980 (Cordera Campos et al., 1989:114).

CHAPTER THREE: THE OAKVIEW BARRIO

1. Several recent publications discuss Mexican immigrants in ways that counter this dehumanizing tendency. One is a compilation of oral histories of Mexican immigrants and their family members conducted by Davis (1990). Other examples are the volume of undocumented immigrants' letters translated and compiled by Siems (1992) and the family study by Álvarez (1987).

2. Fred Villedas (a pseudonym) was instrumental in bringing Mexican bracero farmworkers to Oakview in the late 1940s and early 1950s, and he was mentioned by three of these six men as a key figure in their early settlement. Villedas, a U.S. citizen of Mexican and Italian descent, worked as an agricultural labor contractor in Salinas, California, and when he moved to Oakview to manage a store, he brought several Mexican immigrant men to work with him.

3. These figures are derived from data collected by the Oakview (a pseudonym) School District and presented in a report entitled "Racial/Ethnic Make-up of Schools." School-district records that show country of origin for LEP (limited English proficient) children indicate that by far the vast majority of these children are from Mexico, although there are also representatives from the Philippines and from El Salvador and other Central American countries.

4. See "California Cities: Rich and Poor," *Los Angeles Times*, July 6, 1992, which reports per capita income ranging from $55,721 to $68,236 for these three municipalities. Rank is according to per capita income earned in 1989 and reported in the April 1990 census. These data were compiled by statistical analyst Maureen Lyons and researcher Tracy Thomas.

5. Some classification schemes are based on legal status, dividing legal immigrants from undocumented immigrants and, in the Mexican case, noting the

special circumstances of contract workers (Portes and Bach, 1985). Other typologies of Mexican immigrants make distinctions according to length and frequency of migrant trips, essentially classifying migrants into two groups: short-term sojourner or seasonal migrants, and long-term settler migrants (Mines, 1981; Chavez, 1988). Yet a third typology, which encompasses all U.S. immigrants, uses socioeconomic background and migrant motives to yield four classifications: labor migrants, professional immigrants, entrepreneurial immigrants, and refugees and asylees (Portes and Rumbaut, 1990).

6. In some instances they were married or living with another respondent, and in other cases their spouse or companion was not included in the sample.

7. I was never sure if Dolores Ávila was tired or depressed. The psychological impact of migration and resettlement on women is a topic that deserves profound inquiry. It is also one of the many important topics that arose and that I was unable to pursue over the course of my fieldwork. More than a few women in the study suffered from what they described as *nervios* (excessive nervousness and anxiety), from physical ailments that may reflect psychosomatic manifestations of illness, and several seemed, at times, to be depressed. Conflicting cultural ideals and new patterns of behavior may contribute to depression in Mexican immigrant women, but those who remain in communication with kin in Mexico generally experience fewer depressive symptoms (Vega et al., 1986, 1987). For a review of the psychological stressors created by migration and the implications for psychotherapy with Latina immigrants, see Espín (1987). See also Freidenberg et al. (1988), and Vega et al. (1986, 1987).

8. *Chola* or *cholo* refers to a person who has left her or his society and culture of origin, but who has not acculturated and integrated into the new sociocultural context. In many parts of Latin America, *cholos* refers to indigenous people who live in cities. In Chicano-Mexicano communities in the U.S., the term generally refers to youths who are associated with gangs; in the Oakview barrio, many parents worried about their chilren becoming *cholos*.

9. After having lived with Amador more or less continuously for six years, María Alicia learned in 1991 that he was still married to another woman and was the father of a ten-year-old boy in Mexico.

CHAPTER FOUR: GENDERED TRANSITIONS

1. According to Rouse (1987, 1989), the analytic primacy of the household in migration studies began to occur in the late 1970s. Although Rouse (ibid.) refers to this as the "adaptationist" approach, it is essentially identical to what I call the "household strategies" view. Rouse explains this paradigmatic shift as: (1) an attempt to demonstrate the rationality of research subjects; (2) a reflection of interest in the domestic sphere, stemming from both feminist inquiries into the "private" world of family and home and Marxist-informed approaches which acknowledged labor occurring outside of the market; and (3) an attempt to locate and conceptualize contingent agency (1987:3). The focus on the household was also shaped by the promise of a relatively neat methodological category, one based on coresidence and wage pooling (Fox-Genovese, 1983).

2. Variations of the household strategies model were also widely adopted in fields outside of migration—in studies of education, consumption, and labor-force participation (Wolf, 1990). As commentators have noted, the household model is typically used as a tool for understanding poor people's behavior in third-world settings, or the behavior of poor peasants making the transition to proletarians in countries undergoing industrialization. The household model is not used as a model to understand, say, middle-class families' patterns of educational acquisition, or the "strategies" used by the rich and powerful to perpetuate their family dynasties (Selby et al., 1990; Wolf, 1990). The household strategies approach was shaped by social theorists who, in an attempt to correct previous views that emphasized the victimization of the powerless and the force of social structure over human agency, made extraordinary efforts to rationalize the actions of working people, peasants, women, and migrants.

3. Compare, for example, the migration studies published in the early 1980s by Pessar (1982) and Selby and Murphy (1982) with later publications written, albeit collaboratively, by the same authors (e.g., Grasmuck and Pessar, 1991; Selby et al., 1990.) The later works exhibit a more conditional, tempered usage of the household model and its assumptions of household "moral economy" and utility maximization. These later works question as well the notions of rationality and consciousness embedded in the concept of "household strategies." In a similar vein, Tilly and Scott's classic study on the history of British and French women's work, *Women, Work and Family* (1978), peripherally dealt with migration and utilized a version of the household model called "family strategies." While Tilly and Scott developed one of the more gender-sensitive approaches within the household paradigm, they did not go far enough in analyzing or decomposing gender relations within the family unit, so as to underscore how families arrive at particular strategies. The authors themselves recognize this shortcoming in the introduction to a later edition of their book, in which they note that the processes of arriving at family strategies often involves "contention, bargaining, negotiation, and domination." (1987:9).

4. In some cases, the household is portrayed as sending migrants in order to preserve family integrity or continue with household reproduction (Arizpe, 1981a; Dinerman, 1982; Selby and Murphy, 1982), but again, this behavior is posed primarily as a reaction to external economic forces.

5. In a study of a Mexican village then (1958–61) unaffected by migration, Romanucci-Ross (1973) found many examples of women "abandoning" their husbands. In her study, she cites twenty-three cases of women leaving men, four cases of men leaving women, and two cases of mutually desired separation—figures that she finds suggestive of "the striking independence and defiance of women in this village. Women . . . leave men under varying circumstances—to rejoin their families, to go to their lovers, to live with a man they meet later, or to live and support themselves alone" (1973:62). In the Oakview barrio I never once heard of *hombres abandonados* (abandoned man), whether in the context of international migration or of marital separations due to disagreements. Certainly Mexican popular culture—ballads, movies, jokes (Peña, 1991)—abounds with stories of teacherous women who betray men and leave their husbands. But in Oakview, this was not reflected in social reality. In the Oakview barrio I asked

many people, not just the study participants, if they knew of instances where Mexican women had left their husbands behind to come work in the U.S. No one knew anyone personally who fit that description, but a few people told me they had heard of such women, reputed to have come seeking *libertinaje* (sexual promiscuity). Although it appears to be quite rare, some women do migrate to work in the U.S. while their husbands remain behind in Mexico (see Chavez, 1992:25).

6. These processes may indicate more generalized patterns. In a study of Mexican American families in Texas, sociologist Norma Williams found that working-class married women's ability to develop new, more independent identities depended on their attainment of new social skills, especially those developed in the public sphere. See Norma Williams, *The Mexican American Family: Tradition and Change* (Dix Hills, N.Y.: General Hall, 1990).

7. See Benería and Roldán (1987:116–18) for a discussion of how these practices affect women industrial homeworkers in Mexico City, and LeVine (1993) for an analysis of how these practices shape marital relationships for working-class and lower-middle-class women in Cuernavaca, Mexico.

8. Since it is not possible to observe decision-making processes in migration, these scenarios were reconstructed in the interviews through the study participants' memories, ex post facto rationalizations, and my own interpretations.

9. In Mexico, while women's marital infidelity is routinely condemned, men's extramarital sexual relationships are tolerated so long as the men financially provide for their families (de la Peña, 1984; Romanucci-Ross, 1973; LeVine, 1993).

10. When Mexican women migrate to the U.S. in order to confront their husbands about their extramarital relationships, there is no guarantee that the men will respond as the women wish. Davis (1990:157–66) reports a case where a wife, with her mother-in-law, journeyed from Jalisco to Oregon to find her husband, who had taken up with a woman he wished to marry and with whom he wanted to start a new family. In spite of their face-to-face confrontation with him, and their letters of entreaty to the INS, the American consulate, and a U.S. senator, he did not reunite with his wife and children.

11. The one exception, where the wife's kin did not play a role in facilitating migration, was the Ramírezes, who were a newly married couple at the time of migration.

12. For an analysis of older women "imported" as child minders by immigrant women and families in Quebec, see Deirdre Meintel, Micheline Labelle, Genevieve Turcotte, and Marianne Kempineers, "The New Double Workday of Immigrant Women Workers in Quebec," Women's Studies, 13 (1987): 273–93.

13. Related to both the notion of household adaptation and that of strategies is the issue of household sponsorship of migration. One can take an ex post facto approach and claim that those people in migrant households who stay behind to assume the tasks of daily household reproduction—to work and to care for the children—are in fact "sponsoring" the migrant worker for capitalist production; this approach emphasizes that households in the migrant-sending areas absorb the costs of reproduction generally assigned to capitalist firms in the migrant-

receiving areas. Not uncommonly, though, this line of argument is used to suggest that the household "sends" or "sponsors" a migrant.

14. I am grateful to María Patricia Fernández-Kelly for suggesting the use of this visual tool to illustrate the relationship between these three different levels of analyses.

CHAPTER FIVE: RECONSTRUCTING GENDER THROUGH IMMIGRATION AND SETTLEMENT

1. According to Rouse, Mexican immigrant men are primarily ambivalent about the class transformations that migration brings about because it signifies a loss of their independence as small, peasant producers. Rouse found that men of rural origin who had settled in the United States "were particularly critical of the ways in which the rhythms and routines of proletarian labor impinged on their sense of independence. . . . They also criticized the forces that challenged their authority within the home" (1992:38). In a study of Mexican migrants from the rural village of Las Animas in Zacatecas, Goldring also found that the men expressed strong preferences to return and retire in Mexico, while the women emphasized preferences to stay in the United States. According to Goldring (forthcoming), these divergent views reflect "gendered memory" of rurality and the division of labor by gender; the Mexican village is alluring to the men because it represents the place of retirement, while for the women, it represents not only continued housework responsibilities, but housework that involves more drudgery than in the United States. In Oakview, I found that men from urban as well as rural areas of Mexico expressed a desire to return to Mexico, while their wives did not.

2. Length of separation does not always equal the sum of years from the husband's first departure after marriage until the wife's migration because in some cases the husbands interrupted their U.S. stays by returning home to Mexico to stay for a few years before resuming their migration careers. This pattern was most prevalent among the pre-1965 migrants. Years of marital separation were calculated according to respondents' best estimates. In most cases, this included both the husband's and the wife's estimates.

3. The co-dependency group was organized by a Chicana social worker operating out of the local community center, where the meetings were held. In addition to the Mexican immigrant women, a few immigrant women from Central America and one from South America attended the evening meetings. All of them attended because their spouses, boyfriends, and sons abused alcohol or drugs. The meetings featured open discussion and guest speakers (I once gave an update on changes in IRCA, the Immigration Reform and Control Act). The group's very lively discussions did not rigidly focus only on substance-abuse issues. In fact, a good deal of the time, the discussions resembled feminist consciousness-raising activities.

4. Survey research conducted among return migrants in Mexico showed that while married temporary migrant women had lower employment rates in the U.S. than their single peers, they were more likely to enjoy higher occupational prestige and higher wages than their single counterparts. The positive correlation

of higher wage rates with marriage and childbearing, however, may simply reflect the fact that married women are more likely to have the option of not working (Kossoudji and Ranney, 1984). Single women's lower wages and occupational prestige also reflect their concentration in live-in domestic work, a job that married migrant women are less likely to take.

5. As I approached the completion of fieldwork for this study, I realized that by not including interviews with children and adolescents, I had overlooked their participation in the migration and resettlement processes.

6. Mexican undocumented immigrant women interviewed by Argüelles (1990) in Arizona and New Mexico, and in San Diego and Los Angeles, California, also reported that isolation and loneliness characterized their lives in the United States.

7. In a study of Mexican migrants who work seasonally in the United States, Guendelman and Pérez-Itriaga (1987) found that egalitarian marital relations established when both spouses were working in California reverted back to more patriarchal arrangements when the families moved back to Mexico.

8. In *Family and Social Network*, a seminal study of working-class community life in Britain, Elizabeth Bott (1971) found that spouses shared the same extended family and friendship networks when conjugal roles overlapped, while separate networks prevailed when spouses maintained distinct, separate roles in family life. Among the Mexican immigrants in Oakview, the families that approached what Bott called overlapping "conjugal roles" prior to migration were more likely than other families to share network resources for migration. These networks, however, generally involved the wives' kin.

CHAPTER SIX: WOMEN CONSOLIDATING SETTLEMENT

1. Mexican undocumented immigrant women may have even higher rates of labor-force participation than documented immigrant women. One study conducted in San Diego found employment rates of 47.5 percent for documented women, and 63 percent for undocumented women (Chavez et al., 1986).

2. Women's activities which occur internally in the family may also enhance family social status in the community and, by doing so, indirectly promote settlement. Papanek (1979) has suggested that women's support for the income-earning activities of other family members, socialization of children, and religious and ritual observances constitute "status-production work." Yanagisako (1977) and di Leonardo (1987) examine women's work in solidifying and maintaining kinship ties. This chapter emphasizes women's activities that occur external to the family, and which link the family to U.S. society.

3. Two electronics assembly firms and a few machine shops are located in Oakview, and many others in the nearby Silicon Valley. Few people in the community traveled to the Silicon Valley to work in the electronic assembly firms, and the machine shops that assemble electronics and fabricate and paint plastic parts in Oakview hire mostly citizen women and men, including second-generation Mexican immigrants and Chicanos and Asian immigrants. A Mexican immigrant woman with whom I became friends, but who did not participate in the study, worked at the largest electronics firm in Oakview, where she was also in

charge of recruiting new workers (in fact, she tried to recruit me). Legal resident papers were required, so she had difficulty seeking Mexican employees. Moreover, many Mexican immigrant women did not wish to work in assembly because the pay was lower—starting hourly wages were $5.50 before taxes—than what they might potentially earn by cleaning houses, and assembly workers were frequently subject to layoffs or reduced schedules. When I visited this electronics assembly firm, most of the workers were Asian immigrant women.

4. The men completed the INS legal permanent resident application with an affidavit of support testifying to financial responsibility provided by kin, a close friend, or the employer.

5. Restaurant employers were not the first ones to encourage Mexican migrant workers to stay. Agricultural and railroad-company employers in the late nineteenth and early twentieth centuries also found that encouraging family migration helped to stabilize their male Mexican migrant work force (Taylor, 1929; González, 1983).

6. The husbands of these women obtained legal status through employer certification, and once a husband agreed to sponsor his wife's migration, she too obtained legal status. The men, however, did not always automatically share their legal status.

7. Rollins points out that while census figures show that the domestic occupation is declining, these figures are misleading because of widespread underreporting practices. Census data underestimate the numbers of both African American and immigrant women in the occupation (1985:56–57).

8. As U.S. citizen women have entered paid work, they—not their male partners—remain primarily responsible for either doing or finding someone to do housecleaning and child care (Hertz, 1986; Hochschild, 1989).

9. Margarita Cervantes, for example, found the isolation intolerable after having worked amid friends and kin as a motel maid. She experienced private housecleaning as "nothing but your own thoughts and conversations rumbling around in your head." Although she would earn less as a motel maid, she quit domestic work to return to the social environment of motel cleaning, where kin, friends, and acquaintances from her Zacatecas village worked; eventually she turned to street vending. Her experience, however, is not representative, as most undocumented immigrant women who find a niche in paid domestic work stay with it for long periods of time.

10. Survey data collected among return migrant women in Mexico in 1978 and 1979 also indicate that the pay they receive for domestic work in the U.S. is low: 97 percent of the women who had worked in private households in the U.S. reported earning less than ten dollars a day (Kossoudji and Ranney, 1984:1124–25). These low wage rates, however, were supplemented with "payment in kind" in the form of room and board, as two-thirds of these women had worked in live-in arrangements.

11. In 1993, Bill Clinton's nominations of Zoe Baird and then Kimba Woods for U.S. attorney general failed because these nominees had hired undocumented immigrant women as nannies and domestic workers (Woods did so before employer sanctions went into effect, but this fact did not exonerate her). Legal-service providers in immigrant communities across the nation report that as a result of

the Zoe Baird hearings, many employers requested that undocumented immigrant women working as domestic workers show documents proving legal status (personal communication from Martha F. Davis, attorney at NOW Legal Defense Fund, New York, and from Nancy Cervantes, attorney at CHIRLA, the Coalition for Humane Immigrant Rights in Los Angeles, March 1993). In the wake of these Justic Department fiascos, more public figures, especially those in elite political circles, will no doubt now be reluctant to hire undocumented immigrants as domestic workers.

12. In a study of Mexican migrants in the Midwest, Chavira (1988:71) characterizes the women's activities as "subsidy providers." She found that "women always carry, handle, and store all the family's documents and handle all bureaucratic matters affecting the family. . . . They function, as well, as cultural brokers as they introduce the family to the medical bureaucratic culture." In a study conducted among Mexican immigrant women in Santa Barbara, California, O'Conner (1990:88) found an "increase in all-female networks and their role informing immigrants about government agencies. . . . " O'Conner (ibid.) notes, however, that these "immigrants still do not receive adequate services from formal government and private agencies."

13. Health insurance is generally tied to employment, but even though Latinos have a higher rate of labor-force participation than any other racial-ethnic group in California, they have the lowest rate of health-insurance coverage. Many immigrants and U.S.-born Latinos do not have employer-sponsored health insurance because they work for small firms with fewer than twenty-five employees, or they work in informal-sector jobs (Rodríguez, 1992).

14. Medi-Cal is California's health-care system for low-income Californians. Undocumented Latina immigrant women surveyed in the San Francisco Bay area cited medical care as one of their top three social-service needs (Hogeland and Rosen, 1990), and another study found that 81 percent of Mexican undocumented immigrants surveyed in San Diego County lacked private medical insurance (Rumbaut et al., 1988:159). Eighty-four percent of undocumented respondents in the same San Diego study reported that they had paid for their most recent medical bill out of personal funds (ibid.: 172).

15. Surveyors in a San Francisco study reported of an undocumented immigrant woman, that "when the labor pains started, she felt like crying. Not because of the pains, but thinking in how much the bill was going to be and how they were going to pay for it" (Hogeland and Rosen, 1990:65). Still, many Mexican undocumented immigrant women do give birth in U.S. hospitals. In Los Angeles County, which has the highest concentration of Mexican undocumented immigrants of any U.S. metropolitan area, David Heer (1990) found that 18.6 percent of all births in 1980–81 involved at least one parent of Mexican origin and the mother undocumented.

16. The practice of returning to Mexico for childbirth had the unanticipated, deleterious effect of disqualifying these women for amnesty legalization because it interrupted continuous residence in the U.S. from the cutoff date of January 1, 1982.

17. An important part of new immigrants' consumer activities revolves around their roles as apartment renters. For an analysis of the impact of Latino

immigrant apartment renters on economic and ethnic intergroup relations, see Hagan and Rodríguez (1992).

18. In Oakview, and throughout the San Francisco Bay area, private attorneys charged an average of $1,000 to file the necessary forms for a couple. At the Catholic Charities legalization programs, individuals were charged $300, or special family rates of $480. Together with medical examinations ($70 to $120 per person), INS application fees ($185 per individual or $420 per family), and notarized letters and documents ($10 each), the application procedure was an expensive proposition. In immigrant communities everywhere, an entrepreneurial army quickly positioned itself to reap lucrative profits from amnesty legalization.

19. Foundations made credit available for the amnesty-legalization procedure, but most immigrants preferred the installment payment plan. Many applicants distrusted the credit plans because of the "public charge" clause in the amnesty regulations. Applicants feared that any indicator of their likelihood to become a "public charge" would invalidate their applications.

20. Cárdenas and Flores's (1986:36–37) study of undocumented Mexican immigrant settlers in Houston, Texas, revealed that the majority had purchased television sets, radios, furniture, automobiles, and household appliances.

21. IRCA, along with mandating employer sanctions and a legalization program, also affected the public-assistance eligibility for immigrants. Amnesty-legalization applicants became ineligible to receive most public benefits for five years, until they would become eligible for U.S. citizenship. Under IRCA, the state must also verify the immigration status of all "alien applicants" for AFDC, Medicaid, food stamps, educational grants and housing assistance, and even unemployment compensation. In this nationwide verification system, an applicant must provide his or her alien registration document (the so-called green card) so that the A-number (the "alien" identification number) can be checked through INS computer data-base systems. The INS lobbied on behalf of this program before Congress, arguing that it would be a cost-effective means of saving taxpayers' money. Pilot projects conducted in various states were first implemented in 1984 under the Systematic Alien Verification for Entitlement program, or SAVE. A report issued by the General Accounting Office in 1987 found inconclusive evidence that SAVE did in fact save taxpayer resources (GAO, October 1987). The one area in which SAVE did prove cost-effective was unemployment compensation, which is paid into by potential beneficiaries. Here the GAO reported that in four of the six states where SAVE had prevented undocumented immigrant workers from cashing in on their unemployment compensation, the SAVE costs of computer tracking and verification totalled approximately $127,000 while savings (or the amount denied undocumented workers in unemployment compensation) totaled $3.1 million. The new regulations are rationalized on the basis that the beneficiary of unemployment compensation must be legally available and authorized to work in order to receive benefits.

22. Cornelius's (1981:35) survey of undocumented settlers in California and Illinois found that only 2 to 3 percent had received welfare (usually in the form of AFDC for U.S.-born citizen children); fewer than 3 percent reported receiving

free health care, none reported receiving food stamps, and 4 to 7 percent reported receiving unemployment compensation. In Cárdenas and Flores's
(1986:38) study of eighty-seven long-term undocumented immigrant women in
Houston, Texas, only two women reported ever having received AFDC payments, and none had received unemployment compensation or even assistance
from Catholic charities. A survey of five thousand amnesty applicants enrolled
in English classes in California showed that 90 percent of pre-1982 applicants
stated that they had never collected food stamps, and more than 90 percent said
they had never received General Assistance, AFDC, Social Security benefits or
Supplemental Security Income (Comprehensive Adult Student Assessment System, 1989). The Los Angeles Parents' Survey conducted by David Heer in
1980–81 found higher levels of public-assistance utilization. Heer (1990:157–
159) found that nearly 19 percent of all families where the mother was a
Mexican undocumented immigrant had received some food-stamp income and
AFDC assistance. These families, however, had received substantially smaller
amounts than those families where the mother was a legal immigrant or a U.S.
citizen.

23. One study based on participant observation and interviews in the pov-
erty-stricken region of South Texas found that among 52 Mexican immigrant
households with at least one documented family member, approximately 77 percent had received food stamps, and 25 percent had received other forms of
assistance, such as Social Security, SSI, AFDC, and unemployment compensation
(Briody, 1987:40). A San Francisco survey that employed community workers
found that, of 345 undocumented Latina immigrant women, 29 percent had
never looked for services of any type in the U.S. While the majority of women
reported that fear of deportation prevented them from seeking help, Mexican
women were less likely than Central American women to correlate fear of deportation with fear of seeking services (Hogeland and Rosen, 1990:63).

24. That undocumented immigrants sometimes utilize public assistance first
came to my attention during the early weeks of my field research, when I worked
with a grass-roots neighborhood-based group that organized a public informational forum on IRCA and the amnesty-eligibility provisions. After a basic pres-
entation, we divided the four hundred attendees into different classrooms where
attorneys addressed specific eligibility problems. One classroom was reserved for
prior recipients of public cash assistance, and that session was attended exclusively by women, most of whom came with small children in tow. I learned about
my respondents' past use of public assistance and debt as I assisted with their
legalization applications.

25. Undocumented immigrants are eligible to receive WIC and restricted
Medi-Cal coverage for emergency and pregnancy services, and ineligible undocumented immigrant parents may apply for their U.S.-citizen children to receive
AFDC, food stamps, and SSI. Under WIC, undocumented immigrant women
may receive supplemental food, nutrition counseling, and referrals to health care
if they are pregnant, postpartum, or breast-feeding, and if they or their children
are "at nutritional risk" (National Immigration Law Center, 1991, 1993).

26. None of the people in my study were involved as participants or observers of the local weekend soccer matches. A nephew living in Teresa and

Eudoro Ibarra's household was the only person I met who played in the local soccer league.

27. Participant observation allowed me to learn about associational behavior. Had I relied on only interviews or survey methods, I probably would have obtained less accurate indicators of this involvement. This became evident to me when I worked at the Catholic parish legalization clinic, where together with other volunteers, I assisted in filling out amnesty-legalization applications. One of the questions on the form asked about participation or membership in organizations, political parties, or social clubs. Almost without exception, applicants reported no associational activities, but in fact, many of them participated in some church, school, or community group.

28. In an important essay, di Leonardo introduced the concept of kin work to refer to "the conception, maintenance, and ritual celebration of cross-household kin ties, including visits, letters, telephone calls, presents, and cards to kin; the organization of holiday gatherings; . . . the mental work of reflection about all these activities." (1987:442–43).

29. None of the families in this study were involved in evangelical churches, although at least one family regularly received boxes of food from one of these churches. Many Central American and Mexican immigrants are drawn to the small, storefront evangelical Protestant churches scattered throughout Los Angeles, but these churches were not very popular in the Oakview barrio during the late 1980s. Moore and Vigil (1993) note that in East Los Angles, these storefront evangelical churches provide important sources of social and economic support for poor Mexican immigrants.

30. For an analysis and discussion of liberation theology's impact on Latina feminism and activism, see Isasi-Díaz and Tarango (1988).

CHAPTER SEVEN: GENDERED IMMIGRATION

1. Others who have made this observation suggest retaining a more modified use of the term "household" (e.g., Grasmuck and Pessar, 1991; Rouse, 1987). In a study of Mexican immigration, Roger Rouse (1987) suggests that we use the term "household projects" so as not to privilege collective over individual goals. In a study of young women's employment in Java, Diane Wolf suggests the term "household practices" as a reference to all household members' activities, decisions, and interactions. While the term "household practices" avoids many of the problems with the household-strategies model, it holds little explanatory power for the study of immigration. As Wolf (1992:263) wisely notes, "The most compelling view of the household comes from *unbundling* these relations, interactions, and activities. We should concern ourselves not only with the results of individual or household-level action, but also with the *process* involved in reaching that decision or action."

2. This observation is inspired by Barrie Thorne's (1993) research and perspective of children as actors in their own right.

3. The national conference on immigrant and refugee women, titled "Dreams Lost, Dreams Found: Women Organizing for Justice," was held in Berkeley, California, October 5–7, 1991, and was sponsored by the Family

Violence Prevention Fund and the Coalition for Immigrant and Refugee Rights and Services, a San Francisco Bay–area coalition that includes over eighty-five organizations.

4. Mexican-born youth and U.S.-born youth of Mexican descent do not always socialize together. In a study conducted in East Los Angeles, where recent immigration has "Mexicanized" Chicano neighborhoods, Moore and Vigil (1993) report that the White Fence gang prides itself on recruiting only U.S.-born Chicanos.

5. According to Heisler (1986), the governments of these immigrant-sending countries maintain immigrants' connections to political and social institutions in their home society. Embassies and consulates engage staffs of legal experts, social workers, and teachers who operate special schools in the language of origin for immigrants in Western Europe. Religious organizations, trade unions, and political parties from the immigrants' countries of origin also maintain representation.

References

Acker, Joan. 1992. "From Sex Roles to Gendered Institutions." *Contemporary Sociology*, 21:565–69.

Acuña, Rudolfo. 1981. *Occupied America: A History of Chicanos*. New York: Harper and Row.

Ahern, Susan, Dexter Bryan, and Reynaldo Baca. 1985. "Migration and La Mujer Fuerte." *Migration Today*, 13 (1): 14–20.

Alarcón, Rafael. 1988. "El proceso de 'nortenización': Impacto de la migración internacional en Chavinda, Michoacán." Pp. 337–53 in Thomas Calvo and Gustavo Lopez, editors, *Movimientos de población en el occidente de México*. Zamora, Michoacán, Mexico: El Colegio de Michoacán.

Alba, Francisco. 1978. "Mexico's International Migration as a Manifestation of its Development Pattern." *International Migration Review*, 12:502–13.

Alejo, Franciso Javier. 1983. "Demographic Patterns and Labor Market Trends in Mexico." Pp. 79–89 in Donald L. Wyman, editor, *Mexico's Economic Crisis: Challenges and Opportunities*. Monograph Series, no. 12. La Jolla, Calif.: Center for U.S.-Mexican Studies, University of California at San Diego.

Álvarez, Robert, Jr. 1987. *Familia: Migration and Adaptation in Baja and Alta California, 1880–1975*. Berkeley: University of California Press.

Amado, Pablo Comesana. 1990. "Madres y sacerdotes solicitan trabajo para pandilleros de puerta en puerta." *La Opinión*, May 2.

Argüelles, Lourdes. 1990. "Undocumented Female Labor in the United States Southwest: An Essay on Migration, Consciousness, Oppression and Struggle." Pp. 299–312 in Adelaida R. Del Castillo, *Between Borders: Essays on Mexicana/Chicana History*. Encino, Calif.: Floricanto Press.

Arizpe, Lourdes. 1977. "Women in the Informal Labor Sector: The Case of Mexico City." *Signs: Journal of Women in Culture and Society*, 3:25–37.

———. 1978. *Migración, etnicismo y cambio económico*. Mexico City: Centro de Estudios Sociológicos, El Colegio de México.

———. 1979. *Indígenas en la ciudad de México: El caso de las 'Marías.'* Mexico City: Sep Diana.

———. 1981a. "Relay Migration and the Survival of the Peasant Household." Pp. 187–210 in Jorge Balán, editor, *Why People Move: Comparative Perspectives on the Dynamics of Internal Migration*. Paris: Unesco Press.

———. 1981b. "The Rural Exodus in Mexico and Mexican Migration to the U.S." *International Migration Review,* 15:626–49.

Arizpe, Lourdes, and Josefina Aranda. 1981. "The 'Comparative Advantages' of Women's Disadvantages: Women Workers in the Strawberry Export Agribusiness in Mexico." *Signs: Journal of Women in Culture and Society*, 7:453–73.

Baca, Reynaldo, and Dexter Bryan. 1981. "Mexican Undocumented Workers in the Binational Community: A Research Note." *International Migration Review*, 15:737–48.

———. 1985. "Mexican Women, Migration and Sex Roles." *Migration Today,* 13 (3): 14–18.

Bach, Robert L. 1978. "Mexican Immigration and U.S. Immigration Reforms in the 1960's." *Kapitalistate,* 7:63–80.

Bach, Robert L., and Howard Brill. 1990. "Shifting the Burden: The Impacts of IRCA on U.S. Labor Markets." Interim report to the Division of Immigration Policy and Research, U.S. Department of Labor.

Bach, Robert L., and Lisa A. Schraml. 1982. "Migration Crisis and Theoretical Conflict." *International Migration Review,* 16:320–41.

Balán, Jorge, Harley L. Browning, and Elizabeth Jelin. 1973. *Men in a Developing Society.* Institute for Latin American Studies. Austin: University of Texas Press.

Balderrama, Francisco. 1982. *In Defense of La Raza: The Los Angeles Mexican Consulate and the Mexican Community, 1929–1936.* Tucson: University of Arizona Press.

Barkin, David. 1987. "The End to Food Self-Sufficiency in Mexico." *Latin American Perspectives,* 14:271–97.

Barrera, Mario. 1979. *Race and Class in the Southwest: A Theory of Racial Inequality.* Notre Dame, Ind.: University of Notre Dame Press.

Bean, Frank D., Allan G. King, and Jeffrey S. Passel. 1983. "The Number of Illegal Migrants of Mexican Origin in the United States: Sex Ratio-Based Estimates for 1980." *Demography,* 20:99–109.

———. 1986. "Estimates of the Size of the Illegal Migrant Population of Mexican Origin in the United States: An Assessment, Review and Proposal." Pp. 13–36 in Harley Browning and Rudolfo O. de la Garza, editors, *Mexican Immigrants and Mexican Americans: An Evolving Relation.* Austin: Center for Mexican American Studies Publications, University of Texas Press.

Bean, Frank D., Georges Vernez, and Charles B. Keely. 1989. *Opening and Closing the Doors: Evaluating Immigration Reform and Control.* Santa Monica, Calif., and Washington, D.C.: Rand Corporation and the Urban Institute.

Bean, Frank D., Thomas J. Espenshade, Michael J. White, and Robert F. Dymowski. 1990. "Post-IRCA Changes in the Volume and Composition of Unauthorized Migration to the United States: An Assessment Based on Apprehension Data." Pp. 111–58 in Frank D. Bean, Barry Edmonston, and Jeffrey S. Passel, editors, *Unauthorized Migration to California: IRCA and the Experience of the 1980s*. Washington, D.C.: Urban Institute Press.

Benería, Lourdes. 1979. "Reproduction, Production, and the Sexual Division of Labor." *Cambridge Journal of Economics*. 3:203–25.

———. 1992. "The Mexican Debt Crisis: Restructuring the Economy and the Household." Pp. 83–104 in Lourdes Benería and Shelley Feldman, editors, *Unequal Burden: Economic Crises, Persistent Poverty, and Women's Work*. Boulder, Colo.: Westview Press.

Benería, Lourdes, and Martha Roldán. 1987. *The Crossroads of Class and Gender: Industrial Homework, Subcontracting and Household Dynamics in Mexico City*. Chicago and London: University of Chicago Press.

Benería, Lourdes, and Gita Sen. 1981. "Accumulation, Reproduction, and Women's Role in Economic Development: Boserup Revisited." *Signs: Journal of Women in Culture and Society*, 7:279–97.

Beuchler, Judith-Maria Hess. 1976. "Introduction to 'Women and Migration,'" *Anthropological Quarterly*, 49:1–76.

Blau, F. 1984. "The Use of Transfer Payments by Immigrants." *Industrial and Labor Relations Review*, 37:222–39.

Blood, Robert O., and Donald M. Wolfe. 1960. *Husbands and Wives*. New York: Free Press.

Blumberg, Rae Lesser. 1991. "Introduction: The 'Triple Overlap' of Gender Stratification, Economy and Family." Pp. 7–32 in Rae Lesser Blumberg, editor, *Gender, Family and Economy: The Triple Overlap*. Newbury Park, Calif.: Sage.

Blumstein, Philip, and Pepper Schwartz. 1983. *American Couples: Money, Work and Sex*. New York: William Morrow.

Bogardus, Emory S. 1934. *The Mexican in the United States*. School of Research Studies, no. 5. Los Angeles: University of Southern California Press.

Bohning, W. R. 1972. *The Migration of Workers in the United Kingdom and the European Community*. Published for the Institute of Race Relations. London: Oxford University Press.

Bonacich, Edna. 1990. *Asian and Latino Immigrants in the Los Angeles Garment Industry: An Exploration of the Relationship between Capitalism and Racial Oppression*. Working Papers in the Social Sciences, vol. 5, no. 13. Los Angeles: Institute for Social Science Research, UCLA.

Bott, Elizabeth. 1971. *Family and Social Network*. New York: Free Press.

Brettel, Caroline B., and Patricia A. deBerjeois. 1992. "Anthropology and the Study of Immigrant Women." Pp. 41–63 in Donna Gabaccia, editor, *Seeking Common Ground: Multidisciplinary Studies of Immigrant Women in the United States*. Westport, Conn.: Greenwood Press.

Brettel, Caroline B., and Rita James Simon. 1986. "Immigrant Women: An Introduction." Pp. 3–20 in Rita James Simon and Caroline B. Brettel, editors, *International Migration: The Female Experience*. Totowa, N.J.: Rowman & Allanheld Publishers.

Briody, Elizabeth. 1987. "Patterns of Household Immigration into South Texas." *International Migration Review*, 21:27–47.

Broom L., and J. H. Smith. 1963. "Bridging Occupations." *British Journal of Sociology*, 14:321–34.

Browner, Carole. 1986. "Gender Roles and Social Change: A Mexican Case Study." *Ethnology*, 25:89–106.

Browning, Harley L., and Nestor Rodríguez. 1982. "Mexico-U.S.A. Indocumentado Migration as a Settlement Process and Its Implications for Work." Paper prepared for the Hispanic Labor Conference, University of California at Santa Barbara, February 4–5.

———. 1985. "The Migration of Mexican Indocumentados as a Settlement Process: Implications for Work." Pp. 277–97 in George J. Borjas and Marta Tienda, editors, *Hispanics in the U.S. Economy*. Institute for Research on Poverty Monograph Series. New York: Academic Press.

Brubaker, William Rogers. 1989. "Membership without Citizenship: The Economic and Social Rights of Noncitizens." Pp. 145–65 in William Rogers Brubaker, editor, *Immigration and the Politics of Citizenship in Europe and North America*. Lanham, Md.: University Press of America.

Burawoy, Michael. 1976. "The Functions and Reproduction of Migrant Labor: Comparative Material from Southern Africa and the United States." *American Journal of Sociology*, 81:1050–87.

Bustamante, Jorge A. 1975. *Espaldas mojadas: Materia prima para le expansion del capital norteamericano*. Cuadernos del Centro de Estudios Sociologicos, no. 9. México, D.F.: El Colegio de México.

———. 1990. "Undocumented Migration from Mexico to the United States: Preliminary Findings of the Zapata Canyon Project." Pp. 211–26 in Frank D. Bean, Barry Edmonston, and Jeffrey S. Passel., editors, *Unauthorized Migration to California: IRCA and the Experience of the 1980s*. Washington, D.C.: Urban Institute Press.

Calavita, Kitty. 1989. "The Immigration Policy Debate: Critical Analyses and Future Options." Pp. 151–77 in Wayne A. Cornelius and Jorge A. Bustamante, editors, *Mexican Migration to the United States*. La Jolla, Calif.: Center for U.S.-Mexican Studies, University of California at San Diego.

Camarillo, Albert. 1979. *Chicanos in a Changing Society*. Cambridge, Mass.: Harvard University Press.

Cárdenas, Gilberto, and Estevan T. Flores. 1986. *The Migration and Settlement of Undocumented Women*. Austin: Center for Mexican American Studies, University of Texas.

Cardoso, Lawrence A. 1980. *Mexican Emigration to the United States, 1897–1931*. Tucson: University of Arizona Press.

Carrerras, Mercedes. 1974. *Los Mexicanos que devolvio a la crisis, 1929–1932*. Mexico City: Secretaria de Relaciones Exteriores.

Carrillo, Teresa. 1986. "The Women's Movement and the Left in Mexico: The Presidential Candidacy of Doña Rosario Ibarra." Pp. 96–113 in Teresa Córdova et al., editors, *Chicana Voices: Intersections of Class, Race, and Gender*. Austin: Center for Mexican American Studies, University of Texas.

———. 1990. "Women and Independent Unionism in the Garment Industry." Pp. 213–33 in Joe Foweraker and Ann L. Craig, editors, *Popular Movements and Political Change in Mexico*. Boulder, Colo., and London: Lynne Rienner Publishers.

CASAS (Comprehensive Adult Student Assessment System). 1989. *A Survey of Newly Legalized Persons in California*. Prepared for the California Health and Welfare Agency. San Diego: Comprehensive Adult Student Assessment System.

Castells, Manuel. 1975. "Immigrant Workers and Class Struggle in Advanced Capitalism: The Western European Experiences." *Politics and Society,* 5:33–66.

Chant, Sylvia. 1991. *Women and Survival in Mexican Cities: Perspectives on Gender, Labour Markets, and Low-Income Households*. Manchester and New York: Manchester University Press.

Chavez, Leo R. 1985. "Households, Migration and Labor Market Participation: The Adaptation of Mexicans to Life in the United States." *Urban Anthropology,* 14:301–46.

———. 1988. "Settlers and Sojourners: The Case of Mexicans in California." *Human Organization,* 47:95–108.

———. 1991. *Shadowed Lives: Mexican Undocumented Immigrants*. Case Studies in Cultural Anthropology Series. Fort Worth, Tex.: Harcourt Brace Jovanovich.

Chavez, Leo R., Wayne A. Cornelius, and Oliver William Jones. 1986. "Utilization of Health Services by Mexican Immigrant Women in San Diego." *Women and Health,* 11:3–20.

Chavez, Leo R., Estevan T. Flores, and Marta Lopez-Garza. 1989. "Migrants and Settlers: A Comparison of Undocumented Mexicans and Central Americans in the United States." *Frontera Norte,* 1:49–75.

Chavira, Alicia. 1988. *"Tienes Que Ser Valiente:* Mexican Migrants in a Midwestern Farm Labor Camp." Pp. 64–73 in Margarita B. Melville, editor, *Mexicanas at Work in the United States*. Mexican American Studies Monograph no. 5. Houston, Tex.: University of Houston.

Cockcroft, James D. 1983. *Mexico: Class Formations, Capital Accumulation and the State*. New York: Monthly Review Press.

———. 1986. *Outlaws in the Promised Land*. New York: Grove Press.

Colen, Shellee. 1989. "'Just a Little Respect': West Indian Domestic Workers in New York City." Pp. 171–94 in Elsa M. Chaney and Mary Garcia Castro, editors, *Muchachas No More: Household Workers in Latin America and the Caribbean*. Philadelphia: Temple University Press.

Collins, Patricia Hill. 1990. *Black Feminist Thought*. Boston: Unwin Hyman.

Cordera Campos, Rolando, and Enrique González Tiburcio. 1989. "Percances y damnificados de la crisis economica." In Cordera Campos et al., editors, *México: El reclamo democratico*. México, D.F.: Siglo Veintiuno Editores.

Cornelius, Wayne A. 1976. "Outmigration from Rural Mexican Communities." In *The Dynamics of Migration: International Migration*. Interdisciplinary Communications Program, Occasional Monograph Series, vol. 2, no. 5. Washington, D.C.: Smithsonian Institution.

————. 1982. "Interviewing Undocumented Immigrants: Methodological Reflections Based on Fieldwork in Mexico and the U.S." *International Migration Review,* 16:378–411.

————. 1988. "*Los Migrantes de la Crisis:* The Changing Profile of Mexican Labor Migration to California in the 1980s." Paper presented at the conference, Population and Work in Regional Settings. El Colegio de Michoacán, Zamora, Michoacán, Mexico, November 28–30.

————. 1989a. "Impacts of the 1986 U.S. Immigration Law on Emigration from Rural Mexican Sending Communities." *Population and Development Review,* 15: 689–706.

————. 1989b. "The U.S. Demand for Mexican Labor." Pp. 25–47 in Wayne A. Cornelius and Jorge A. Bustamante, editors, *Mexican Migration to the United States.* La Jolla, Calif.: Center for U.S.-Mexican Studies, University of California at San Diego.

————. 1992. "From Sojourners to Settlers: The Changing Profile of Mexican Immigration to the United States." Pp. 155–95 in Jorge A. Bustamante, Clark W. Reynolds, and Raúl A. Hinojosa Ojeda, editors, *U.S.-Mexico Relations: Labor Market Interdependence.* Stanford, Calif.: Stanford University Press.

Cornelius, Wayne A., Leo R. Chavez, and Oliver William Jones. 1982. *Mexican Immigrants and Southern California: A Summary of Current Knowledge.* La Jolla, Calif.: Center for U.S.-Mexican Studies, University of California at San Diego.

Corwin, Arthur F., and Lawrence A. Cordoso. 1978. "Vamos al Norte: Causes of Mass Mexican Migration," Pp. 38–66 in in Arthur F. Corwin, editor, *Immigrants—and Immigrants: Perspectives on Mexican Labor Migration to the United States.* Westport, Conn.: Greenwood Press, 1978.

Corwin, Arthur F., and Johnny M. McCain. 1978. "Wetbackism since 1964: A Catalogue of Factors." Pp. 67–107 in Arthur F. Corwin, editor, *Immigrants—and Immigrants: Perspectives on Mexican Labor Migration to the United States.* Westport, Conn.: Greenwood Press, 1978.

Cromwell, R. E., and R. A. Ruiz. 1979. "The Myth of Macho Dominance in Decision-Making within Mexican and Chicano Families." *Hispanic Journal of Behavioral Sciences,* 1:355–75.

Cross, Harry E., and James A. Sandos. 1981. *Across the Border: Rural Development in Mexico and Recent Migration to the United States.* Institute of Governmental Studies, University of California at Berkeley.

Crummet, María de los Angeles. 1987. "Rural Women and Migration in Latin America." Pp. 239–64 in Carmen Diane Deere and Magdalena León de Leal, editors, *Rural Women and State Policy: Feminist Perspectives on Latin American Agricultural Development.* Boulder, Colo., and London: Westview Press.

Curry-Rodríguez, Julia E. 1988. "Labor Migration and Familial Responsibilities: Experiences of Mexican Women." Pp. 47–63 in Margarita B. Melville, editor, *Mexicanas at Work in the United States.* Mexican American Studies Monograph no. 5. Houston, Tex.: University of Houston.

Dagodag, Tim W. 1975. "Source Regions and Composition of Illegal Mexican Immigration to California." *International Migration Review,* 9:499–511.

Davis, Marilyn. 1990. *Mexican Voices, American Dreams*. New York: Henry Holt and Company.

de la Peña, Guillermo. 1984. "Ideology and Practice in Southern Jalisco: Peasants, Rancheros and Urban Entrepreneurs." Pp. 204–34 in Raymond T. Smith, editor, *Kinship and Practice in Latin America*. Chapel Hill: University of North Carolina Press.

de la Torre, Adela, and Beatríz M. Pesquera, editors. 1993. *Building with Our Hands: New Directions in Chicana Studies*. Berkeley: University of California Press.

Delgado, Héctor L. 1993. *New Immigrants, Old Unions: Organizing Undocumented Workers in Los Angeles*. Philadelphia: Temple University Press.

Deutsch, Sarah. 1987. *No Separate Refuge: Culture, Class and Gender on an Anglo-Hispanic Frontier in the American Southwest, 1880–1940*. New York and Oxford: Oxford University Press.

di Leonardo, Micaela. 1987. "The Female World of Cards and Holidays: Women, Families, and the Work of Kinship." *Signs: Journal of Women in Culture and Society*, 12:440–53.

Dinerman, Ina R. 1978. "Patterns of Adaptation among Households of U.S.-bound Migrants from Michoacán, Mexico." *International Migration Review*, 12:485–501.

———. 1982. *Migrants and Stay-at-Homes: A Comparative Study of Rural Migration from Michoacán, Mexico*. Monograph Series, no. 5. La Jolla, Calif.: Center for U.S.-Mexico Studies, University of California at San Diego.

Donato, Katharine M. Forthcoming. "Current Trends and Patterns of Female Migration: Evidence from Mexico." *International Migration Review*.

Donato, Katharine M., Jorge Durand, and Douglas S. Massey. 1992. "Stemming the Tide? Assessing the Deterrent Effects of the Immigration Reform and Control Act." *Demography*, 29:139–57.

Durand, Jorge, and Douglas S. Massey. 1992. "Mexican Migration to the United States: A Critical Review." *Latin American Research Review*, 27:3–42.

Elu de Leñero, María del Carmen. 1980. "Women's Work and Fertility." Pp. 46–68 in June Nash and Helen Icken Safa, editors, *Sex and Class in Latin America*. South Hadley, Mass.: Bergin & Garvey (first published 1976 by Praeger, New York).

Escobar Latapí, Agustín, and Mercedes González de la Rocha. 1988. "Microindustria, informalidad y crisis en Guadalajara, 1982–1988." *Estudios sociológicos*, 6:553–81.

Escobar Latapí, Agustín, Mercedes González de la Rocha, and Bryan Roberts. 1987. "Migration, Labor Markets, and the International Economy: Jalisco, Mexico and the United States." Pp. 42–64 in Jeremy Eades, editor, *Migrants, Workers, and the Social Order*. London: Tavistock.

Espín, Olivia M. 1987. "Psychological Impact of Migration on Latinas." *Psychology of Women Quarterly*, 11:489–503.

Esteva, Gustavo. 1980. *La batalla en el México rural*. México, D.F.: Siglo Veintiuno Editores.

Fatemi, Khosrow. 1987. "The Undocumented Immigrant: A Socioeconomic Profile," *Journal of Borderlands Studies*, 2:85–99.

Fernández-Kelly, María Patricia. 1983. *For We Are Sold: I and My People.* Albany: State University of New York Press.

———. 1989. "Broadening the Scope: Gender and International Economic Development." *Sociological Forum,* 4:611–35.

Fernández-Kelly, María Patricia, and Anna Garcia. 1990. "Power Surrendered, Power Restored: The Politics of Work and Family among Hispanic Garment Workers in California and Florida." Pp. 130–49 in Louise A. Tilly and Patricia Gurin, editors, *Women, Politics and Change.* New York: Russell Sage Foundation.

———. Forthcoming. "Economic Restructuring in the United States: The Case of Hispanic Women in the Garment and Electronics Industries of Southern California," in Wayne A. Cornelius, editor, *The Changing Role of Mexican Labor in the U.S. Economy: Sectoral Perspectives.* La Jolla, Calif.: Center for U.S.-Mexican Studies, University of California at San Diego.

Flores, Estevan T. 1984. "Research on Undocumented Immigrants and Public Policy: A Study of the Texas School Case." *International Migration Review,* 18:505–23.

Fox-Genovese, Elizabeth. 1983. "Antebellum Southern Households: a New Perspective on a Familiar Question." *Review,* 7:215–54.

Freeman, Gary P. 1986. "Migration and the Political Economy of the Welfare State," Pp. 51–63 in Martin Heisler and Barbara Schmitter Heisler, editors, "From Foreign Workers to Settlers?: Transnational Migration and the Emergence of New Minorities." Special issue of *Annals of the American Academy of Political and Social Science,* 485:76–86.

Freidenberg, Judith, Graciela Imperiale, and Mary Louise Skovron. 1988. "Migrant Careers and Well-Being of Women." *International Migration Review,* 22:208–25.

Galarza, Ernesto. 1964. *Merchants of Labor: The Mexican Bracero Story.* Santa Barbara, Calif.: McNally and Loftin.

Gamio, Manuel. 1971a. *The Mexican Immigrant: His Life Story.* New York: Dover Publications (first published 1930 by the University of Chicago Press).

———. 1971b. *Mexican Immigration to the United States.* New York: Dover Publications (first published 1930 by the University of Chicago Press).

García, Brígida, and Orlandina de Oliveira. 1991. "Economic Recession and Changing Determinants of Women's Work." Paper presented at the Sixteenth International Congress of the Latin American Studies Association, Washington, D.C., April 4–6.

García, Mario. 1981. *Desert Immigrants: The Mexicans of El Paso, 1880–1920.* New Haven, Conn., and London: Yale University Press.

García y Griego, Manuel. 1983. "The Importation of Mexican Contract Laborers to the United States, 1942–1964: Antecedents, Operation, and Legacy." Pp. 49–98 in Peter G. Brown and Henry Shue, editors, *The Border That Joins: Mexican Migrants and U.S. Responsibility.* Totowa, N.J.: Rowman and Littlefield.

Glenn, Evelyn Nakano. 1986. *Issei, Nisei, Warbride.* Philadelphia: Temple University Press.

Goldring, Luin. 1992. "Blurring the Border: Migration, Social Movement, and the Construction of Transnational Community." In *New Perspectives on Mexico-U.S. Migration,* proceedings of the conference organized by the Center for Latin American Studies and the Mexican Studies Program at the University of Chicago, October 23–24.

———. Forthcoming. "Gendered Memory: Reconstruction of a Rural Place of Origin by Mexican Transnational Migrants." In Melanie Du Puis and Peter Vandergeest, editors, *Nature, Rurality and Culture: The Social Construction of Rural Development and Environmental Conservation.*

González, Rosalinda M. 1983. "Chicanas and Mexican Immigrant Families 1920–1940: Women's Subordination and Family Exploitation." Pp. 59–83 in Lois Scharf and Joan M. Jensen, editors, *Decades of Discontent: The Women's Movement 1920–1940.* Westport, Conn.: Greenwood Press.

González de la Rocha, Mercedes. 1988. "Economic Crisis, Domestic Reorganisation and Women's Work in Guadalajara, Mexico." *Bulletin of Latin American Research,* vol. 7, no. 2.

———. 1989. "El poder de la ausencia: Mujeres y migración en una comunidad de los Altos de Jalisco." Paper presented at XI Coloquio de Antropología e Historia Regionales, Zamora, Michoacán, Mexico, October 25–27.

Grasmuck, Sherri. 1991. "Bringing the Family Back In: Towards an Expanded Understanding of Women's Subordination in Latin America." Paper presented at the Sixteenth International Congress of the Latin American Studies Association, Washington, D.C., April 4–6.

Grasmuck, Sherri, and Patricia R. Pessar. 1991. *Between Two Islands: Dominican International Migration.* Berkeley: University of California Press.

Grindle, Merilee. 1986. *State and Countryside: Development Policy and Agrarian Politics in Latin America.* Baltimore, Md.: Johns Hopkins University Press.

Griswold del Castillo, Richard. 1984. *La Familia: Chicano Families in the Urban Southwest, 1848 to the Present.* Notre Dame, Ind.: University of Notre Dame Press.

Guendelman, Sylvia, and Auristela Pérez-Itriaga. 1987. "Double Lives: The Changing Role of Women in Seasonal Migration." *Women's Studies,* 13:249–71.

Gutiérrez, Carlos González. 1993. "The Mexican Diaspora in California: Limits and Possibilities for the Mexican Government." Pp. 221–35 in Abraham F. Lowenthal and Katrina Burgess, editors, *The California-Mexico Connection.* Stanford, Calif.: Stanford University Press.

Gutman, Herbert G. 1977. *Work, Culture and Society in Industrializing America: Essays in American Working-Class and Social History.* New York: Vintage Books.

Hagan, Jacqueline Maria, and Nestor D. Rodríguez. 1992. "Recent Economic Restructuring and Evolving Inter-group Relations in Houston." Pp. 145–71 in Louise Lamphere, editor, *Structuring Diversity: Ethnographic Perspectives on the New Immigration.* Chicago and London: University of Chicago Press.

Hamilton, Nora, and Timothy F. Harding, editors. 1986. *Modern Mexico, State, Economy, and Social Conflict.* Beverly Hills, Calif.: Sage Publications.

Handlin, Oscar. 1973. *The Uprooted*. Boston and Toronto: Little Brown and Company (first edition, 1951).

Hardy-Fanta, Carol. 1993. *Latina Politics, Latino Politics: Gender, Culture and Political Participation in Boston*. Philadelphia: Temple University Press.

Hartmann, Heidi I. 1976. "Capitalism, Patriarchy, and Job Segregation by Sex." Pp. 137–70 in M. Blaxall and B. Reagan, editors, *Women and the Work Place*. Chicago: University of Chicago Press.

———. 1981. "The Unhappy Marriage of Marxism and Feminism: Towards a More Progressive Union." Pp. 1–41 in Lydia Sargent, editor, *Women and Revolution*. Boston: South End Press.

Hawley, Ellis. W. 1966. "The Politics of the Mexican Labor Issue, 1950–1965," *Agricultural History*, 40:157–76.

Hayes-Bautista, David E., Werner O. Schink, and Jorge Chapa. 1988. *The Burden of Support: Young Latinos in an Aging Society*. Stanford, Calif.: Stanford University Press.

Heer, David M. 1990. *Undocumented Mexicans in the United States*. Cambridge and New York: Cambridge University Press.

Heer, David M., and Jeffrey S. Passel. 1987. "Comparison of Two Methods for Computing the Number of Undocumented Mexican Adults in Los Angeles County." *International Migration Review*, 21:1,446–73.

Heisler, Barbara Schmitter. 1986. "Immigrant Settlement and the Structure of Emergent Immigrant Communities in Western Europe." In Heisler, Martin, and Barbara Schmitter Heisler, editors, "From Foreign Workers to Settlers?: Transnational Migration and the Emergence of New Minorities." Special issue of *Annals of the American Academy of Political and Social Science*, 485: 76–86.

Hertz, Rosanna. 1986. *More Equal Than Others*. Berkeley: University of California Press.

Hewitt de Alcántara, Cynthia. 1976. *Modernizing Mexican Agriculture: Socioeconomic Implications of Technological Change, 1940–1970*. Geneva: United Nations Institute for Social Development.

Hochschild, Arlie, with Anne Machung. 1989. *The Second Shift: Working Parents and the Revolution at Home*. New York: Viking.

Hoffman, Abraham. 1974. *Unwanted Mexican Americans in the Great Depression: Repatriation Pressures, 1929–1939*. Tucson: University of Arizona Press.

Hogeland, Chris, and Karen Rosen. 1990. *Dreams Lost, Dreams Found: Undocumented Women in the Land of Opportunity*. San Francisco: Coalition for Immigrant and Refugee Rights and Services.

Hondagneu-Sotelo, Pierrette. 1992. "Overcoming Patriarchal Constraints: The Reconstruction of Gender Relations Among Mexican Immigrant Women and Men, *Gender & Society*, 6:393–415.

———. 1994. "Regulating the Unregulated? Domestic Workers' Social Networks," *Social Problems*, 41:50–64.

———. Forthcoming. "Working 'without Papers' in the U.S.: Toward the Integration of Legal Status in Frameworks of Race, Class and Gender." In Elizabeth Higginbotham and Mary Romero, editors, *Women and Work: Race, Ethnicity and Class.* Newbury Park, Calif.: Sage Publications.

Hondagneu-Sotelo, Pierrette, and Michael A. Messner. 1994. "Gender Displays and Men's Power: The 'New Man' and the Mexican Immigrant Man." Pp. 200–218 in Harry Brod and Michael Kaufman, editors, *Theorizing Masculinities.* Newbury Park, Calif.: Sage Publications.

Hossfeld, Karen J. 1990. "'Their Logic Against Them': Contradictions in Sex, Race and Class in Silicon Valley." Pp. 149–78 in Kathryn Ward, editor, *Women Workers and Global Restructuring.* Cornell University Press.

Horowitz, Ruth. 1983. *Honor and the American Dream.* New Brunswick, N.J.: Rutgers University Press.

Isasi-Díaz, Ada María, and Yolanda Tarango. 1988. *Hispanic Women, Prophetic Voice in the Church: Toward a Hispanic Women's Liberation Theology.* San Francisco: Harper and Row.

Jelin, Elizabeth. 1977. "Migration and Labor Force Participation of Latin American Women: The Domestic Servants in the Cities." *Signs: Journal of Women in Culture and Society,* 3:129–41.

Jenkins, J. Craig. 1977. "Push-Pull in Recent Mexican Migration to the U.S." *International Migration Review,* 11:178–89.

Jensen, Leif. 1988. "Patterns of Immigration and Public Assistance Utilization, 1970–1980." *International Migration Review,* 22:51–83.

Jones, Richard C. 1984. "Macro-Patterns of Undocumented Migration between Mexico and the United States." Pp. 33–57 in Richard C. Jones, editor, *Patterns of Undocumented Migration: Mexico and the United States.* Totowa, N.J.: Rowman and Allanheld.

Kandiyoti, Deniz. 1988. "Bargaining with Patriarchy." *Gender & Society.* 2:274–90.

Kaplan, Elaine Bell. 1987. "'I Don't Do No Windows': Competition between the Domestic Worker and the Housewife." Pp. 92–105 in Valerie Miner and Helen Longino, editors, *Competition: A Feminist Taboo?* New York: Feminist Press.

Katzman, David. M. 1981. *Seven Days a Week: Women and Domestic Service in Industrializing America.* Urbana: University of Illinois Press (first published 1978 by Oxford University Press).

Keely, Charles B. 1974. "Immigration Composition and Population Policy." *Science,* 185:587–93.

Keely, Charles B., and Patricia J. Elwel. 1983. "International Migration: Canada and the United States." Pp. 181–207 in Mary M. Kritz, Charles B. Keely, and Silvano M. Tomasi, editors, *Global Trends in Migration: Theory and Research on International Population Movements.* Staten Island, N.Y.: Center for Migration Studies.

Kibria, Nazli. 1993. *Family Tightrope: The Changing Lives of Vietnamese Americans.* Princeton, N.J.: Princeton University Press.

King, Deborah. 1988. "Multiple Jeopardy, Multiple Consciousness: The Context of a Black Feminist Ideology." *Signs: Journal of Women in Culture and Society,* 14:42–72.

Kiser, George C., and Martha Woody Kiser, editors. 1976. *Mexican Workers in the United States*. Albuquerque: University of New Mexico Press.

Kossoudji, Sherrie A. 1992. "Playing Cat and Mouse at the U.S.-Mexican Border." *Demography*, 29:159–77.

Kossoudji, Sherrie A., and Susan I. Ranney. 1984. "The Labor Market Experience of Female Migrants: The Case of Temporary Mexican Migration to the U.S." *International Migration Review*, 18:1,120–43.

Lamphere, Louise. 1987. *From Working Daughters to Working Mothers*. Ithaca, N.Y., and London: Cornell University Press.

Lancaster, Roger N. 1992. *Life Is Hard: Machismo, Danger, and the Intimacy of Power in Nicaragua*. Berkeley: University of California Press.

Lee, Everett S. 1966. "A Theory of Migration." *Demography*, 3:47–57.

LeVine, Sarah (in collaboration with Clara Sutherland Correa). 1993. *Dolor y Alegría: Women and Social Change in Urban Mexico*. Madison: University of Wisconsin Press.

Logan, Kathleen. 1984. *Haciendo Pueblo: The Development of a Guadalajaran Suburb*. Tuscaloosa: University of Alabama Press.

———. 1990. "Women's Participation in Urban Protest." Pp. 150–59 in Joe Foweraker and Ann L. Craig, editors, *Popular Movements and Political Change in Mexico*. Boulder, Colo., and London: Lynne Rienner.

Lomnitz, Larissa. 1977. *Networks and Marginality: Life in a Mexican Shantytown*. New York: Academic Press.

Macías, Anna. 1982. *Against All Odds*. Westport, Conn.: Greenwood Press.

McBride, Theresa. 1976. *The Domestic Revolution: The Modernization of Household Service in England and France, 1820–1920*. New York: Holmes & Meir.

McLemore, S. Dale, and Ricardo Romo. 1985. "The Origins and Development of the Mexican American People." Pp. 3–32 in Rodolfo O. de la Garza, Frank D. Bean, Charles M. Bonjean, Ricardo Romo, and Rodolfo Alvarez, editors, *The Mexican American Experience: An Interdisciplinary Anthology*. Austin: University of Texas Press.

McWilliams, Carey. 1968. *North from Mexico: The Spanish-Speaking People of the United States*. New York: Greenwood Press.

Martin, Joann. 1990. "Motherhood and Power: The Reproduction of a Woman's Culture of Politics in a Mexican Community." *American Ethnologist*, 17:470–90.

Martin, Philip L., and J. Edward Taylor. 1988. "Harvest of Confusion: SAWs, RAWs, and Farmworkers." Working Paper no. PRIP-UI-4. Program for Research on Immigration Policy. Washington, D.C.: Urban Institute.

Massey, Douglas S. 1981. "Dimensions of the New Immigration to the United States and the Prospects for Assimilation." *Annual Review of Sociology*, 7:57–85.

———. 1986. "The Settlement Process among Mexican Migrants to the United States." *American Sociological Review*, 51: 670–85.

Massey, Douglas S., Luin Goldring, and Jorge Durand. 1992. "Continuities in Transnational Migration: An Analysis of 13 Mexican Communities." In *New*

Perspectives on U.S.-Mexico Migration, proceedings of the conference organized by the Center for Latin American Studies and the Mexican Studies Program, University of Chicago, October 23–24.

Massey, Douglas S., and Zai Liang. 1989. "The Long-Term Consequences of a Temporary Worker Program: The U.S. Bracero Experience." *Population Research and Policy Review,* 8:199–226.

Massey, Douglas S., Rafael Alarcón, Jorge Durand, and Humberto Gonzalez. 1987. *Return to Aztlán: The Social Process of International Migration from Western Mexico.* Berkeley: University of California Press.

Massey, Douglas S., Katharine M. Donato, and Zai Liang. 1990. "Effects of the Immigration Reform and Control Act of 1986: Preliminary Data from Mexico." Pp. 183–210 in Frank D. Bean, Barry Edmonston, and Jeffrey S. Passel., editors, *Unauthorized Migration to California: IRCA and the Experience of the 1980s.* Washington, D.C.: Urban Institute Press.

Mines, Richard. 1981. *Developing a Community Tradition of Migration: A Field Study in Rural Zacatecas: Mexico and California Settlement Areas.* Monograph Series, no. 3. La Jolla, Calif.: Center for U.S.-Mexico Studies, University of California at San Diego.

Moore, Joan, and James Diego Vigil. 1993. "Barrios in Transition." Pp. 27–49 in Joan Moore and Raquel Pinderhughes, editors, *In the Barrios: Latinos and the Underclass Debate.* New York: Russell Sage Foundation.

Morales, Rebecca, and Paul Ong. 1990. "Immigrant Women in Los Angeles." Working Papers in the Social Sciences, vol. 5. Los Angeles: Institute for Social Science Research, UCLA.

Moreno, Angelina Casillas. 1986. *La mujer en dos comunidades de emigrantes (Chihuahua).* México, D.F.: Secretaría de Educación Pública.

Morokvasic, Mirjana. 1984. "Birds of Passage Are Also Women . . . " *International Migration Review,* 18: 886–907.

Mummert, Gail. 1988. "Mujeres de migrantes y mujeres migrantes de Michoacán: Nuevo papeles para las que se quedan y las que se van." Pp. 281–95 in Thomas Calvo and Gustavo Lopez, editors, *Movimientos de población en el occidente de México.* México, D.F., and Zamora, Michoacán: Centre d'Etudes Mexicaines et Centraméricaines and El Colegio de Mexico.

———. 1991. "Negotiating Gender Identities and Economic Roles: Public and Private." Paper presented at the 90th Annual Meeting of the American Anthropological Association, Chicago, November.

———. Forthcoming. "Del Metate al Despate: Rural Mexican Women's Salaried Labor and the Redefinition of Gendered Spaces and Roles." (To appear in an anthology on rural Mexican women.)

Naples, Nancy A. 1991. "'Just What Needed to Be Done': The Political Practice of Women Community Workers in Low-Income Neighborhoods." *Gender & Society,* 5:478–94.

National Immigration Law Center. 1991. *Overview of Alien Eligibility for Public Benefits.* Los Angeles: National Immigration Law Center.

———. 1993. *Guide to Alien Eligibility for Federal Programs.* 2d ed. Los Angeles: National Immigration Law Center.

Niembro Díaz, Laura. 1988. "El papel de la mujer en la autoconstrucción de vivienda, zona metropolitana de Guadalajara." Pp. 167–79 in Luisa Gabayet Ortega et al., editors, *Mujeres y sociedad: Salario, hogar y acción social en el occidente de México*. Guadalajara: CIESAS del Occidente, El Colegio de Jalisco.

North, David S., and Marion F. Houstoun. 1976. *The Characteristics and Role of Illegal Aliens in the U.S. Labor Market: An Exploratory Study*. Washington, D.C.: Linton.

Oakview, Calif. (pseudonym), School District. 1981. "Racial/Ethnic Make-up of Schools." CBED Survey.

O'Conner, Mary I. 1990. "Women's Networks and the Social Needs of Mexican Immigrants." *Urban Anthropology*, 19:81–98.

Oliveira, Orlandina de. 1990. "Empleo feminino en México en tiempos de recesión económica: Tendencia recientes." Pp. 31–54 in Neuma Aguiar, editor, *Mujer y crisis: Respuestas ante la recesión*. Caracas, Venezuela: Editorial Nueva Sociedad.

Ortega, Luisa Gabayet. 1988. "Antes eramos mayoria . . . Las mujeres en la industria textil de Guadalajara." Pp. 91–105 in Luisa Gabayet Ortega et al., editors, *Mujeres y sociedad: Salario, hogar y acción social en el occidente de México*. Guadalajara: CIESAS del Occidente, El Colegio de Jalisco.

Papanek, Hannah. 1979. "Family Status Production Work: The 'Work' and 'Non-Work' of Women." *Signs: Journal of Women in Culture and Society*, 4:775–81.

Pardo, Mary. 1990. "Mexican American Women Grassroots Community Activists: 'Mothers of East Los Angeles.'" *Frontiers*, 11:1–7.

Park, Robert. 1969. "The City: Suggestions for the Investigation of Human Behavior in the Urban Environment." Pp. 91–130 in Richard Sennett, editor, *Classic Essays on the Culture of Cities*. New York: Appleton-Century, Crofts (reprinted from *American Journal of Sociology*, 20:1916).

Passel, Jeffrey S. 1985. "Undocumented Immigrants: How Many?" *Proceedings of the Social Statistics Section, American Statistical Association*, 1985:65–72.

———. 1986. "Undocumented Immigration." *Annals of the American Academy of Political and Social Science*, 487:181–200.

Passel, Jeffrey S., and Karen A. Woodrow. 1984. "Geographical Distribution of Unauthorized Immigrants: Estimates of Unauthorized Aliens Counted in the 1980 U.S. Census by State." *International Migration Review*, 18:642–75.

———. 1987. "Change in the Undocumented Alien Population in the United States, 1979–83." *International Migration Review*, 21:1,304–23.

Peattie, Lisa Redfield. 1968. *The View from the Barrio*. Ann Arbor: University of Michigan Press.

Pedraza, Silvia. 1991. "Women and Migration: The Social Consequences of Gender." *Annual Review of Sociology*, 17:303–25.

Pedraza-Bailey, Silvia. 1985. *Political and Economic Migrants in America: Cubans and Mexicans*. Austin: University of Texas Press.

Peña, Manuel. 1991. "Class, Gender and Machismo: The 'Treacherous-Woman' Folklore of Mexican Male Workers," *Gender & Society*, 5:30–46.

Perlman, Janice. 1976. *The Myth of Marginality: Urban Poverty and Politics in Rio de Janeiro*. Berkeley: University of California Press.

Pessar, Patricia R. 1982. "The Role of Households in International Migration and the Case of U.S.-Bound Migration from the Dominican Republic." *International Migration Review*, 16:342–64.

———. 1984. "The Linkage between the Household and Workplace in the Experience of Dominican Women in the U.S." *International Migration Review*, 18:1,188–1,212.

———. 1986. "The Role of Gender in Dominican Settlement in the United States." Pp. 273–94 in June Nash and Helen Safa, editors, *Women and Change in Latin America*. South Hadley, Mass.: Bergin & Garvey.

Piore, Michael J. 1979. *Birds of Passage: Migrant Labor and Industrial Societies*. New York: Cambridge University Press.

Portes, Alejandro. 1978. "Migration and Underdevelopment." *Politics and Society*, 8:1–48.

Portes, Alejandro, and Robert L. Bach. 1985. *Latin Journey: Cuban and Mexican Immigrants in the United States*. Berkeley: University of California Press.

Portes, Alejandro, and Rubén G. Rumbaut. 1990. *Immigrant America*. Berkeley: University of California Press.

Rapp, Rayna. 1978. "Family and Class in Contemporary America: Notes toward an Understanding of Ideology." *Science and Society*, 42:278–300.

Reichert, Joshua S. 1981. "The Migrant Syndrome: Seasonal U.S. Wage Labor and Rural Development in Central Mexico." *Human Organization*, 40:56–66.

Repak, Terry A. 1990. "Economic Change and International Migration: The Case of Central Americans in Washington, D.C." Unpublished paper, Emory University.

Rix, Sara E., editor. 1990. *The American Woman, 1990–1991: A Status Report*. New York and London: W. W. Norton and Company.

Rodríguez, Carlos. 1992. *The Health Care Crisis in the Latino Community*. Report prepared by Latino Issues Forum and West Coast Regional Office of Consumers Union. San Francisco: Tortuga Press.

Rodríguez, Nestor, and Rogelio T. Nuñez. 1986. "An Exploration of Factors That Contribute to Differentiation between Chicanos and Indocumentados." Pp. 138–56 in Harley L. Browning and Rodolfo O. de la Garza, editors, *Mexican Immigrants and Mexican Americans: An Evolving Relation*. Austin: Center for Mexican American Studies Publications, University of Texas Press.

Rollins, Judith. 1985. *Between Women: Domestics and Their Employers*. Philadelphia: Temple University Press.

Romanucci-Ross, Lola. 1973. *Conflict, Violence, and Morality in a Mexican Village*. Palo Alto, Calif.: National Press Books.

Romero, Mary. 1987. "Domestic Service in the Transition from Rural to Urban Life: The Case of La Chicana." *Women's Studies*, 13:199–222.

———. 1988a. "Chicanas Modernize Domestic Service." *Qualitative Sociology*, 11:319–34.

———. 1988b. "Sisterhood and Domestic Service: Race, Class and Gender in the Mistress-Maid Relationship." *Humanity and Society*, 12: 318–46.

———. 1992. *Maid in the U.S.A.* New York and London: Routledge.

Romo, Ricardo. 1983. *East Los Angeles: History of a Barrio.* Austin: University of Texas Press.

Rosado, Georgina. 1990. "De campesinas inmigrantes a obreras de la fresa en el valle de Zamora, Michoacán." Pp. 45–71 in Gail Mummert, editor, *Población y trabajo en contextos regionales.* Zamora, Mexico: El Colegio de Michoacán.

Rosaldo, Michelle Zimbalist. 1974. "Woman, Culture, and Society: A Theoretical Overview." Pp. 17–42 in Michelle Zimbalist Rosaldo and Louise Lamphere, editors, *Woman, Culture and Society.* Stanford, Calif.: Stanford University Press.

Rouse, Roger. 1987. "Migration and the Politics of Family Life: Divergent Projects and Rhetorical Strategies in a Mexican Transnational Migrant Community." Unpublished Paper, Center for U.S.-Mexican Studies, University of California at San Diego.

———. 1989. "Mexican Migration to the United States: Family Relations in the Development of a Transnational Migrant Circuit." Ph.D. dissertation, Department of Anthropology, Stanford University.

———. 1990. "Men in Space: Power and Appropriation of Urban Form among Mexican Migrants in the United States." Paper presented at the Residential College, University of Michigan, Ann Arbor, Michigan, March 14.

———. 1992. "Making Sense of Settlement: Class Transformations, Cultural Struggle, and Transnationalism among Mexican Migrants in the United States." Pp. 25–51 in Nina Glick Schiller, Linda Basch, and Cristina Blanc-Szanton, editors, *Towards a Transnational Perspective on Migration.* Annals of the New York Academy of Sciences, vol. 654. New York: New York Academy of Sciences.

Ruiz, Vicki L. 1987. "By the Day or the Week: Mexicana Domestic Workers in El Paso." Pp. 61–76 in Vicki L. Ruiz and Susan Tiano, editors, *Women on the U.S.-Mexico Border: Responses to Change.* Boston: Allen and Unwin.

———. 1992. "The Flapper and the Chaperone: Historical Memory among Mexican-American Women." Pp. 141–57 in Donna Gabaccia, editor, *Seeking Common Ground: Multidisciplinary Studies of Immigrant Women in the United States.* Westport, Conn.: Greenwood Press.

Rumbaut, Rubén G., Leo R. Chavez, Robert J. Moser, Sheila M. Pickwell, and Samuel W. Wishik. 1988. "The Politics of Migrant Health Care: A Comparative Study of Mexican Immigrants and Indochinese Refugees." *Research in the Sociology of Health Care,* 7:143–202.

Salas, Elizabeth. 1990. *Soldaderas in the Mexican Military.* Austin: University of Texas Press.

Salazar, Gloria González. 1980. "Participation of Women in the Mexican Labor Force." Pp. 183–201 in June Nash and Helen Icken Safa, editors, *Sex and Class in Latin America.* South Hadley, Mass.: Bergin & Garvey.

Salzinger, Leslie. 1991. "A Maid by Any Other Name: The Transformation of 'Dirty Work' by Central American Immigrants." Pp. 139–60 in Michael Burawoy et al. editors, *Ethnography Unbound: Power and Resistance in the Modern Metropolis.* Berkeley: University of California Press.

Samora, Julian. 1971. *Los Mojados: The Wetback Story.* Notre Dame, Ind.: University of Notre Dame Press.

Sánchez, George J. 1990. "'Go after the Women': Americanization and the Mexican Immigrant Woman, 1915–1929." Pp. 250–63 in Ellen Carol DuBois and Vicki L. Ruiz, editors, *Unequal Sisters: A Multicultural Reader in U.S. Women's History.* New York and London: Routledge.

Sassen-Koob, Saskia. 1978. "The International Circulation of Resources and Development: The Case of Migrant Labour." *Development and Change,* 9:509–45.

————1982. "Recomposition and Peripheralization at the Core." Pp. 88–100 in Marlene Dixon and Susanne Jonas, editors, *The New Nomads: From Immigrant Labor to Transnational Working Class.* San Francisco: Synthesis Publications.

————. 1984. "The New Labor Demand in Global Cities." Pp. 139–71 in Michael P. Smith, editor, *Cities in Transformation.* Beverly Hills, Calif.: Sage Publications.

————. 1988. *The Mobility of Labor and Capital: A Study of International Investment and Labor Flow.* Cambridge and New York: Cambridge University Press.

Schmidt, Katharine A. 1991. "Domestic Workers Note Abuse, Low Pay." *Santa Monica Outlook,* November 5.

Schumacher, August. 1981. *Agricultural Development and Rural Employment: A Mexican Dilemma.* La Jolla, Calif.: Center for U.S.-Mexican Studies, University of California at San Diego.

Segura, Denise A. 1988. "Familism and Employment among Chicanas and Mexican Immigrant Women." Pp. 24–32 in Margarita B. Melville, editor, *Mexicanas at Work in the United States.* Mexican American Studies Monograph no. 5. Houston, Tex.: University of Houston.

Selby, Henry A., and Arthur D. Murphy. 1982. *The Mexican Urban Household and the Decision to Migrate to the United States.* ISHI Occasional Papers in Social Change, no. 4. Philadelphia: Institute for the Study of Human Issues.

Selby, Henry A., Arthur D. Murphy, and Stephen A. Lorenzen with Ignacio Cabrera, Aida Castaneda, and Ignacio Ruiz Love. 1990. *The Mexican Urban Household: Organizing for Self-Defense.* Austin: University of Texas Press.

Siems, Larry, editor. 1992. *Between the Lines: Letters between Undocumented Mexican and Central American Immigrants and Their Families and Friends.* Hopewell, N.J.: Ecco Press.

Simon, Rita J., and Margo Corona DeLey. 1984. "The Work Experience of Undocumented Mexican Women Migrants in Los Angeles." *International Migration Review,* 18:1,212–29.

Sirola, Paula. 1992. "Beyond Survival: Latino Immigrant Street Vendors in the Los Angeles Informal Sector." Paper presented at the Seventeenth International Congress of the Latin American Studies Association, Los Angeles, Calif., September 24–27.

Soldatenko, Maria Angelina. 1991. "Who Is Organizing Latina Garment Workers in Los Angeles?" *Aztlán: Journal of Chicano Studies Research,* 20 (1 and 2).

Solórzano-Torres, Rosalía. 1987. "Female Mexican Immigrants in San Diego County." Pp. 41–60 in Vicki L. Ruiz and Susan Tiano, editors, *Women on the U.S.-Mexico Border: Responses to Change*. Boston: Allen and Unwin.

Sosa Riddell, Adaljiza. 1986. "The Status of Women in Mexico: The Impact of the International Year of the Woman." Pp. 305–24 in Lynne B. Iglitzin and Ruth Ross, editors, *Women in the World 1975–1985: The Women's Decade*. Second, revised edition. Santa Barbara, Calif.: ABC-CLIO.

Soto, Shirlene. 1986. "Tres modelos culturales: La Virgen de Guadalupe, la Malinche y la Llorna." *Fem* (Mexico City), no. 48: 13–16.

Stacey, Judith, and Barrie Thorne. 1985. "The Missing Feminist Revolution in Sociology." *Social Problems*, 32:301–16.

Stephen, Lynn. 1991. *Zapotec Women*. Austin: University of Texas Press.

Stevens, Evelyn P. 1973. "*Marianismo:* The Other Face of Machismo in Latin America." Pp. 89–101 in Ann Pescatello, editor, *Female and Male in Latin America*. Pittsburgh: University of Pittsburgh Press.

Taylor, Paul. 1929. "Mexican Labor in the United States: Migration Statistics." Pp. 237–55 in Carl C. Plehn, Ira B. Cross, and Melvin M. Knight, editors, *University of California Publications in Economics*, Berkeley: University of California Press.

———. 1983. "Mexicans North of the Rio Grande." Pp. 1–16 in Paul Taylor, *On the Ground in the Thirties*, Salt Lake City: Peregrine Smith Books (originally published in 1931).

Thadani, Veena N., and Michael P. Todaro. 1984. "Female Migration: A Conceptual Framework." Pp. 36–59 in James T. Fawcett, Siew-Ean Khoo, and Peter C. Smith, editors, *Women in the Cities of Asia: Migration and Urban Adaptation*. Boulder, Colo.: Westview Press.

Thomas, Robert J. 1985. *Citizenship, Gender, and Work: Social Organization of Industrial Agriculture*. Berkeley: University of California Press.

Thomas, W. I., and Florian Znaniecki. 1927. *The Polish Peasant in Europe and America*. New York: A. A. Knopf.

Thompson, E. P. 1966. *The Making of the English Working Class*. New York: Vintage Books.

Thorne, Barrie. 1982. "Feminist Rethinking of the Family: An Overview." Pp. 1–24 in Barrie Thorne with Marilyn Yalom, editors, *Rethinking the Family: Some Feminist Questions*. New York: Longman.

———. 1993. *Gender Play: Girls and Boys in School*. New Brunswick, N.J.: Rutgers University Press.

Tienda, Marta, and Karen Booth. 1991. "Gender, Migration and Social Change." *International Sociology*, 6:51–72.

Tienda, Marta, and Leif Jensen. 1985. "Immigration and Social Program Participation: Dispelling the Myth of Dependency." *Social Science Research*, 15:372–400.

Tilly, Louise A., and Joan W. Scott. 1978. *Women, Work and Family*. New York: Holt, Rinehart and Winston (1987 edition published by Methuen).

Todaro, Michael P. 1969. "A Model of Labour Migration and Urban Unemployment in Less Developed Countries," *American Economic Review*, 59:138–48.

————. 1976. *Internal Migration in Developing Countries: A Review of Theory.* Geneva: International Labor Organization.

UNICEF. 1991. *The State of the World's Children.* Oxford: Oxford University Press.

U.S. Census. 1991. P.L. 94-171 File, March.

U.S. Congress. Senate. Immigration Commission. 1911. *Immigration Commission Report.* 61st Congress, 3d session.

U.S. General Accounting Office (GAO). 1987. *Immigration Reform: Verifying the Status of Aliens Applying for Federal Benefits.* Report to Congressional Committees. GAO/HRD-88-7, October.

U.S. Immigration and Naturalization Service. 1983. *1980 Statistical Yearbook of the Immigration and Naturalization Service.* Washington D.C.: Government Printing Office.

————. 1989. *Immigration Statistics: Fiscal Year 1988.* Washington D.C.: Government Printing Office.

————. 1991. *Statistical Yearbook of the Immigration and Naturalization Service, 1990.* Washington, D.C.: Government Printing Office.

————. 1992. "Legalization Applicants (I-687 and I-700) by Type of Application, Date of Application, and Status. Female applicants only; Table 3, data generated February 13." Washington, D.C.: Legalization Application Processing System and Statistics Division.

Valdés, Dennis Nodín. 1991. *Al Norte: Agricultural Workers in the Great Lakes Region, 1917–1970.* Austin: University of Texas Press.

Van Arsdol, Maurice D., Joan W. Moore, David M. Heer, and Susan Pauliver Haynie. 1979. *Non-apprehended and Apprehended Undocumented Residents in the Los Angeles Labor Market: An Exploratory Study.* Final Report of Contract No. 20–06–77–16 to the Employment and Training Administration, U.S. Department of Labor. Los Angeles: University of Southern California Population Research Laboratory.

Vega, William A., Bohdan Kolody, and Juan Ramon Valle. 1987. "Migration and Mental Health: An Empirical Test of Depression Risk Factors among Immigrant Mexican Women." *International Migration Review,* 21:512–29.

Vega, William A., Bohdan Kolody, Juan Ramon Valle, and Richard Hough. 1986. "Depressive Symptoms and Their Correlates among Immigrant Mexican Women in the United States." *Social Science and Medicine,* 22:645–52.

Villar, Maria de Lourdes. 1990. "Rethinking Settlement Processes: The Experience of Mexican Undocumented Migrants in Chicago." *Urban Anthropology,* 19:63–79.

Wallace, Steven P. 1988. "Central American and Mexican Immigrant Characteristics and Economic Incorporation in California." *International Migration Review,* 22:375–93.

Ward, Kathryn, editor. 1990. *Women Workers and Global Restructuring.* Ithaca, N.Y.: International Labor Relations Press, Cornell University.

Warren, Robert, and Jeffrey S. Passel. 1987. "A Count of the Uncountable: Estimates of Undocumented Aliens Counted in the 1980 United States Census." *Demography,* 24:375–93.

Weber, Devra Anne. 1989. "*Raiz Fuerte:* Oral History and Mexicana Farmworkers." *Oral History Review,* 17:47–62.

Wiest, Raymond E. 1983. "Male Migration, Machismo, and Conjugal Roles: Implications for Fertility Control in a Mexican Municipio." *Journal of Comparative Family Studies,* 14:167–81.

Wirth, Louis. 1938. "Urbanism as a Way of Life." *American Journal of Sociology,* 44:1–24.

Wolf, Diane L. 1990. "Daughters, Decisions and Domination: An Empirical and Conceptual Critique of Household Straegies." *Development and Change,* 21:43–74.

———. 1992. *Factory Daughters: Gender, Household Dynamics and Rural Industrialization in Java.* Berkeley: University of California Press.

Woo, Ofelia Morales. 1993. "Migración internacional y movilidad transfronteriza: El caso de las mujeres mexicanas que cruzan hacía Estados Unidos." *Mujer y frontera,* 8:115–46. Mexico: El Colegio de la Frontera Norte y Universidad Autónoma de Ciudad Juárez.

Wood, Charles. 1982. "Equilibrium and Historical-Structural Perspectives in Migration." *International Migration Review,* 16:298–319.

Woodrow, Karen A., and Jeffrey S. Passel. 1990. "Post-IRCA Unauthorized Immigration to the United States: An Assessment Based on the June 1988 CPS." Pp. 33–75 in Frank D. Bean, Barry Edmonston, and Jeffrey S. Passel, editors, *Unauthorized Migration to California: IRCA and the Experience of the 1980s.* Washington, D.C.: Urban Institute Press.

Wrigley, Julia. 1991. "Feminists and Domestic Workers" (review essay), *Feminist Studies,* 17:317–29.

Yanagisako, Sylvia Junko. 1977. "Women-centered Kin Networks in Urban Bilateral Kinship." *American Ethnologist,* 4:207–26.

———. 1979. "Family and Household: The Analysis of Domestic Groups." Pp. 161–205 in Bernard J. Siegel, Alan R. Beals, and Stephen A. Tyler, editors, *Annual Review of Anthropology.* Palo Alto, Calif.: Annual Reviews.

Yans-McLaughlin, Virginia. 1977. *Family and Community: Italian Immigrants in Buffalo, 1880–1930.* Ithaca, N.Y.: Cornell University Press.

Ybarra, Lea. 1982. "Marital Decision-Making and the Role of Machismo in the Chicano Family." *De Colores,* 6:32–47.

———. 1983. "Empirical and Theoretical Developments in the Study of Chicano Families." Pp. 91–110 in Armando Valdez, Alberto Camarillo, and Tomás Almaguer, editors, *The State of Chicano Research on Family, Labor and Migration.* Proceedings of the First Stanford Symposium on Chicano Research and Public Policy. Stanford, Calif.: Stanford Center for Chicano Research.

———. 1988. "Separating Myth from Reality: Socio-economic and Cultural Influences on Chicanas and the World of Work." In Margarita B. Melville, editor, *Mexicanas at Work in the United States.* Mexican American Studies Monograph no. 5. Houston, Tex.: University of Houston.

Young, Eva, and Mariwilda Padilla. 1990. "Mujeres unidas en acción: A Popular Education Process." *Harvard Educational Review,* 60:1–18.

Young, Grace Esther. 1987. "The Myth of Being 'Like a Daughter.'" *Latin American Perspectives*, 14:365–80.

Zabin, Carol. 1992. "Binational Labor Markets and Segmentation by Gender: The Case of Agriculture and the North American Free Trade Agreement." Paper presented at the Seventeenth International Congress of the Latin American Studies Association, Los Angeles, Calif., September 24–27.

———, editor. 1992. *Mixtec Migrant Farmworkers in California Agriculture: A Dialogue among Mixtec Leaders, Researchers, and Farm Labor Advocates.* Working Paper no. 9. Davis, Calif.: California Institute for Rural Studies.

Zavella, Patricia. 1987. *Women's Work and Chicano Families: Cannery Workers of the Santa Clara Valley.* Ithaca, N.Y.: Cornell University Press.

Zinn, Maxine Baca. 1979. "Political Familism: Toward Sex Role Equity in Chicano Families." *Aztlán*, 8:13–26.

———. 1980. "Employment and Education of Mexican American Women: The Interplay of Modernity and Ethnicity in Eight Families." *Harvard Educational Review*, 50:47–62.

———. 1992. "Race and the Reconstruction of Gender." Center for Research on Women Research Paper no. 14. Memphis, Tenn.: Memphis State University.

Zinn, Maxine Baca, Lynn Weber Cannon, Elizabeth Higginbotham, and Bonnie Thornton Dill. 1986. "The Exclusionary Practices in Women's Studies." *Signs: Journal of Women in Culture and Society*, 11:290–303.

Index

Compositor:	Fog Press
Printer:	Maple-Vail Book Mfg. Group
Binder:	Maple-Vail Book Mfg. Group
Text:	10/13 Sabon
Display:	Sabon